About the author

John Hayes retired in 1997 after a working life in British secondary schools. Since then, he and his wife Mary have divided their lives between the small North Devon town of Torrington and the village of Neohori in southern Greece's Mani peninsula. *Greco Files* is his first book.

GRECO
FILES

A Brit's-Eye View of Greece

Καλή Ανάγνωση!

John Hayes *John*

24.11.21.

Matador
9 Priory Business Park,
Wistow Road, Kibworth Beauchamp,
Leicestershire. LE8 0RX
Tel: 0116 279 2299
Email: books@troubador.co.uk
Web: www.troubador.co.uk/matador
Twitter: @matadorbooks

ISBN 978 1800464 995

British Library Cataloguing in Publication Data.
A catalogue record for this book is available from the British Library.

Printed and bound by CPI Group (UK) Ltd, Croydon, CR0 4YY
Typeset in 11pt Adobe Garamond Pro by Troubador Publishing Ltd, Leicester, UK

Matador is an imprint of Troubador Publishing Ltd

For my grandchildren: Jakey, Zoë, Mia and Jamie.

Their love of Greece is already well-developed. My hope is that this book will enhance their understanding and appreciation of why their paternal grandparents chose to establish a second home there.

Snow-covered peaks of the Taygetos Mountains from the village of Aghia Sophia, West Mani.

CONTENTS

Introduction

Three events spread over six years conspired to create the setting for *Greco Files*. The first occurred in 1991 when my wife, Mary, and I opted for a Sunmed package holiday to Stoupa, an emerging seaside resort on the Mani Peninsula of southern mainland Greece; unremarkable in itself but a pivotal first step. The other two were less commonplace and owed as much to good fortune as to opportunism. Three years later, we surprised ourselves by purchasing an old, run-down stone house in the village of Neohori that overlooks Stoupa; and in 1997, our voluntary redundancies and early retirements enabled us, much sooner than expected, to take the plunge and move to Greece part-time. *Greco Files* is part memoire, part commentary that integrates accounts of our personal experiences with background information about Greece and its people.

During our years living part-time in Greece, I have tried hard to master the language, assimilate the traditions and customs, digest the history and current affairs, and travel widely in order to better appreciate and understand my adoptive country. I have always been a restless individual with scant regard for trifling matters and a strong desire to occupy my time with activities and projects that present a challenge, that require learning new skills and ultimately result in personal development and something to show for the commitment of time and effort. Learning the language, renovating our traditional village house, creating a pleasure garden from a derelict site, and setting up and running a boutique olive oil business for ten years are examples of how I have preferred to occupy my time. These experiences, and more, feature throughout this book.

My decision to embark on writing *Greco Files* was made in 2016. Mary and I had just wound up our olive oil and olive business and I was looking for another challenge. Our North Devon friends and neighbours, Bob and Moira, had both written and self-published books in retirement and I suspect their experiences, which they shared freely with us, were partly responsible for triggering the notion that I might use my renewed freedom to do likewise. Whether it should be fiction or non-fiction barely registered; my storytelling credentials are limited, whereas my literary strengths (such as they are) and employment experiences had prepared me in several ways with the skills and know-how to write a non-fiction book. The subject matter was never in doubt either; our Greek experience had much to offer. My only doubts concerned my ability to compose something that was well-written and well-informed, and at the same time interesting and entertaining enough to attract a readership.

The background material for *Greco Files* has been accumulated in predictable ways. I have visited many parts of Greece, often with friends Judy and Kevin, and gathered information from assorted media, both hard copy and digital. I must also acknowledge the tens of people of diverse nationalities who, during ordinary everyday conversations over the last fifty-five years, have unwittingly furnished me with stories and material which have informed this book.

Since the very start of our Greek adventure, Mary and I have kept diaries – we have just completed our twenty-third. They have proved an indispensable source of often long-forgotten information. Another invaluable source has been the fortnightly letters I wrote from Greece to my elderly mother in the UK between 1997 and her death in 2010 at the age of 103. I found them systematically stored in a shoebox while sorting through her effects. I regret I have kept so few of her replies. Even so, some of her acute observations have not gone unheeded in this book.

Torrington, April 2021

Acknowledgements

A great many people have helped me to write *Greco Files* and I thank them all for their involvement, big or small. I am especially indebted to my wife Mary, who throughout the long process has been a regular source of reference, encouragement and constructive criticism. Over a four-year period, she was always the first person to read through the early drafts, as well as comment on my subsequent re-working of chapters. Her comments and suggestions have been responsible for refining both the content and the grammatical correctness of this book. She has also been most patient and understanding of my regular self-imposed exiles to our home office. Without her unequivocal support, *Greco Files* would have remained a pipe-dream.

Several others have kindly accepted my requests to review chapters in their draft forms and have provided me with invaluable critiques, insights and reminders of matters that might otherwise have been overlooked. I am especially grateful to my sister and brother-in-law, Anna and Ashok Sethi, Bob and Moira Brewer, George Hadjimatheou and Helen Suddards, and David and Lorraine Matthews for their contributions in this respect. I am also indebted to Marina and Socrates Galineas and to Neohori friends, Vangellis Tsouleas and Koula and Sophia Pterneas, who have always been willing to discuss and explain Greek matters that I have not properly understood. Another Neohoritis, John Phipps, has gladly provided me with photos, data, background information and invaluable insights.

To fail to acknowledge my debt to six newspapers and their websites for being the source of so much of the contemporary information found in *Greco Files* would be an unforgiveable omission. Two are Greek national dailies, *Ethnos* and *Kathimerini*; two are Kalamata dailies, *Eleftheria* and *Tharros*; one is the now defunct *Athens News,* and the other is British, *The Guardian*. I especially wish to thank Helena Smith, *The Guardian*'s Athens correspondent, who has kept me appraised of Greek matters for more than a quarter of a century. Two large plastic boxes full of well-ordered cuttings are a measure of the value I place on her well-informed and insightful reporting.

I must also acknowledge the important role Wikipedia has played in facilitating easy access to and cross-checking of information, as well as providing invaluable lists of references that have often led me to more detailed original sources. On many occasions, my thoughts have turned to those authors in the past whose only recourse was to spend hours in libraries seeking the information they required. For most contemporary equivalents, the process is quick, straightforward and effortless by comparison.

A Bibliography identifies those books that have also provided me with much detailed background information and many diverse interpretations of Greece and Greekness. The online *Guardian and Observer style guide* proved an indispensable aid when clarification of grammar, spelling and idioms was needed.

Finally, thanks go to my younger son Peter, for the time he has spent configuring and enhancing the photos contained in *Greco Files*.

Torrington, April 2021

Notes to Readers

Generally speaking, foreigners find many Greek words difficult to pronounce. Even transliteration – converting printed or written Greek letters into their English equivalents – can still render some Greek words difficult to read or say. In this book, I have deliberately used many common Greek words in transliterated form. They appear in italics but one critical aid is missing: stress marks above the syllable that should be emphasised when speaking the word. The Greeks call them τόνοι (ton-ee). Stressing the wrong syllable can make a correctly-sounded word difficult to understand for many Greeks. So be warned!

I have also adopted three other protocols which require a little explanation. When the term Mediterranean occurs with a capital M it refers specifically to the region encompassing the Mediterranean Sea. Where it exists without a capital M it refers to mediterranean lands in a more general, global sense to include parts of Australia, South Africa, Chile and California, for example. Historically, I have chosen to adopt the abbreviations BCE (Before Christian Era) and CE (Christian Era) instead of the more conventional BC and AD.

When referring to my British compatriots, whether they are tourists or settlers, I have chosen to refer to them using the shorthand 'Brits'. I am not attracted to any of the alternatives. 'Expats' is often a pejorative term, 'Britons' seems to be overloaded with historical connotations while 'English' misrepresents those many folk who hail from Scotland, Wales or Northern Ireland.

List of Photographs

With the exception of the cover photograph and photos (i), (ii) and (iii), photos occur opposite the start of each chapter that they are intended to represent.

Front Cover: 'Neohori Dreaming' – an automaton by Paul Tennant – *Jayne Poole Photography*

(i)   Snow-covered peaks of the Taygetos Mountains from the village of Aghia Sophia, West Mani.

(ii) Monks at the Great Meteoron monastery in central Greece.

(iii) Great Mulleins on the roadside, near Nomitsi, West Mani.

1.   Our home in Neohori, West Mani.

2.   Our pleasure garden in Neohori.

3.   Gathering storm over the Gulf of Messinia.

4   *Ifigeneia* moored in Stoupa harbour.

5.   A wildfire wilderness – *courtesy of John Phipps*.

6.   A rack of Greek newspapers on display outside a kiosk – *Terry Harris/Alamy stock photo*.

7.   Traditional Mani olive harvest – *courtesy of John Phipps*.

8.   Mary slitting Kalamata olives.

9.   Euro 2004 Champions – *PA Images/Alamy stock photo*

10. Heroes of the Greek Revolution 1821 – *courtesy of the artist, Kostas Louzis, aka Skitsofrenis*.

Unless stated otherwise, photographs are the property of the author.

Greek History – A Simple Timeline

Cycladic & Minoan Cultures		2000 BCE	
(3000 - 1050 BCE)		1900	1st palace at Knossos, Crete (c 1900 BCE)
		1800	
		1700	
		1600	Volcanic eruption of Santorini (c 1600 BCE)
Mycenaean		1500 BCE	
Civilisation		1400	
(1600 – 1100 BCE)		1300	
		1200	? Siege of Troy (c 1200 BCE)
		1100	
	A	1000 BCE	
Greek Dark Ages	N	900	
(1100 – 750 BCE)	C	800	
	I	700	1st Olympic Games (776 BCE)
Archaic Period	E	600	
(800 – 480 BCE)	N	500 BCE	Building of the Parthenon (525 BCE)
	T	400	Sea Battle of Salamis (480 BCE)
Classical Period (510 – 323 BCE)		300	Death of Alexander the Great (323 BCE)
		200	
Hellenistic Period	G	100	
(323 BCE – 146 CE)	R	0	
	E	100	
	E	200	Roman sacking of Corinth (146)
Roman Period (146 – 395)	C	300	
	E	400	Byzantium renamed Constantinople (330)
		500 CE	
		600	
		700	
Byzantine Empire		800	
(324 – 1453)		900	Mt Athos declared the Holy Mountain (885)
		1000 CE	
		1100	Great Schism (1054)
		1200	
Frankish,		1300	Fourth Crusade (1204)
Latin &		1400	
Venetian		1500 CE	Fall of Constantinople (1453)
occupations / Ottoman		1600	
(1204 – 1797) / Empire		1700	
(1453 – 1821)		1800	
Independent		1900	Sea Battle of Navarino (1827)
Greece		2000 CE	Great Fire of Smyrna (1922)
(1821 – present)		2100	

Map 1 - Greece & its Neighbours

Map 2 – The Peloponnese

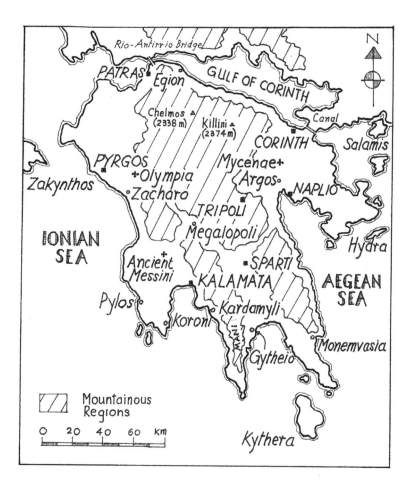

Map 3 - The Mani Peninsula

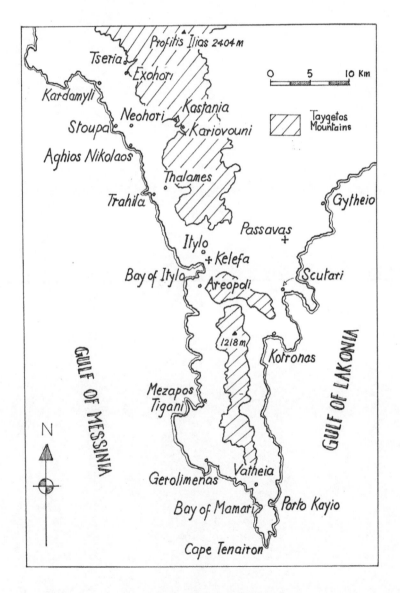

Our home in Neohori, West Mani.

Chapter 1

STONES, TILES & MORTAR

Whatever For?

Building work was the last thing on my mind in October 1997 as I reversed down the perilously narrow street to our Greek house in the village of Neohori. A small contingent of our new neighbours had gathered to observe my nervous progress, no doubt intrigued by this unannounced arrival of strangers in a large white van with British number plates. Mary and I had just completed our first European road trip from the UK to Greece: a journey of seven days, full of adventure, new experiences and a few dodgy moments. The Leyland DAF van, purchased a few days before departure specifically for removing stuff to our new Greek home, was rammed full to bursting: camping gear, tools, building equipment, furniture, kitchen paraphernalia, bedding, clothing, books etc. – all surplus to requirements in the UK or begged and borrowed from friends and family – and guaranteed to attract the scrutiny of customs officials at ferry ports.

The house had been unoccupied and unattended for ten years prior to our arrival and, apart from viewing it before purchase in 1994 and a single visit to take photos and measure up twelve months

1

later, we were still largely ill-prepared for what we encountered. Our intention to camp inside the house while assessing and organising what building work was necessary soon fell foul of some unexpected existing residents: a family of rodents, who were understandably dismayed at our arrival. We were no match for them and, after a third night when their antics were so disturbing that we decamped to sleep on the open-air terrace, we sought refuge in rented rooms in Stoupa, the nearby seaside resort.

"Whatever for?" had been my elderly mother's reaction when confronted with the news that Mary and I had purchased a second home in Greece. Other family members, friends and acquaintances were equally intrigued. Right from the start of our relationship in the mid-'60s, Mary and I had been fortunate enough to enjoy regular Mediterranean holidays. The combination of sun, sea and mountains, the relaxed, outdoor lifestyle and healthy diet persistently beckoned us back for more. Thus, in the summer of 1991, with our sons keen to make their own independent summer holiday plans, we chose to spend two weeks on a Greek package holiday in Stoupa, on the west coast of the Mani Peninsula in the southern Peloponnese. Chosen from a Sunmed brochure, Stoupa appeared to be a quiet, relaxing, traditional kind of seaside resort, only recently on the tourist map and just what we were looking for to recharge our batteries. With direct flights from Gatwick to Kalamata Airport and no long onward transfers involving coaches or ferries, it seemed ideal . . . . . and so it proved.

Although I had occasionally viewed run-down Breton cottages with some interest during summer camping holidays in France with our sons, they were only passing fancies, and Mary and I had never even raised, let alone considered, the prospect of a second home abroad. So, we somewhat surprised ourselves when we noted down a phone number from a flier pinned to a noticeboard in the Sunmed office in Stoupa while queuing to book tickets for a day trip to Ancient Olympia. The number belonged to an Englishwoman called Susan Shimmin, ('Suzanna' to the Greeks), longtime resident in Greece, who specialised in uniting foreigners with Greek property for sale. During three consecutive summer visits – we had fallen in love with Stoupa – Sue drove us around the district for a day at a time, viewing old stone houses in various states of disrepair. With her immaculate Greek, impressive network of local connections, dogged driving skills, encyclopedic knowledge of the Mani and her relaxed, engaging manner, these pleasurable trips of exploration and discovery allowed us to assimilate the local geography and history and gradually refine our requirements and preferences.

In the years before emails and smartphones allowed easy and instant communication of texts and images, Sue had to rely on traditional means of producing and circulating her lists of available property to potential customers. A typewriter and ink duplicating machine generated the hard copy (always on cream-coloured, headed A4 paper), a camera produced tiny 'thumbnail' photos that were attached to the description of each property, and various European postal services did the rest. The 1991 list came in two parts, Spring and Autumn, and contained 44 properties for sale with prices that mostly ranged from £10,000 to £50,000. The most expensive was a £125,000 beach-side property in Stoupa; an absolute bargain by today's standards. Prices were accompanied by an asterisked rider that indicated they were all *'estimates based on what the owner said he wanted when the property first went on the market, and can fluctuate up and down depending on inflation, exchange rates and so on'*. Sue's succinct and idiosyncratic descriptions of properties always aroused some mirth amongst customers. For me, her most memorable line was *'all the stones are here'* at the end of a scarcely disguised account of a roofless house in an advanced state of ruin. The phrase suggested the house could be reassembled with relative ease, stone by stone, in a Lego kind of way.

The Neohori house Sue introduced to us for the first time in August 1994 had a bold, official number 122 fixed to the street-side wall but the villagers knew it as *to spiti tou koufou* (the house of the deaf man). Sue was confident it would meet with our approval and even declared that she would be interested in buying it herself if we turned it down, but this could have just been sales talk. Previously we had seriously considered two other properties in the area but neither purchase had materialised. Competing buyers beat us to the first one in Katafigio (Tseria) and the owner of the second in Koutifari (Thalames) hiked the price at the last minute, putting it beyond our budget. Both experiences, rather than deter us, had made us more determined than ever, and the Neohori house seemed to fit the bill. It was a traditional stone property in reasonable condition, it had sea views, it was a five-minute drive from the beach at Stoupa and was located in a 'living' village, where our neighbours would be working Greek families. According to Sue's experienced eye, the property possessed much potential and, most important of all, it came within our £20,000 budget. It took us less than twenty-four hours to decide to buy, and we have never regretted it. The few photos of the exterior and interior of the house that we later showed to friends and family prompted a range of reactions. Builder friends quickly appreciated the potential, while others, by the look of barely disguised horror on their faces, were bemused that their normally rational friends had embarked on what appeared to be such an unpromising project.

To spiti tou koufou had been the home of Yiorgos Pterneas. Yiorgos' deafness, attributed to a wartime accident while on active service, had prevented him from becoming a schoolteacher and had left him reliant on tutoring youngsters from the village, who would come to his house for extra mathematics lessons. The house, which had been unoccupied since Yiorgos' death in 1987, had been his daughter's dowry when she married Yiannis Haliotis. Thus, it was to the Haliotises' new house on the edge of the village that we went with Susan Shimmin on August 4th 1994 to kick-start the process of purchase. Sat on their shaded balcony, nibbling icing sugar 'submarines' in glasses of chilled water – a traditional Greek summertime refreshment – we confirmed the price of six million drachmas (£16,305) and agreed to pay a 350,000 drachmas deposit. Sue then hastily produced handwritten agreements in both Greek and English that both parties signed, we shook hands and the deal was done. However, it was two more months before the house and its freehold became legally ours. There were formal procedures to navigate.

The most pressing was to hand over the deposit in cash before our imminent return to the UK at the end of our holiday. This involved a bus trip to Kalamata and the Trapeza Pisteos (Credit Bank) on Stadiou Avenue, where, with the aid of a credit card, we were able to withdraw the deposit, that was roughly equivalent to £1000. It was supplied in 5000-drachma notes; seventy of them in two bulging envelopes that Mary tucked into her handbag, which she guarded tenaciously as we walked back to the bus station. Although Sue would take care of most of the other outstanding matters at the Greek end, there was one she could not undertake without us. It involved a visit to the *Poleodomio* in Kalamata – regional home of the government planning and building control authority – to agree with specialist civil servants the 'taxable value' of the house. With the aim of obtaining a valuation close to the price we had agreed with the vendor, it was necessary to under-declare the price. The reason for this standard subterfuge is quite simple: the Greek authorities expect applicants to quote a property price that is less than they paid, so if you were 100% honest you might well end up with a taxable value that exceeded the actual cost, and that would just not do.

Mary and I watched intently as Sue engaged in a question and answer session, all the time translating into English for our benefit and occasionally referring to us for answers. When we had provided sufficient information about the location, size and condition of the house, the civil servant consulted a huge ledger to seek details of similar properties in Neohori and their taxable values, before seeking the opinion of a more senior colleague. We were relieved when the agreed taxable value turned out much the same as the actual price and, with the property purchase tax then at a rate of 9%, we paid the Greek government just over 460,000 drachmas (£1,250). With other costs that included payments to a surveyor, lawyer, notary public and

Sue's fee, the total cost just exceeded our budget of £20,000, which we had decided to raise with the aid of a building society loan when we returned to the UK. The whole process had been quicker and less convoluted than we had imagined.

Our Greek Home

There are many villages called Neohori in Greece. It is probably the most common place name of all and simply means 'new village'. Where there are several Neohoris in the same region it is sometimes necessary to distinguish them, one from the other. To the Greek postal service, the Neohori where our house is located is known officially as *Neohori Lefktrou* – meaning the Neohori of Lefktro, Lefktro being the name of its ancient predecessor nearby. It is located on the west-facing side – originally known as the 'shady' side – of the Mani Peninsula, which was historically divided into two parts: the Outer Mani in the north and Inner or Deep Mani in the south. The modern equivalents comprise parts of the prefectures of Messinia and Lakonia and administrative units known as *Dytiki* (West) Mani and *Anatoliki* (East) Mani respectively. Our Neohori is in West Mani.

The original core of Neohori stretches along the edge of a slightly sloping sandstone plateau about 200 metres above sea level and no more than two kilometres from the sea. The steep, winding descent gives access to the narrow, low-lying coastlands below that border the Gulf of Messinia and contain the tourist resorts of Kardamyli, Stoupa and Aghios Nikolaos. Towering up, not far behind, are the Taygetos Mountains, which gaze out across the Gulf to the relatively subdued profile of the Messinian peninsula beyond. As the name Neohori suggests, and judging from the marble date stones that adorn older properties, the original village does not possess a long history, and probably dates from the mid-18th century. Rumour suggests that its original settlers were forced to abandon their homes further south, near the village of Nomitsi, when earth movements dried up their spring water supply. In winter, Neohori contains about 250 permanent inhabitants – many more than in higher villages, where post-war depopulation has left just a handful of pensioners – but many less than the 400 or so who occupied Neohori at its peak in the 1950s and '60s. In summertime the population is considerably enlarged by Greeks returning temporarily to their place of birth and upbringing, to stay with their parents and grandparents, reconnect with old friends and neighbours, and enjoy the many outdoor opportunities the area provides.

The heart of Neohori is a curious mix of buildings. Some original stone houses – few with towers – have been abandoned and are in an accelerating state of disrepair. Some have deteriorated further and are just overgrown mounds of collapsed tiles and stones, while others have been restored and renovated and given a new lease of life. Squeezed in between are more modern 20th-century houses, distinguishable by their greater height and girth, their larger windows, and their rendered exterior walls. Almond, fig, mulberry, lemon and pomegranate trees, as well as occasional rampant grape vines, give shade to gardens and secluded courtyards hiding behind tall stone walls. Old Neohori is a maze of crooked narrow streets followed inexorably by poles carrying electricity and telephone cables, and street lights. The streets are interspersed by mini squares (*rougges*), often accompanied by stone benches for engaging in evening chatter and street taps that bring fresh spring water from the mountains. Neohori has two churches. The more modern *Vaggelistra* dominates the village with its imposing dome, bell tower and illuminated cross, and possesses a large forecourt used for festivals and celebrations. The other, dedicated to St Nicholas, is much more ancient and stands on the other side of the village alongside the cemetery and ossuary. It is much smaller and simpler in style and its barrel-vaulted interior contains an array of primitive, faded frescos telling bible stories, which are in sharp contrast to their stunning contemporary equivalents in *Vaggelistra*.

Although there is no longer a proper *taverna*, two coffee shops (called *cafeneio*) serve food as well as drinks and, along with two bakeries – one also a *zacheroplasteio* making cakes and biscuits as well as bread – and a mini-market selling everything from newspapers to toilet brushes, they provide a better range of services than in most villages. There is also a well-used community centre in the former primary school and two olive presses: one privately owned and the other operated by the village farmers' cooperative. The building boom, which started in the mid-1990s, lasted for fifteen years until the economic crisis took hold, and has revived since 2018, has seen Neohori expand on all sides. Many of these new stone houses occupy former olive groves, small arable fields and grazing land, and were built mainly for foreigners as holiday or retirement homes. Their locations above, below and alongside Neohori have one thing in common: they all have stunning sea views.

Our Neohori home is located in the heart of the village and is a traditional Mani stone property, but without a tower. Although there are clear signs that it was built in three stages, its crudely engraved marble date stone, located high on an outside wall, declares its year of construction as 1764. At that time, Greece was still straining under the occupation of the Ottoman Turks; it would be nine more years before the Boston Tea Party shook the foundations of the British colony of America, and in France, festering unrest would lead to a bloody Revolution twenty-five years later. It must be one of the oldest houses in Neohori.

Its basic form can be imagined as three shoe boxes. Two are aligned side by side and represent the ground floor while the first floor is formed by the third box, positioned squarely on top of one of the others, with the uncovered one being an open terrace. Each 'shoe box' is rectangular in shape and roughly twelve metres long and five metres wide. The thick outer walls are made of roughly-faced mixed stone with marble quoins and sandstone door and window frames, all bonded with lime mortar. The foundations rest on solid sandstone bedrock, which was levelled before a large-capacity cistern (*isterna*) for collecting rainwater and a smaller cesspit (*vothro*) were excavated; the latter on the downslope side of the former, for obvious reasons.

This vital preparation work provided valuable building material in situ.

With earthquake resistance a foremost consideration, it is a simple but solid structure. The ground floor walls contain two impressive parallel stone arches (*kamares*) that have the appearance of mini tunnels and are sometimes referred to as barrel vaults. They occupy almost the entire length and width of both adjoining 'shoe boxes' and have been infilled with rubble and soil from above to provide additional structural strength and to support the overlying solid floors. Made of close-fitting sandstone blocks, this double-vaulted ground floor once provided a cooking area, storage space and occasional livestock accommodation. The twin arches, which are linked by a narrow, arched passageway – a difficult structural feature and a considerable achievement for the builders – were originally only accessed from a small outside yard.

For former inhabitants, the first floor living and sleeping quarters must have been cramped, confined to just two rooms – barely fifty square metres in total – and the small open terrace, which was reached by climbing a steep exterior flight of marble steps directly from the street. The pitched roof was covered by traditional Byzantine-style earthenware tiles (known mischievously as 'monks' and 'nuns') fastened with lime mortar. The doorways were low, the ceilings high with cypress roof timbers and cane insulation exposed, while the walls were plastered and painted with limewash. One floor was made of pine planks – surely 20th-century replacements for the originals – while the other was solid and surfaced with a traditional mortar known as *koursani*, a mixture of sand, slaked lime and crushed tile that was also used for lining walls. Household utilities were extremely limited, even primitive in some cases. Wintertime heating had probably been provided by a rudimentary cast iron stove with temporary chimney pipes, but all that remained was a blackened stone hearth. The property had been connected to mains water and electricity as late as the 1970s, the former getting no further than the outside terrace. Located over a substantial solid marble sink, the single brass tap was attached to the wall of a brick-made outside toilet that resembled a rudimentary sentry box. It was linked via a long drop soil pipe to the cesspit below. How toilet functions were executed prior to its construction in the 1950s or '60s is a mystery, better not dwelt on. Two electric lights did little to illuminate the interior, which was gloomy even at midday because the windows were small and few in number. The single electric socket was probably an underused luxury.

Maniot Styles

The Classical Age in Greece, with its magnificent temples and theatres and its Doric, Ionic and Corinthian styles, is judged by many to have been the pinnacle of Greek architectural achievement, but it found little expression in the Mani Peninsula. Remote and inaccessible, with an unforgiving mountainous terrain and rocky, unwelcoming coastline, its inhabitants were consumed with the basic process of survival in a harsh and challenging environment with limited resources. Yet, from earliest times, the Mani was well populated with a dense network of traditional settlements scattered across the countryside. The earliest Maniot dwellings are thought to date from the Mycenaean Age (1600 to 1100 BCE), which predated the Classical Age by at least 500 years. They were modest in the extreme compared with some contemporary constructions elsewhere, like the citadel of *Mykini* (Mycenae) in the northeast Peloponnese that became King Agamemnon's royal capital and boasted Cyclopian walls, the famous Lion Gate, sumptuous palaces, rich treasuries and innovative beehive tombs.

Nothing even remotely comparable was constructed in the Mani Peninsula. Dwellings were primitive and often arranged in loose clusters, ideally on a gently sloping hillside where precious fresh water and soil were present. The earliest Maniot dwellings were made of local, roughly hewn stone, arranged in a rectangular shape, and sometimes comprised two floors: the basement partly excavated into underlying rock for the livestock, with living quarters on top. The roofs were flat, composed of massive slabs of stone laid horizontally on top of the walls and infilled with smaller wedge-shaped stones and clay. Inside would have been remarkably hot in summer and dank and chilly in winter. Until the middle of the 19th century, when slaked lime and thus efficient mortar became available to bond the stones, the height and width of buildings were limited. Construction was almost always a communal build involving members of the extended family.

A few dwellings from Mycenaean times were accompanied by massive rectangular fortified towers, beginning an architectural tradition for which the Mani has become well-known. Although villages dominated by stone towers are common, Vatheia in the deep south of the peninsula is the most spectacular expression of this custom, a veritable 'mini-Manhattan'. It occupies a strategic site on top of a steep-sided hill with commanding views of the Gulf of Messinia, the coastlands and the parched mountains that form the backbone of the peninsula. An enemy would have needed exceptional confidence to even contemplate an attack. But Vatheia's fortified towers were not only constructed to resist attack by outsiders, they were also an internal security measure. Family feuds were common enough in the past for an American travel blogger to nickname Vatheia 'vendettaville'. It was dominated by four main clans, each of which occupied a separate part of the village. The biggest clan was the Mickalakiani, made up of sixteen different but closely aligned families. Disputes over land, water, suspected theft or disrespectful behaviour could often deteriorate into acts of revenge, honour beatings and killings, and wholesale inter-clan conflict. When he came across the village in 1805, Colonel William Leake – an English military surveyor and acute observer of Greek life and customs – was informed by his Maniot guides that Vatheia had been at internal war for over forty years, resulting in some 100 deaths.

Vatheia today has a sad, haunted feel about it. More than one third of today's ninety or so ruined buildings are the remains of multi-storey tower houses that were constructed between 1840 and 1900, when the total population was at its peak: between 300 and 400 inhabitants. All buildings were densely packed together and often in adjoining groups, largely self-contained and thus all the better to defend in times of inter-clan conflict. Adjacent to the dwellings of each clan were churches, cisterns, olive presses, *rougges* (mini squares), and *alonia* (threshing circles), all contained within a tight-knit area and linked by a network of roughly-paved alleys and pathways. Beyond were cemeteries, outbuildings and stone-walled small fields for livestock and cultivation; some containing prickly pears, which were considered much more valuable in those days. In its heyday Vatheia might have been a dangerous place to live, but it was also a vibrant and self-sustaining community. Today, the almost total absence of inhabitants, the majority of dwellings abandoned and in a state of ruin, the overgrown pathways, the dilapidated outbuildings and crumbling field boundary and terrace walls combine to create a sombre mood of reflection in most visitors. Despite the efforts of the Greek tourist board in the early 1990s, and the piecemeal efforts of some enterprising locals, Vatheia remains a decrepit remnant of a bygone age, photographed by passing tourists on their way to somewhere else. Without some concerted intervention, it will surely continue to disintegrate, and this iconic Mani village of towers will become nothing more than anonymous piles of stone, overgrown with prickly pear.

Although stone towers represent the defining architectural image of the Mani Peninsula, the presence of castles (*kastro*) reflects its long and chequered history. They may be fewer in number, scattered, and sometimes even more dilapidated than the tower villages, but their size and spectacular strategic sites make them difficult to ignore. There are ten of them in all, if you include the castles at Kalamata and Vardounia – both on the northern fringes of the Mani – and they form a strategic cordon on both sides of the Taygetos Mountains. Whether their purpose was to control movement, resist invasion, restrain an uppity local population or simply to impose authority, the choice of natural sites that could be easily fortified was of paramount military importance. Two contrasting examples of classic defensive sites in the Mani are occupied by the castles of Passavas and Grande Magne. Situated high on a hill overlooking a deep, narrow, rocky gorge, the garrison of Passavas castle was able to control passage through the foothills of east Mani, from Gytheio and the lowlands of the Evrotas river to Areopolis and the Deep Mani. By contrast, the fabled Frankish castle of Grande Magne was located on the upstanding headland at the tip of the narrow, rocky promontory known as Tigani (frying pan), which stretches out into the Bay of Mezapos. Virtually impregnable to attack by land or sea, its primary weakness was its unreliable water supply, dependent solely on intermittent winter rainfall and human-made cisterns.

All Mani castles have experienced chequered histories involving construction, destruction, re-construction and modification by a succession of occupants over several hundred years. Passavas has existed for more than 2,000 years and is a prime example. It was first fortified by the Spartans in the pre-Christian era, then inherited by the Laconians, occupied by the Byzantines and completely re-built by the Franks in 1254. Subsequently, it was regained by the Byzantines, captured, rebuilt and reinforced by the Ottoman Turks, and finally conquered in 1684 by the Venetians, who laid waste to the castle and settlement, intending it should never be used again. Later on, the Maniots, resisting Ottoman occupation and fighting for their independence, had other ideas and used it as an arsenal and safe haven.

Most Mani castles are today in an advanced state of ruin, with only the size and extent of their perimeter walls bearing testimony to their eventful pasts. Once abandoned, they were often pillaged for their stone and other building materials, and little of value was left untouched. The skeletons of buildings, many since collapsed, are all that remain. The castle of Kelefa is a good example. Especially visible in late afternoon sunshine, it is still bounded by thick marble and limestone walls, five mighty circular bastions and two fortified gateways, which enclose a rectangular area measuring 120 by eighty metres. It was built by the Ottoman Turks as late as 1679 and occupies a gently sloping site bounded by steep, rocky slopes on two sides, and overlooks the small town of Itylo to the north and the large, safe anchorage of the Bay of Itylo to the west. Its primary purpose was to provide a secure base for the garrison to impose Ottoman authority on its resentful Maniot subjects and curtail their burgeoning human trafficking. It also served to intimidate any hostile shipping thinking of using the Bay of Itylo, and to control passage through the Taygetos Mountains.

Closer inspection of the Kelefa reveals more destruction than is evident from a distance. Whereas the perimeter walls are surprisingly intact, with the seaward ramparts and bastions accessible by the original stone steps, the same cannot be said of the one-hectare area inside the walls, which in its heyday housed a mosque with minaret, barracks, an ordnance depot and gunpowder magazine. Today it is dominated by abandoned, overgrown olive trees and unchecked undergrowth that conceals randomly scattered piles of stones and building rubble, the remains of former buildings. Just a few isolated, free-standing walls have resisted the passage of time, piercing the green canopy but giving few clues as to their original function. The whole site is an obstacle course for anyone wishing to explore. With just a few exceptions, restoration of these castles dating from the Middle Ages has been largely ignored by the Greek authorities, even though they represent significant chapters in Greek history. Maybe it's not surprising that the focus has been on the more famous structures dating from Classical Antiquity.

Renovation

In stark contrast to anything featured on British TV's *Grand Designs*, the restoration of our Neohori property and its conversion into a second home was a modest, small-scale, low-budget affair. Right from the outset, Mary and I decided that our expenditure on restoration would not exceed what we paid for the house and so, to keep costs down and occupy ourselves gainfully, we intended to play a significant, hands-on role in its transformation. For the five years between 1994 and 1999, this project regularly occupied our thoughts and conversations, and in the latter two years when we were 'on task' in Greece, it dominated our every waking hour. From the moment the property became ours, we agreed we would bide our time, consider all the implications, make plans and preparations, and be ready to respond to any change of circumstances that would permit us to embark on our ambitious project. Neither of us was in any hurry.

Only on rare occasions did Mary and I have any doubts or second thoughts. We were excited at the prospect but realistic enough to know that planning and patience were necessary. On occasional winter evenings at home in Torrington, North Devon, when work and other commitments allowed, I began the process of converting raw measurements, photos and the outcome of our discussions into accurate drawings. Scale plans, cross-sections and 3D sketches were created to show what existed and how it might be reconfigured to provide us with a modern home within an historical stone carcass. The opportunity in 1997 for both of us to take voluntary redundancy and early retirement from our jobs in secondary schools in North Devon was eagerly grasped with both hands. It provided the chance to tackle the renovation of our Greek house much sooner than anticipated.

Discussions with builder friends, Terry and Paul, designed to elicit practical building renovation advice, rapidly transformed into an unlikely fantasy, instantly code-named 'Johnny and the Argonuts'. It involved them abandoning their wives and families for three months, and us driving across Europe in a builder's van rammed with tools and equipment and undertaking the essential structural work on our Neohori house. Sadly, it never worked out and they have never quite forgiven me for 'pulling the plug' on this far-fetched scheme. While attracted by the prospect in some respects, I could not countenance the negative message our plans were bound to have on our Greek neighbours – yet unmet – and Greek builders in Neohori. It would surely have been a bad start to our life in the village.

The more prudent alternative was to employ a local builder, and Susan Shimmin recommended Takis Spyropoulos from Verga, near Kalamata. He had formerly led a team renovating old houses for a discredited Kalamata-based architect and had recently chosen to set up on his own. Attracted by his reputation for sensitivity with building renovation, we had little hesitation in engaging him and his team. A short delay while he completed his existing project allowed us time to obtain a building permit, undertake some clearing work and find alternative accommodation while building work was in progress.

Proof that our house was connected to mains electricity and water, and a carefully selected photo clearly showing it possessed a roof, doors and windows allowed us to persuade the authorities at the local government planning and building control department in Kalamata that the necessary building work was simply remedial and thus only required a basic, free permit. This enabled us to proceed without detailed professional drawings and supervision by an architect or structural engineer, and thus expensive additional fees were avoided. However, knowing that the roof would probably need replacing, both Takis and Sue were somewhat uneasy with this outcome, fearing that neighbours might protest, the free permit be declared invalid and the whole building process come to a premature halt. As it turned out, there was no need to worry. Somewhat delayed, the building permit was delivered by Sue on November 6th 1997, and work began early the following day when Takis and his team stripped the roof of all its tiles, lime mortar and canes, depositing the considerable volume of debris in the street below. Suddenly the whole first floor was exposed to the elements and thus, with winter approaching, a rapid assessment of what work was required before the roof could be reconstructed was urgent.

Greek building regulations demand that any restoration of an old property must involve the installation of a steel-reinforced concrete ring beam around the top of the walls to help the structure resist any seismic activity. To add to that, some of the old cypress beams and rafters needed replacement and we wanted a fireplace, so construction of a chimney had also to be taken into account. By the end of November, Takis and his team had undertaken these preliminary tasks and completed the roof, despite several days of intermittent heavy rain that delayed progress. New replacement roof timbers had been attached to the rigid ring beam and the rafters clad with thin planks; we didn't want traditional cane. Then a mix of tiles – new underneath and recycled originals on top to preserve the roof's historical appearance – were cemented into place on top of nine-centimetre thick insulation boards lying on a waterproof membrane. We were delighted with the outcome; the whole process had taken less than three weeks and our new Greek home was weatherproof once again – just in time for the onset of winter.

Whereas Takis had replaced a roof several times before, the other major task we required of him would be a first. We wanted him to create an interior link between the first floor and the *kamares* below, which we planned to convert into two bedrooms and a bathroom. The reason for choosing this 'upside down' arrangement was simple: the *kamares* were partly excavated into solid rock and would remain cooler – sometimes 8°C cooler in high summer – than any other part of the house. My drawings envisaged linking upstairs and downstairs by excavating a large hole in the solid upstairs floor, carefully deconstructing a small section of the vaulted arch and building some stone steps. Takis was understandably somewhat apprehensive at the prospect, mainly because he recognised, more than most, how important the arch was to the structural integrity of the whole building.

The crucial question was how Takis should tackle this job: should it be 'top down' or 'bottom up'? It didn't take him long to decide to start from below. He built a stone pillar on one side and constructed stone steps on the other, both right up to the underside of the *kamara* and designed to reinforce those parts that would remain intact. All this was done in the semi-gloom of a single light bulb at the end of a long extension lead. The rest of the operation – the deconstruction of the unsupported central portion of the arch from the top down – went like clockwork, dispelling any initial doubts Takis might have harboured. Once the dust had settled, the stone steps were raised to the floor level above and the ends of the truncated *kamara* secured, we had the internal link between floors that we desired. Takis and his team completed several other less demanding jobs, such as constructing the stone fireplace, before they cleared up and left on December 6th 1997. The following day we set off on our road journey back to the UK. It had been an eventful couple of months but so far, so good!

Although Takis returned a couple of times in the first half of 1998 to lay concrete floors in the *kamares* and build a dividing brick wall to separate bathroom from bedroom, it was other Greek tradesmen who now took centre stage. Yiorgos, our plumber from the nearby village of Riglia, surely faced the sternest test. His challenge was to convert a single cold tap and a primitive 'long drop' toilet, both located on the outside terrace, into a modern, integrated hot and cold water supply system, with drainage of 'grey water' directed into the large cistern beneath the house, and toilet water into the small cesspit. This was demanding enough in itself but especially arduous in a solidly built, 230-year-old stone house. Intermittently during the summer of 1998, Yiorgos toiled with various gauge hammer drills to penetrate concrete floors, sandstone blocks, bedrock and stone walls to make passage for an assortment of copper and plastic pipes, which he then connected up to the bathroom and kitchen facilities that had been installed previously. It was hot, physical and sometimes unrewarding work, especially in the gloomy *kamares*, illuminated solely by artificial light. Yiorgos' final job for us was to install an electric water heater, later replaced by a solar panel, releasing him to celebrate one of the most eagerly awaited national and religious holidays in Greece – the

Dormition, or Assumption of the Virgin Mary – on August 15th, the following day. We have no doubt he was glad to see the back of *to spiti tou koufou* but the plumbing system he installed remains intact and has never let us down.

During the period when the plumbing was taking place, Vangellis, a congenial electrician from Stoupa, was engaged in converting a rudimentary system of one socket and two lights into a modern, comprehensive electric circuit, spanning both levels. His end-of-job report to DEH (the Greek national electricity company, pronounced 'dayee') was vital: it would determine whether a permit was issued and mains electricity officially reconnected. Although Vangellis and his brother Elias were able to take advantage of holes through floors and walls that Yiorgos had already created, plenty of channelling of brick, plaster and solid floors was necessary to make way for plastic trunking that would eventually carry the electric cables. It would be mid-September 1998 before the final adjustments were completed, all our lighting and sockets installed and our cooker and water heater connected to the electricity supply. At last we could abandon use of the camping stove and enjoy the luxury of hot showers; hitherto it had been cold showers in the outside yard.

Several other tradesmen also contributed to the renovation process. Kostas, a seasoned joiner from Stoupa, made and installed new windows, a replacement front door and a large glazed unit containing a door, which was squeezed into the arched entrance to the *kamara* that would become our bedroom. Odysseas – surely not his real name? – was the first of several Albanian tradesmen we employed. Many Albanians came to Greece to seek work in the building trade during the 1990s, bringing with them a reputation for hard work and well-honed masonry and stone-working skills. Odysseas plastered the rough stone walls supporting the *kamara* arch in our bedroom with a flamboyant Balkan style that involved flicking the very fluid white plaster – a mix of lime and marble dust – onto the wall before rendering it flat and smooth. That he was a skilled plasterer was in little doubt, but a tidy workman he definitely was not. Without copious coverings of polythene – we had been forewarned – the clearing-up, which was left entirely to us, might have taken several days.

Byzantine Churches

While our humble Neohori house was being transformed into a second home, the state of a small 12th-century church dedicated to Aghios Petros (St Peter) and located in the nearby village of Kastania was causing serious concern. Perched on a narrow terrace carved out of a steep rocky slope, this Byzantine gem occupies a vantage point at the top of this West Mani village of winding narrow streets and densely packed traditional stone dwellings. Scattered amongst them are eleven other Byzantine churches; surely a sign that the early Maniots were God-fearing folk.

The Mani Peninsula possesses an impressive collection of Byzantine churches. Most are found within the confines of towns and villages but others are dispersed in the most unexpected places: in olive groves, beside caves, on cliff tops, deep in ravines, and beside wells and fountains. Sometimes the reason for their location is hard to fathom. Many of the rural Byzantine churches in Mani date from the revival of Christianity under the Byzantines that began in the 8th century. They all possess an easily recognisable standard form: they are small and simple, rectangular in shape with barrel roofs, and orientated east-west. They are constructed of local faced stone, occasionally augmented by pillaged stone from nearby older and abandoned structures. Sometimes the stonework is decorated with repeated patterns of tile or small brick known as *clisonné*, a distinctive mark of Byzantine style. Lintels, quoins, and door and window frames are frequently of marble and sometimes decoratively carved in what appear to be arbitrary forms. Bell towers, which are commonly attached to churches in outer Mani, are thought to have come later, during the Venetian occupation.

Over 900 years old, Aghios Petros' very existence was being put in jeopardy by the relentless forces of nature. Its precipitous site was undermining its structural stability and ingress of moisture was damaging the many wall and ceiling frescoes. It had originated as a simple cruciform church with four columns supporting an octagonal central dome. Two later additions altered its appearance: a portico was constructed at the entrance in the 13th century and a bell tower added in 1813. Furthermore, previous attempts at maintenance and repair did not warrant the approval of modern experts. Thus in 2013, with the generous financial backing of private sponsors Thanasis and Maria Martinos, and under the supervision of two prominent non-government organisations, a wholesale restoration of Aghios Petros began. It represented a massive undertaking on a cramped, difficult to access site, involving a dedicated team of archaeologists, structural engineers, stone masons, roofers and fresco restorers, all experienced and skilled in their particular field of ecclesiastical restoration. The outcome of their sixteen months of unstinting endeavor was recognised as outstanding in May 2016, when one of the European Commission's 'Europa Nostra' prizes for restoration was awarded to Aghios Petros, declaring it 'a model for the preservation of cultural heritage'.

This ambitious project started with major structural works to stabilise the foundations. Two reinforced concrete retaining walls clad with natural stone were constructed on the upslope and downslope sides of the church. The exterior walls, decorated with elaborate *clisonné*, were repaired, repointed, refreshed and cleaned, and the somewhat permeable roof, previously clad with *tikles* – irregularly shaped, thick stone slates – replaced with specially made, wide earthenware tiles. Hand in hand with the exterior structural work, high level, adjustable stainless steel bars were inserted within the church to hold the most vulnerable walls in place. Meanwhile, previous internal restoration work deemed to be substandard was removed and the delicate and painstaking process of exposing and refreshing the exceptional frescoes began. Working in cramped, uncomfortable conditions, often perched high on scaffolding and illuminating their tasks with head torches, the restorers worked their alchemy, reviving the frescoes in a way few could have imagined possible. The figures of Christ, the Virgin Mary and assorted saints, along with representations of bible stories, have been brought back to life. Once again, they provide a vivid pictorial backcloth for the rare marble iconostasis, topped with a large gilded cross seemingly borne aloft by ferocious green griffins. The decorative capitals of the marble columns and the scene depicted on the half-moon shaped marble lintel over the doorway linking the portico and the nave suggest that the early Orthodox Christian religion possessed a primitive, almost pagan, dimension. What that carving represents always promotes lively discussion.

Doing It Ourselves

Any visit with guests to admire the many charms of Kastania always starts with a visit to Aghios Petros. Even in its previous forlorn state, it never failed to make a deep impression, and now, fully restored to its former glory, it is a great joy to behold, no matter how many times we return. With its miniature form, its primitive simplicity, its calm and its historical links with early Christianity, it makes a sharp contrast with the size, opulence and splendour of many Gothic and Renaissance churches and cathedrals in other parts of Europe. And yet, even for a non-believer, it possesses a strong spiritual dimension that has been enhanced, not diminished, by the restoration. Yet for me, the achievements of those teams of highly skilled workmen and women who have turned back the clock and recreated a place of worship in its original form often eclipses the holy essence of Aghios Petros that they have managed to preserve. I rarely leave Kastania without wondering what a better job we might have made of renovating our Neohori home if we had possessed half the know-how, experience and resources of those restorers.

Although we accepted from the outset that large, demanding

restoration jobs on our Neohori home would be done by builders and tradesmen, we were determined to do as much building and DIY work as our skills allowed. We were not complete novices; some experience had been gained previously, doing DIY and helping build an ambitious extension to our family home in Torrington. I had also 'learnt on the job' while labouring for Mike, an experienced and multi-skilled builder friend, during three consecutive post-retirement winters. There was never any intention of undertaking significant structural work, plumbing or electrics ourselves, but we were confident that there were plenty of other less demanding jobs we could manage. It was going to be 'hands-on' wherever possible.

During and long after the period when our builders and tradesmen were active on site, Mary and I undertook various tasks, sometimes in tandem, sometimes independently. I spent a lot of time making mortar, sometimes two mixes a day when the temperatures were cooler and I was feeling energetic or driven to finish a task. In the early years, before I belatedly purchased a cement mixer, I mixed it all by hand with a long-handled shovel, often in the street outside, laying myself open to comment and opinion from everyone who passed. As well as sand and cement, Greek mortar contains a magic ingredient I had not encountered before. The Greeks call it *asvesti* – slaked lime in paste form – purchased in robust polythene bags from any builders' yard. It makes the mortar pliable and easier to use in every situation and made me feel more like a seasoned professional, especially when rendering walls, when it helps the mortar stick like glue. I built stone and brick walls, laid paving stones – grey/blue *Karistou* and cream-coloured *Artas* – and I eventually developed the confidence and know-how to build two free-standing stone pillars and a stone arch. I also tiled floors and walls. Meanwhile, Mary did a lot of stripping back crumbling lime plaster on the first floor to expose some handsome sandstone arches over the windows, two niches and what might have been a blocked-up window. She also cleaned sandstone blocks, which formed the *kamares* downstairs, pointed stone, grouted tiles and did most of the wall painting and the staining and varnishing of the undersides of the roof. It was undeniably a team effort. We learned lessons from observing our builders at work and asking them questions; we got to know local builders' yards and what they offered; we took inspiration from one or two other foreigners undertaking their own renovations; and we gained confidence from our own achievements. Slowly we convinced ourselves that we could tackle some bigger jobs on our own.

The unwanted brick sentry box of a toilet in the corner of the terrace proved my most daunting demolition job. The core of the problem was the one and a half metres square flat roof that was made of fifteen-centimetre thick concrete, over-reinforced with steel bars to a degree that might have allowed it to withstand a nuclear blast. With hindsight, my approach to its demolition was seriously flawed, but at the time it seemed sound enough. It involved systematic deconstruction of three of the supporting brick walls by hand, leaving the offending roof propped by the remaining back wall and two sturdy wooden props at the unsupported corners. My plan was to remove the props – one by one, at a safe distance, with the aid of a rope – which would flip the roof onto the abandoned plot of land five metres below, where it could easily be broken up. But no matter how hard I tugged, the second prop would not budge. It needed encouragement with a sledgehammer, and that's when the sudden collapse of the heavyweight roof nearly took me with it. A very close escape left me gasping for breath with my heart thumping and barely able to admit to Mary my near-death experience. Added to that was the ignominy of having to explain to our next-door neighbours that the falling concrete slab had brought down their telephone line.

Mary's biggest achievement involved the tedious and repetitive task of cleaning and then repointing the 200 sandstone blocks that form the tall, elegant *kamara* arch in what would become our bedroom. These beautifully faced, beige-coloured stones that fit together so perfectly had been blackened over time by the frequent use of fires for cooking. And it wasn't just surface discolouration; it was a hard veneer of soot and flakes of ash bound together with a tenacious glue of steam, cooking oil fumes and wood smoke. A scrubbing brush proved useless – even a wire brush had little impact – so Mary resorted to a toothed hammer that turned out to be the only effective alternative. This toil lasted over three months in the early summer of 1998. Perched on a stepladder, with headscarf and protective glasses in place, holding on with one hand and gently working the hammer with the other, it was slow, arm-aching, back-breaking work.

Nibbling away bit by bit at the offending veneer, Mary was constantly showered by dust, sand and small bits of stone. She set herself a target of six blocks per session, each block taking about twenty minutes to clean, after which there was the crumbling lime mortar pointing to remove. She claimed the best thing about the job was that she could always see the progress she had made, the newly cleaned stone contrasting vividly with the blackened blocks still awaiting her attention. By the time she had finished, Mary had little appetite to tackle the delicate repointing of the blocks, but she was eventually persuaded otherwise. Her first experimental efforts left the pointing flush with the surface of the stones, which didn't look right, so another pointing style was adopted, which left the mortar proud. This proved much more demanding of Mary's novice skills but the outcome was much more agreeable to the eye. I wasn't sure whether it was deep relief that she had finally finished or a flush of pride at her achievement that dominated her feelings as she downed her tools after the final session of pointing. The unreserved compliments Mary received from a host of visitors encouraged her, after a six-week break, to start cleaning and repointing the other *kamara* that was destined to become our guest bedroom. Fortunately, this was a more straightforward task because the stone had not been blackened and the arch was lower and more accessible.

The most ambitious job Mary and I undertook jointly was in the autumn of 2001, when we constructed a veranda on our first floor terrace to replace the bamboo-clad pergola we had erected previously. Purchasing the adjoining land and having our terrace extended provided the opportunity to construct a more permanent covered outside space, a vital means of surviving a Greek summer. Step one was to construct an end wall and two sandstone block pillars to support the roof. The pillars proved more difficult than I imagined; getting them vertical was straightforward enough with the aid of a plumb line and spirit level, but avoiding them twisting slightly was more demanding. On two occasions I deconstructed my previous day's work in order to get the pillars absolutely right.

Simultaneously we searched for timber to match the beams and rafters inside the house. Cypress is a strong, durable softwood that we expected to find locally. In the event, it involved a phone call by builder friend Daniel and a visit to a wood yard just outside the city of Sparti, on the other side of the Taygetos Mountains and nearly two hours from Neohori. Following the briefest of introductions, the businesslike owner led me to an enormous, well-seasoned cypress tree trunk lying supine in his yard, where, with a piece of chalk, he quickly divided the cut end of the trunk into the cross-sectional dimensions I required. In no time he was reassuring me that the tree trunk would provide all the timber I needed, that it would be sawn the following morning and delivered by the end of the week. I was flabbergasted; even more so when the arrangement worked out exactly as he had promised.

With the end wall and pillars complete and the timber delivered, it was time to assemble the roof itself – the biggest, most complicated piece of construction Mary and I had ever undertaken on our own. For several months I'd taken every opportunity to observe local roofers in action, taking photos of their unfinished work when they'd gone home at the end of the day. I was pretty confident that I knew the correct sequencing of jobs and understood the importance of each step in obtaining a sound roof. The first involved creating the timber framework that would support the roof tiles. Cutting, assembling and fixing the beams and rafters in warm sunshine was one of the most satisfying and rewarding of tasks, but not without its difficulties. The spicy aroma of sawn cypress will always remind me of cutting each rafter to an individual length to accommodate the irregular house wall to which the framework would be attached. The pitch of the roof also presented a problem. Even tucking it in tightly under the eaves of the existing house roof on the upside, while keeping it high enough on the downside for a normal-sized person to avoid ducking every time they passed underneath, left its pitch barely tolerable. With the framework installed and looking the part, Mary and I clad it with tongue and groove planks – another satisfying job – before covering them with a waterproof membrane. Then we nailed down uniformly-spaced battens at right angles to the rafters and nailed modern overlapping roof tiles to them. It was at this juncture that we, unknowingly, made a crucial error.

There is a saying in Greece: *'Build your first roof for an enemy, the second for a friend and the third for yourself'*; the implication being that you never get it absolutely right first time, and maybe not even second time round. This certainly applied to our efforts, and the first time the veranda roof was subjected to heavy rain and high winds, several leaks materialised. I was devastated. How was this happening after all the care we had taken? What made it worse was, despite some close examination of various possible points of ingress and the application of sealant, the problem didn't go away. Frustrated and irritated in equal measure by my inability to comprehend the root cause of the leaks, we decided we should strip off some of the tiles, nailed in place just six months previously. Within half an hour all was revealed. Because of the minimum pitch of the roof, I had expected some rainwater penetration of the tiles under certain extreme conditions, but I hadn't figured that the battens would restrict the free escape of this rainwater to the guttering. Actually, they ponded back the water and, as water always does, it had found a way out and leaked through nail holes in the waterproof membrane and cladding onto the terrace below. It was a novice roofer's error.

There seemed little choice. We needed to strip the roof and start all over again. We removed all the battens and replaced all the waterproof membrane (just in case), this time securing it with thin battens nailed along the rafters, which we had judged were the crucial missing element first time round. We then re-fixed the main battens, which were now raised sufficiently above the waterproof membrane to allow any unwanted ingress of rainwater to flow away freely. The tiles went on more snugly than first time round and after ten days we had completed the second version of our veranda roof. It has never leaked since and provides us with welcome daytime shade in summer and warmth and protection from the elements in winter. Recovering from a replacement knee operation in autumn 2008, several after-dark sessions of physiotherapy on an exercise bike were conducted on the veranda, accompanied solely by stunning displays of thunder and lightning out across the Gulf of Messinia and the reassuring gurgle of rainwater draining into the aluminium guttering. Neither electric light nor music device were deemed remotely necessary. The entertainment was Mother Nature's own, and no hint of a leak.

We have now lived part-time in our Neohori home for twenty-three years, almost a third of our lifetimes. We have hosted numerous guests: family, friends and even friends of friends, who have all found staying in our 'upside-down' house a unique and memorable experience – and mainly for the right reasons. Of course, its location within an authentic Greek village, its tranquility, its tree-green outlook, the antics of acrobatic swallows and little owls, its views of the sea and its sunsets all make an impact. But the house – and garden too – also make a deep impression. Judging from the reactions of guests, two things stand out. They all enjoy spending much of their stay outside in the open air, in full sun or shade depending on their mood and inclination, and they all find the guest bedroom a little intimidating. They appreciate the natural summer coolness that comes with its semi-subterranean setting, but the absence of a window ensures a complete blackout after lights-out. One of our earliest guests woke up in the night and genuinely thought she had gone blind, and since that disturbing episode we have provided a soft night light. Sleeping underneath a vaulted arch made of large sandstone blocks can also be a little unnerving, especially on the first night of a visit when we have appraised our guests of the drill in the unlikely event of an earthquake. Guests also find coping with the heat during summer months somewhat counterintuitive. The fact that we close shutters, windows and doors during the afternoon and evening to keep the heat out and leave them wide open overnight and in the morning, with secure mesh screens in place to let in the cool air and keep out the mosquitoes, takes some getting used to.

For us, the most rewarding aspect of anyone staying for the first time is if they show an interest in how the house has been transformed. That is especially so if they had been unsure of our sanity when they first learned of our plans to buy and restore a run-down Greek village property. Trying to explain how the jigsaw of jobs combined to create the home they are holidaying in would be impossible without a trawl through the photo albums in which Mary has kept an exact annotated pictorial record of all the work done by builders, tradesmen and ourselves. The photos never fail to generate genuine appreciation and recognition – and in some cases, mild incredulity – at what we have managed to achieve. The photo of me standing in our living room entirely open to a blue Greek sky the morning after the roof had been completely removed in November 1997 always produces a spontaneous reaction of "*Bloody Hell!*" or similar. Of course, our family and friends are particularly interested in seeing evidence of the jobs that Mary and I have worked on exclusively, but we are always adamant that we were just supporting cast to the Greek stars of the show: Takis and his building team, Yiorgos the plumber, Vangellis the electrician, Kostas the joiner, and the rest. Without their experience, skills and hard work, our Greek haven would never have materialised and provided us with so much pleasure over so many years. We take great satisfaction and some pride in having been part of the process and it annoys us to hear people boast, "*We built a house, blah, blah, blah*", "*We restored a village cottage, blah, blah, blah*" when we're sure they never once mixed cement, constructed a stone wall, sawed a piece of wood or tiled a floor.

Our pleasure garden in Neohori.

Chapter 2

NATURE GENTLY MANIPULATED

Myth and Legend

Greek mythology is well endowed with stories that feature flowers, plants and nature. As well as providing a rich source of information about the indigenous flora of 2,500 years ago, it provides an insight into the ancient Greeks' elementary understanding of nature before scholars like Theophrastus began to suggest alternative explanations. Plants and flowers were used in various illustrative ways in Greek mythology: they provided the setting for mythological events, they helped to explain the origins and creation of mythological characters, and symbolised their metamorphosis from one form to another. Some plants and flowers were also attributed with significant curative and religious properties.

The story of Persephone, daughter of Zeus and Demeter, is a well-known Greek myth in which flowers, fruit and nature play important roles. Persephone's beauty had entranced Hades, the god of the underworld, for a long time before he abducted her while she was gathering wild flowers with Artemis and Athena. Her mother Demeter was incensed by the kidnapping, and after undertaking exhaustive but abortive searches on Earth, she concluded that her daughter must be detained somewhere in the Underworld. To force Hades' hand, she used her powers as goddess of agriculture to immediately halt all growth on Earth until Persephone was released. A kind of post-nuclear winter prevailed, which soon provoked the desired response. Hades released Persephone, and Demeter duly restored Mother Nature. The story would have ended there were it not for one thing: Persephone had tasted the food of Hades, in particular the pomegranate. This determined two outcomes: she was required to spend every winter in the underworld, but her return in springtime was marked by germination, regrowth and blossoming. Thus, as well as being queen of the underworld through her entanglement with Hades, she also became the goddess of spring. A most unlikely combination.

While the hoi polloi – from the Greek *οι πολλοί*, meaning 'the many' or 'the mass of ordinary people' – were content to rely on their personal observations of how nature worked, borrowing from mythology when their own practical experiences let them down, certain scholars were seeking alternative explanations. Theophrastus (372–287 BCE) was a pioneer of the natural sciences and became known as the 'Grandfather of Botany'. He studied a wide range of subjects, first under Plato and then Aristotle, and became Aristotle's successor as leader of the Lykeion School. Few of his published works survive, but the two most noteworthy that remain, entitled *Enquiry into Plants* and *Growth of Plants*, were groundbreaking works. *Enquiry into Plants* contained the first ever classification of plants, dividing them into four main groups: trees, shrubs, sub-shrubs and herbs. It considered for the first time, and in some detail, the morphology of plants, how they reproduce, the natural conditions that favour different plants, their economic uses and their medicinal and restorative qualities. It was a significant scientific work of its age and a considerable academic achievement. Thanks to translations into Latin and later printed editions with illustrative woodcuts, the importance of these two treatises lasted nearly 2,000 years; right up until the Swedish scientist Carl Linnaeus' innovative research and classification in the 18th century fundamentally changed the way scientists appreciated the botanical world.

Suburban sprawl, so common in westernised countries today, was absent in Ancient Greece. There was a relatively clear division between urban and rural. Towns were densely occupied and often enclosed within a fortified wall, hence there was little space for gardens. Planted and irrigated areas within towns were rare and took the form of public open spaces rather than private gardens. Outside the town walls things were different, especially where there was a source of water. Vegetable and fruit gardens were common, requiring considerable toil for those who earned their living supplying the nearby townsfolk. Approximating to modern-day parks, sacred groves surrounded sanctuaries, temples and burial places. They were planted with all kinds of trees, most common among which were olives, planes, pines, cypresses and laurels. The most famous gardens in Ancient Greece were located outside Athens' city walls. Known as the Gymnasia, they housed three venerable education establishments, the Academia, the Lykeion and the Kynosarge, which contained the celebrated schools of philosophy associated with Plato and Aristotle. The gardens were located alongside the rivers Kephissos, Eridanos and Ilissos, and were believed to be inhabited by gods and spirits, and the haunt of nymphs and satyrs. Today it's hard to imagine, when hurtling along the noisy and heavily congested, elevated Kifissos Avenue in an airport shuttle bus, with a concrete jungle of apartment blocks flashing by, that in Classical times this was the site of a peaceful and very rural sacred grove and garden.

Alexander the Great's prowess and achievements as a great military leader are well known. In just twelve years, between 335 and 323 BCE, he used the might of his armies to extend his kingdom of Macedon, in what is now northern Greece, as far east as the river

Indus and the foothills of the Himalayas, and south to the fringes of the Sahara Desert. Had he lived longer, Alexander might have instigated a fundamental change in the attitude of Greeks, especially prosperous and influential ones, towards ornamental or leisure gardens. The location and very existence of the Hanging Gardens of Babylon is the subject of conjecture and disagreement amongst modern scholars. It is unknown if Alexander ever witnessed them, although he is known to have camped with his army in Babylon and Ninevah, both considered places where the Hanging Gardens may have been. It seems that Alexander was impressed with some aspects of the sophisticated cultures and civilisations he conquered. Although content to destroy the palaces and plunder their treasuries, he was enchanted by the many royal gardens he visited and slowly embraced this innovative gardening concept, which involved adapting 'nature' in a way hitherto unappreciated in the West.

Alexander was particularly impressed by King Cyrus' royal garden at Pasargardae, near Persepolis, in modern-day Iran. Built as an integral part of the imperial capital and symbolic heart of the Persian Empire, it incorporated a formal geometric design dividing it into four parts, all watered by a sophisticated irrigation system, incorporating stone pathways and pavilions and adorned with pomegranate and mountain cherry trees, rose bushes, irises, lilies and ornamental grasses. But Alexander's dream that this Persian garden should become the template for gardens of the rich and powerful in his homeland never materialised. His premature and controversial death in Babylon at the age of thirty-two saw to that. The popularity of Persian-style gardens would have to await the rise of the Roman Empire. Only then did gardens borrowing much from these so-called 'Paradise Gardens' of the East that had so enchanted Alexander begin to appear in Italy. These were in the form of the irrigated pleasure gardens of private Roman villas belonging to the wealthy upper classes. Filled with trees, shrubs and flowers and adorned with fountains, decorative earthenware pots and statuary, they represented, albeit 300 years later, what Alexander had had in mind for Greece.

Neohori Dreaming

From the moment in August 1994 when Mary and I first glimpsed the old stone house in Neohori that was to become our Greek home, we coveted the adjoining plot of land. We knew that more space, particularly outdoor space, would make a big difference to our lives there, principally in summer. However, this plot wasn't especially ideal: it was larger than we needed, highly irregular in shape, contained the remains of a derelict stone house, and had been used as the neighbourhood rubbish dump during the years since it was abandoned by its owners in the 1950s. Several layers of assorted detritus had accumulated, making it difficult to judge what potential existed underneath. On the other hand, it lay directly between our house and a view of the sea, and the prospect of someone else buying the land and building on it caused us some disquiet, not least because that might deprive us of the magical sunsets that no visitor fails to remark on.

The plot also contained some mature trees: two almonds, two citrus and a fig, overlooked by a huge carob tree on an adjacent property. As well as fruit and nuts, they give us a verdant outlook from March to December and shield us from more modern, concrete-framed buildings nearby. We cherish this green vista with a blue fringe – the latter more sky than sea – and the much-valued shade that comes with it. However, what charmed us most was a giant, buttressed, free-standing stone arch, which seemed just one earthquake away from collapse. Formerly the site of a flour mill that had fallen into disuse and disrepair, it had the potential, once strengthened and restored, to provide a regal centrepiece to the plot and bestow a distinctive source of shade and shelter, whatever the season. Even before it became ours, we felt a strange responsibility to preserve this magnificent and rare monument that had the potential to become a unique architectural feature of a future garden. But all that would have to wait: we had the house to restore and make habitable first. And anyway, we were reluctant to commit ourselves to any more expenditure until we were sure that our decision to live part-time in Greece was working out as planned.

As it turned out, events overtook us. In October 1998 – barely a year after we had arrived in Neohori – we were approached by a senior member of the plot's owners; a family who lived on the other side of the village. As its immediate neighbours, it must have been obvious that we might be interested in buying the land. With hindsight, our immediate reaction was probably far too enthusiastic and, in a matter of days and with the help of Nikos, a Greek-American friend who lived in the village, we negotiated a price and shook hands on a deal. Although Mary and I were shortly due to return to the UK for the winter, the offer of a deposit was declined and we agreed to finalise the deal when we returned in the spring. To reassure the vendor of our genuine intent, Nikos half-jokingly declared in both Greek and English that, *"An Englishman's word is his bond!"* Unfortunately, these concluding words would backfire on us.

By the time we returned to Neohori in February 1999, the price of the land had shot up. We were dismayed but promptly declined to pay more than we had agreed four months earlier. Nikos was even more indignant but urged us to be patient and wait for the vendor to see sense and realise that we were the sole neighbours with the urge and resources to purchase this plot of land. It took six months of waiting but then things moved rapidly. Eleni, the youngest of nine and the only female member of the family, took charge. The original price was restored, the plot surveyed and the deal closed at a meeting with the notary public in nearby Kardamyli on October 26th 1999. We drove there in our car with Mary in the front passenger seat clutching a plastic shopping bag full of wads of 5,000-drachma notes and Eleni in the back. After lengthy formalities that involved the contract being read out aloud in Greek and English, witnesses gathered from the street, signatures and official stamps, the money was counted, first by the notary, then by the vendor. When all was seen to be in order, we headed home, but this time it was Eleni clutching the bag of money.

It was another five years before we seriously began to research and plan the hard landscaping and the trees, shrubs and plants that might convert our adjoining land into a garden. We had both grown up in families sustained by fruit and vegetables from gardens assiduously worked by our fathers, and Mary's father had been a professional gardener for assorted landed gentry for most of his working life. However, neither Mary nor I were confident we had absorbed sufficient gardening knowledge to successfully transform a run-down, semi-derelict plot into a pleasure garden, in a climate zone we were still coming to terms with. I had accumulated some gardening experience through jointly working an allotment in south-east London during the 1970s and subsequently with a long thin garden in Torrington that I had reclaimed from the semi-wild. But equally, this experience was confined almost exclusively to producing fruit and vegetables. Fortunately, a couple of post-retirement winters working on North Devon projects with friend Colin, a landscape gardener with a background at Kew and RHS Rosemoor, introduced me to a range of temperate flowering plants, ornamental grasses and trees, shrubs and climbers. The challenge was to research and find Mediterranean equivalents.

Nature's Garden

Greece is one of the world's biodiversity hotspots, with a range of flora unsurpassed for such a small country. More than 600 species are unique. A springtime visit reveals the abundance of flowering plants decorating the roadsides, fields, shorelines and mountainsides with an artist's palette of natural colour. Colour is also the main ingredient for less indigenous plants that prosper in pots on crowded urban balconies, in brightly painted discarded olive cans on whitewashed village walls, and on steps, doorways and courtyards throughout the country. Most Greeks take advantage of their obliging climate and decorate their home environs in these simple but effective ways. Yet Greece's authentic biodiversity is found elsewhere: in the wildscapes of Greece where human interference with nature has been minimal and where a range of natural habitats and ecosystems can be found that have evolved slowly over thousands of years.

'*The predominance of evergreen trees and shrubs; the abundance of small, often grey-leaved aromatic shrubs; the short-lived flush of brightly coloured annuals and bulbous plants in spring, followed by another flush when rains return in early winter*' is how Oleg Polunin – one of the foremost British botanists of his generation – summarises Mediterranean natural vegetation in his 1980 seminal book, *Flowers of Greece and the Balkans*. More specifically, he identifies the natural vegetation of the Mani Peninsula as a combination of evergreen forest, maquis, frigana (traditionally spelt phrygana in English) and pseudo-steppe, thus aligning it with that of other coastal regions of southern and central Greece, and many of the islands. The distribution of these different vegetation zones depends on a host of factors. Foremost are altitude, geology, aspect, gradient and soil depth, while prolonged human activity and repeated wildfires have dramatically altered what grows in some areas.

Maquis and frigana are the two commonest types of natural vegetation in the Mani Peninsula. Whereas botanists can readily distinguish one from the other, for the average layperson their different identities are not easy to appreciate. Both are dense scrubland and almost impenetrable for humans. They occupy similar habitats, which stretch from the upper margins of cultivated areas where conditions have dissuaded farmers from claiming more land from the wild, right up to an altitude of about 900 metres where evergreen forests begin to dominate. Two differences stand out. The maquis is taller, reaching two to three metres high, and composed of hard-leaved evergreen shrubs like laurel, juniper, myrtle, broom and heather. Except when it exhibits a blush of springtime colour, it remains a uniform green. Frigana, on the other hand, has a more grey-green colour and is composed of more scattered, low-growing shrublets with small, leathery leaves on short spiny branches. Its plants are typically thickset and compact and include varieties of cistus, vetch, daphne and phlomis, along with thyme, spurge, oregano, lavender and sage. Some are aromatic but few reach more than fifty centimetres in height. It is these frigana plants in flower in springtime that are responsible for the stunning displays of colour on Greek hillsides.

Above 900 metres in the Mani, maquis and frigana merge into evergreen forest of Aleppo and Calabrian pines underlain by tall shrubs like kermes and holm oaks, carob and wild olive. Higher still are large, mature stands of Black Pine and Cephalonian Fir; while on the summits of the Taygetos Mountains, which reach 2,404 metres at their highest point, scattered alpine plants re-emerge amongst the bare rock and loose stones, once the winter snows have melted. This is the pseudo-steppe zone Polunin refers to. These zones of natural vegetation take a long time to establish but can be quickly destroyed if the delicate balance within their environments is fundamentally changed by natural or human forces. In these cases, other more mixed, less distinctive zones of vegetation can evolve. The small stands of tall, pencil thin cypress trees that tourists often associate with Greece are native to the islands of the eastern Aegean and Crete, but elsewhere they are probably introduced or naturalised. In recent years they have been liable to attack by a virulent canker that results in dieback and eventual death. Sadly, the evidence is widespread.

For North Europeans, the seasons in southern Greece can be somewhat bemusing. Of course, the sequence is the same and there is no reversal of summer and winter months as in the southern hemisphere, but somehow they require a reappraisal of what happens when. Most fundamentally, it is coming to terms with the heat and drought of the Greek summer being the equivalent of the cold and wet of the North European winter and the season when plant growth is at a standstill. The first rains of autumn, as well as generating a universal sigh of relief amongst the population, have a profound effect on the Greek countryside, triggering a rapid reawakening of Mother Nature, known to Greeks as their 'Second Spring'. Grasses revive, seeds germinate and slowly some colour returns to the hitherto parched waysides, fields and olive groves. In the Mani, sea squills send their slim flowering stalks skywards from huge bulbs, and the bush-like tree spurges, seemingly drained of life and nondescript throughout the summer, show the first tiny signs of revival. At surface level, clumps of golden sternbergias, pale pink crocuses and purple-pink cyclamen confirm the restart of nature's annual cycle.

Except in the mountainous interior, Mani winters are usually short-lived, with only a few days and nights when temperatures hover close to freezing point. The peaks of the Taygetos Mountains can sometimes retain a covering of snow until April but at sea level signs of spring arrive early – sometimes within just a few weeks of the winter solstice – and creep upwards and inland as days lengthen and average temperatures increase. The blossom on almond trees, which ranges from pure white to bold pink, is an early sign. A single mature almond tree in full bloom on a distant hillside, spotlighted by a ray of morning sunshine and viewed against the background of a purple-black threatening sky, remains one of the most vivid and enduring images of my first Mani spring in 1998. It was like a glistening diamond set in a black velvet-lined box. Springtime in Greece is a botanist's dream: a cornucopia of flowering plants carpets fields, olive groves, islets, hills and mountainsides. Even abandoned industrial sites and wasteland are rapidly transformed. Who needs gardens when nature provides colour and form in such wild profusion?

The stunning sequence of natural colour in springtime features a cast of thousands, too numerous to be mentioned individually. For me, the stars of the show are Bermuda buttercups (oxalis) that cover the floors of olive groves with a carpet of sunshine-induced, dazzling bright yellow. They are aggressive colonisers but where they fail to establish total domination, small patches of scarlet and purple anemones and poppies interrupt the monochrome. On wayside verges and abandoned farmland, candelabra-like asphodels cast their rheumy eyes over orchids, irises, fritillaries, grape hyacinths, dainty field marigolds, daisies and wild aubrietia that favour less competition. As spring progresses, hitherto anonymous, low-growing evergreen bushes and shrubs of the maquis and frigana declare their presence. Swathes of gold-flowered Jerusalem sage and purple-flowered common sage compete to dominate the flanks of hills and mountains, and tree spurges adopt their bright green 'pin-cushion' climax forms. The first flowerings of the imperious verbascum or great mullein signal the beginning of the end of springtime. Standing tall above other vegetation and especially common on road verges and waysides, its yellow flowers slowly blossom from bottom to top of a single rod-like stalk. Groups of great mullein in full flower never fail to grab the attention of passers-by.

Summer is heralded by the flowering of clumps of purple thyme, of bright yellow spiny spurges with their dense network of wire netting-like stems, and of rock roses, confusingly members of the cistus, not the rosa, family. Found growing in rocky nooks and crannies at mid-altitudes and adorned with pink and white flowers with eye-catching yellow centres, rock roses are low-growing, aromatic evergreen shrubs that embrace bright sunshine. High summer in Greece is a period of dormancy for many flowering plants. They adapt to the heat and drought in a variety of ways: annuals die but not before dispersing their seed, while bulbs hide below soil level, having accumulated nutrients and water during their growing period. Some plants have evolved specialised leaves that perform a variety of sun-repelling and water conservation features, while others lose their leaves entirely, becoming no more than skeletons.

However, there are some plants that seem to relish the onset of the unrelenting heat and drought of the Greek summer. The roadside verges between Neohori and Stoupa exhibit a curious summer mix – not necessarily typical – of both native plants and exotic intruders. Almost certain to be a candidate for the leading role when Disney makes an animated movie of the plant world's fight-back against humanity, the giant prickly pear is a member of the cactus family. With its egg-shaped fruit perched precariously on the edge of its leathery, paddle-shaped, prickly stems, it has no trouble surviving – one of the reasons it is so invasive when not kept under control. The chaste tree, more a shrub than a tree and resembling a huge, blue-rinsed porcupine, with its abundant aromatic flower spikes, is another roadside adornment in summer. It gets its name from the supposed anti-aphrodisiac properties of its seeds, which were used by priests and monks in the past to curb their carnal instincts. Oleanders are in their spectacular floriferous prime in summer. Many are planted as colourful and effective natural screens, but others have self-seeded from within the long pods that hang from these bushes in autumn. Two tropical intruders, probably escapees from cultivation, also seem to relish summer conditions. The exotic-looking castor oil plant with its large, glossy, star-shaped leaves and its upright, bristly red flower heads never fails to attract the attention of passing tourists. But beware – its seeds are poisonous, as is the milky sap of the oleander. The other common interloper is the Marvel of Peru, or four o'clock plant, one of my roadside favourites. Rarely growing beyond fifty centimetres tall, it is thick with flowers that open in late afternoon. Thanks to its ability to self-seed profusely, this roadside adornment has developed an amazing range of bright colours.

A summer stroll through the parched olive groves around Neohori in the relative coolness of early morning contrasts starkly with household gardens, yards and walls in the nearby village, bursting with showy summer colour in the form of bougainvillea, plumbago, jasminiums and pelargoniums. Although bereft of wild plants in flower, the summertime olive grove has its compensations: the blend of aromas that emanate from trodden dried grasses and wild herbs is certainly one. And if you time your walk to follow a burst of summer rain, the scent is almost intoxicating.

Greek Gardens

Although many Greeks, especially those living in rural communities, would rightly claim to be gardeners, their focus has always been on growing vegetables and tree fruit for family consumption. A few pot plants (flowers and herbs) and some easily tended climbers are often considered sufficient outdoor decoration. The widespread cultural norm in temperate Europe for householders to create an ornamental or pleasure garden on their property is not common in Greece, even where the opportunity exists. Garden centres – such big business in Northern Europe – were few and far between when Mary and I first moved to southern Greece in 1997. Today, there are many more and they are well stocked and often run by horticulturalists, able to offer advice and obtain more specialist plants. Things are changing.

Wealthy Greeks who possess large properties and have perhaps been influenced by visiting botanic gardens abroad are investing more time and money in the design and style of their gardens. However, this welcome trend is subject to a shortage of professional landscape designers and gardeners in Greece, which is also the case in several Mediterranean countries. Whereas many Greek universities offer degree courses in agriculture and horticulture, landscape and garden design is under-represented and remains an obscure profession, largely unrecognised by the Greek public at large. Furthermore, Greece has no equivalent of the Royal Horticultural Society in the UK, with its half a million members and £76 million annual budget. The Mediterranean Garden Society, with its headquarters in Athens but branches worldwide, does not even come close to matching it. The RHS, with its flagship garden and research facilities at its Wisley headquarters, its three – soon to be four – regional gardens, its plant awards system, its training and education programmes and its famous annual flower shows, like those at Chelsea and Tatton Park, is a powerful force in promoting gardening and horticulture in the UK.

Nor does Greece possess many outstanding botanic gardens. Europe contains about 2,000, of which Greece is home to just fifteen, owned and operated by universities, local authorities, foundations, research institutes and environmental societies. For a country acknowledged as a biodiversity hotspot, it is surprising that Greece has relatively few botanic gardens. Maybe it can be partly explained by the well-known cliché that the whole of Greece is a garden.

Variously described as 'the lungs of the city', 'a peaceful, green refuge' and 'a lush oasis', the National Garden is probably the most well-known of Greece's botanic gardens. Commissioned as a Royal Garden in 1838 by Queen Amalia, it occupies a flat, twenty-four-hectares site in Central Athens that in antiquity was part of the sacred grove of Lykeion. Although small compared with many city gardens and parks – Central Park in New York City is 341 hectares and London's Hyde Park is 142 hectares – it provides a haven from the noise, the endless traffic, the hustle and bustle and the harsh concrete and asphalt cityscape that surrounds it. Both Athenians and tourists value its calm, its shade, its wildlife and its all-pervading greenness. Joggers escape traffic fumes, old men play chess, grannies supervise boisterous children and office workers munch their lunches. The National Garden appeals in simple ways to almost everyone.

The original design and planting of the Gardens was undertaken by a French horticulturist, Ludovik Baro, who took advantage of his royal patronage to make use of the Greek Navy to accumulate over 15,000 plants from around the world. The King of Egypt donated palm trees, the Queen of Spain rose bushes from Granada, the emperor of Brazil seventy-five New World trees and shrubs, and the municipality of Sparti gave 300 grafts of lemon, orange and mandarins. Those that survived the journey and the unanticipated rigours of the Attica climate provide the highlight of any visit. Today the National Garden contains over 7,000 trees belonging to 519 species and varieties. Some of the original plantings still exist and are known as 'plant monuments' because of their size and age. The lines of slender, sky-reaching Washingtonia palms, the tall spreading Trees of Heaven and the swollen trunk and huge canopy of the Ombu trees are just a few of the original specimen trees offering botanical interest. As well as exotica, indigenous trees, shrubs and plants are also well represented. While today's National Garden bears more than a passing resemblance to its original form, it has inevitably undergone change and evolution in the 183 years since its inception. The challenge of maintaining the National Garden as a place of harmony and balance as well as botanic merit is a considerable responsibility for the City of Athens authorities.

Realising Our Dream

Four years passed before the restoration of our Greek home in Neohori was complete and Mary and I could begin to turn our attention to converting part of the adjoining land we had purchased in 1999 into a pleasure garden. Three issues loomed large: we were unsure what clearing the site of detritus would reveal, we had limited experience of Mediterranean plants, and we had little appreciation of what variety of weather the Mani's particular brand of Mediterranean climate might bring throughout the year.

Where to start? We needed to establish first principles and decide what kind of garden we wanted. We had vague notions, shaped by summer holiday visits to Mediterranean countries and to prized UK gardens like Christopher Lloyd's at Great Dixter in Sussex and the Beth Chatto Gardens in Essex. We consulted several books and manuals that specialised in mediterranean and dry gardening and slowly a blueprint emerged. We wanted a low maintenance, water-wise garden with some focal points – some hard, some soft; some existing, some to be created. We wanted to use some of the better plants we had already accumulated as well as obtain a range of mainly drought-tolerant perennials, which would include succulents and some indigenous Greek plants. Some hot, summer colour was also desirable. Above all we wanted our garden to have a personality of its own, but at the same time be able to withstand annual periods of neglect while we spent time in our UK home.

The priority, before too many decisions were made, was to clear the site and reveal what lay underneath the mound of building debris and household waste that had accumulated over several decades.

Sometimes working like amateur archaeologists, Mary and I slowly sifted through the layers of detritus, uncovering many discarded items in varying states of decay, which together formed an intriguing tale of 20th-century Greek village life. They included a large number of rubber and plastic shoe soles (the canvas uppers had disintegrated over time), plastic bags containing human hair (the remains of DIY hairdressing?), several cast iron keys, an old-fashioned alarm-clock ravaged by rust except for its brass workings, and, dating back to the 19th century, a battered flintlock pistol minus its stock. We gradually exposed a platform of sandstone bedrock in which a large, neat oval depression had been excavated. Its purpose was revealed after consultation with Yiannis, our elderly Greek neighbour. It had been a flour mill in the past and the human-made depression had housed two horizontal millstones, turned by a donkey or mule in harness. The depth of the depression was shallower than we would have liked – it ranged from just ten to sixty-five centimetres – and we feared it might restrict our future choice of plants. Fortunately, a smaller, more natural depression nearby was somewhat deeper, and it contained some recyclable soil. Apart from pots and some newly constructed raised beds, these depressions would represent the focus of our future plantings.

The next step was to figure out what hard landscaping was necessary. Some things were obvious. The free-standing arch intended as a focal point needed restoring and strengthening, and the dilapidated stone walls on three sides of the site required reconstruction. Furthermore, in order to give the centre of the site some modest height, we planned to build a hollow stone wall in a mock-derelict style (nooks, crannies, ledges and all), and, to make some of the uneven bedrock safe to walk on, we proposed some paving stones and pea gravel. With the occasional – but not inconsiderable – help of two friends, Keith and Kevin, all this was achieved within eighteen months during 2004 and 2005. We put trust in our combined building experiences, used a huge assortment of stone (mostly recycled from within the property) and mixed considerable quantities of mortar. For the most part it was hot, heavy, energy-sapping toil, with sweat-sodden T-shirts the daily norm. At the same time, it was creative and rewarding.

We were keen to preserve and recycle the sandy soil we found in the hollows and depressions of the sandstone bedrock and Mary systematically sifted through it to remove unwanted foreign matter. However, the cubic metre or so we retrieved was considerably less than we needed; and anyway, we were unsure about its quality, even when improved by adding wood ash and easily obtainable goat manure. Fortunately, with a local building boom in full swing, every builders' yard could offer a limited selection of soils – the product of excavating land to construct foundations. In the end we took delivery of two cubic metre bags of contrasting local soils, one of a light brown sandy soil and the other of *terra rossa* – the red, clayey soil so common in limestone areas of the Mediterranean and highly valued. We hoped that we could take advantage of their different qualities. All that remained was the exhausting task of barrowing three tonnes of soil the 100 metres from the small square at the top of our narrow street, where the bags had been delivered, followed by filling the sandstone depressions, the newly constructed raised beds and four giant earthenware pots in time for the winter rains to do their work.

By now it was time to source the plants we needed, get them in the ground and watch them grow. If only it had turned out to be that simple. At the time, the range of plants at Kalamata garden centres was limited and predictable, and only a few featured on our wish list. So, we took a gamble and resorted to bringing bare-rooted plants, bulbs and rhizomes from the UK, carefully prepared and packed in hand luggage. The speed of modern air transport was a critical factor. Provided the plants were reunited with soil, light and air within forty-eight hours, they seemed to survive the trauma with minimal signs of stress. Most of these were brightly coloured, summer-flowering perennials: kniphofias, crocosmias, dahlias, watsonias, tulbaghias, agapanthus, achilleas, cannas and day lilies. All had been comprehensively researched and we were optimistic that they would prosper in their new environment, provided they made a good start. Along with a selection of plants we had received as gifts (mostly succulents) and plants like lavenders, cape honeysuckle and plumbago, which we were able to source from local garden centres, we embarked on a predetermined planting scheme during a month-long stay in Neohori in February 2006. Another gamble was then returning to the UK for nine weeks and neglecting our new plantings as they established themselves.

We also brought with us many packets of seeds from UK suppliers, figuring that seeds germinated and grown on in Greece would more readily adapt to the conditions. These included rudbeckias, salvias, lychnis, knautias, eryngiums, verbenas and zauschnerias, all apparently suited to a Mediterranean climate. Early autumn sowing is the common practice in southern Greece; seeds germinate quickly, easily survive the short, mild winter and – with a little help – have become robust enough by the onset of summer to survive the heat and drought. Or that's the theory. We took a chance with sowing seeds in trays in February 2006 and leaving them with friend Christina to look after in our absence. Thanks more to her assiduous care than our timing, a sufficient number of seedlings survived, which we carefully harboured over the summer before planting them out after the first autumn rains in the spaces that had been left for them.

We returned to Neohori late at night on May 20th 2006, anxious to discover if our gamble, which had seemed increasingly reckless during our nine-week exile, had paid off. Still sleepy-eyed after a strangely restless night, our first impressions from the terrace above were disquieting. The main beds seemed a mass of green growth without any instantly recognisable form, and the deliberate layout of February's careful transplanting proved impossible to identify. Profiting from a warm, wet spring, weeds had taken over, and from a distance, our precious plants were scarcely discernible. However, closer inspection, accompanied by some frantic weeding, quickly revealed that most of them had survived; in fact, healthy growth appeared to have been the norm, with very few casualties. Once fully cleared of weeds, a thick mulch of pea gravel applied and a watering regime installed, we watched these plants grow and develop with heightened expectations. The first summer's display was predictably underwhelming but the stunning show of flowering that followed twelve months later exceeded our wildest dreams. It was just like a TV makeover; even Alan Titchmarsh would have been impressed. Had we been lucky or was our research and decision-making paying off?

Sparoza

Our efforts to create a pleasure garden from the rubbish-strewn site of a former flour mill would have benefitted considerably if Mary and I had known about the Mediterranean Garden Society before we started making plans and putting them into practice. With its worldwide membership, quarterly journal and comprehensive website, the MGS offers its members a host of opportunities to learn from and engage with each other, and to visit other mediterranean gardens of note. The MGS's focal point is Sparoza, a small Greek garden that has inspired many people.

Overlooking the rich, agricultural plain of Spata and only six kilometres from Athens International Airport, Sparoza was fashioned out of an unpromising Attica hillside in the early 1970s. Rectangular in shape, three times as long as it is wide and barely a hectare in size, Sparoza is a miniature gem of a garden, located on an exposed, rocky, limestone slope, tilted towards the south and east. Originally inhabited by dense, prickly, indigenous shrubs as well as scrawny, randomly scattered olive trees, it is relentlessly hot, arid and windy in summer. Even in winter, drought can sometimes be as common as rainfall and severe cold snaps just as debilitating, while the sun-baked alkaline soil – where it occurs – has little to offer. Sparoza was founded by Jaqueline Tyrwhitt. When she died in 1983, the site was bequeathed to the Goulandris Museum of Natural History and subsequently it has been curated by the Mediterranean Garden Society. It has remained at the heart of the MGS ever since.

When Jaqueline Tyrwhitt retired in 1969, she moved from North America, where she had been lecturing in regional and town planning at Toronto and Harvard universities, to her newly constructed house at Sparoza. She had spent many previous summers in Greece and this experience, along with her early training as a horticulturist, inspired her to create a garden from the wild. Jaqueline quickly established a plan of action that included four priorities: to exclude grazing livestock, to sink a borehole to provide irrigation water (so vital if young plants were to survive in their first year), to plant native and exotic trees that would eventually provide shade and shelter from winds as well as create valuable microclimates, and to improve and add to the sparse, thin soil. It might seem a straightforward enough list, but it was not without its challenges. The introduction of trees often required the use of dynamite to break up the bedrock and create planting holes, while soil improvement by strictly organic means involved persuading a local winery to part with the leftovers from grape pressing and a nearby chocolate factory to relinquish the crushed shells from its cocoa bean raw material. By these means, she obtained two additives that enhanced Sparoza's soils in a natural, if somewhat unconventional, way.

It was never Jaqueline's intention to pamper her plants; she was more interested in establishing a test bed in unfavourable conditions for both native and exotic mediterranean plants. *Anything that grew under the difficult conditions prevailing here would be certain to grow better elsewhere*, she declared. However, she knew well enough that giving plants a good start was essential to their survival and the long-term viability of her project. The general layout of the garden has remained virtually intact for almost fifty years. An intensively cultivated middle section surrounding the house and containing an eclectic mix of plants, shrubs and trees from Greece and elsewhere is sandwiched between the northern and southern extremities, where more natural, indigenous environments have been developed. Jaqueline's creative journey, collated in her 1985 book *Making a Garden on a Greek Hillside*, has provided inspiration for all those other gardeners, both Greek and foreign, who have followed in her footsteps.

Following Jaqueline's death in 1983, nine years passed without anything of great note happening to Sparoza. It had not been neglected, neither had it been developed. The late Sally Razelou found the garden 'tidy but limited' when she took up residence as custodian in 1992. The evolution of Sparoza in the twenty-nine years since her arrival has been a labour of love for Sally, resulting in a garden of which her predecessor would surely have been immensely proud. Jaqueline's generous endowment has become Sally's legacy. *'An oasis of beauty, simplicity and horticultural interest and a haven for the annual and perennial flora of Attica'* is how Sally described Sparoza. One of her former garden assistants adds that it possesses *'a sense of nature being gently manipulated to make it more accessible'*.

A sun-blessed personal springtime tour of Sparoza in 2018 was an enlightening and inspirational experience. Sally, then in her eighties but as spritely as someone half her age, led Mary and me slowly through the tree-shaded terraces, highlighting noteworthy plants, of which there are plenty. As well as indicating their botanical names and their native countries, she was able to describe exactly when and how they came to Sparoza and their subsequent growth and flowering history. Sally reminded me of an old-style village schoolmistress proudly introducing each of her varied class of cherished pupils to a visitor. Her encyclopaedic knowledge, her acute memory for detail and her infectious enthusiasm were both inspiring and humbling.

Although Sally was the mainstay of Sparoza's evolution, she would have been the first to admit the important role played by garden assistants and volunteers. Professional gardeners from all over the world come for several months or more as live-in garden assistants, eager to expand their knowledge and experience, both in an environment and with plants hitherto unfamiliar. Others, often local members of the Mediterranean Garden Society – which was founded at Sparoza by Sally and early volunteers – contribute their time, labour and expertise on a regular basis. Many parts of Sparoza bear the imprint of hours of toil by volunteers: plantings, paths, terraces, ponds, the nursery and shade sheds, just to mention a few.

Jennifer Gay was one of the earliest garden assistants. Following postgraduate training at the RHS Rosemoor Gardens in North Devon, she came to Sparoza in 1999 after a spell at the Botanical Gardens in Jerusalem. She stayed for two years and, hand-in-hand with Sally and the band of volunteers, made a significant contribution to Sparoza's development: 'a permanent legacy' is how Sally described it. Jennifer first came to my notice through her articles for the gardening page of the weekly *Athens News*, and the subsequent publication of *Greece, garden of the Gods*, her comprehensive gardening manual that brought together much of the gardening wisdom and knowledge that Jennifer was regularly sharing with her newspaper readership. Although she would probably downplay her contribution, Jennifer is quick to attribute her Sparoza experience as a crucial factor in setting up her and her partner's landscaping business, which is gathering a growing reputation in Greece. She and Piers Goldson (also a former garden assistant at Sparoza) have been involved in several ambitious garden and landscaping projects, including Cephalonia Botanica, the Kassiopia Estate and Rou Estate gardens on Corfu, and the Holy Gardens of Patmos. Her encyclopaedic knowledge of Mediterranean plants and her unerring instinct for successfully merging existing indigenous plants with imported exotics have served her well.

What Went Wrong?

Mary and I were astounded at the impressive display of garden colour in the late spring and early summer of 2007 that resulted from our initial plantings in February 2006. All our tireless excavation of the site, our importing of soil, our research and planning, and our decision to bring packets of seeds and bare-rooted plants from the UK seemed to have been vindicated. But this euphoria was short-lived. The succession of garden colour in the spring and summer of

2008 never matched the previous year's. A number of plants failed to survive their second winter and of those that did, few flowered with the same vigour as previously. This pattern continued in the fourth year with dwindling numbers and lacklustre displays. What had happened to our well-laid plans for a jamboree of summer colour in our Neohori garden? It was turning out to be more like a winter wake than a summer party.

There are survivors that have repaid our trust. They include the small fremontodendron tree festooned with orange-coloured blossom every spring, the two sweetly scented climbing roses (*rosa banksiae*) and the majestic canna lilies in their pots. The royal blue agapanthus responded well to being transferred from ground to pots, while the clumps of achilleas and tulbaghias have adapted successfully and continue to thrive. The only seedlings to survive have been the scarlet lychnis coronaria that flowers and self-seeds so profusely, but only thanks to regular watering throughout the arid summer. Disappointingly, the intended stars of the show – the crocosmias, the dahlias, the kniphofias, the day lilies and the watsonias – all perished, leaving scarcely a trace but prompting much soul-searching on our part.

During those years of disappointment, we searched desperately for quick fixes, like moving plants in early spring to where they might profit from less direct sunlight or more slowly draining soil, and filling gaps with replacements from our own modest plant nursery. But gradually we came to accept that our strategy was flawed and that a different approach was necessary. So, what had gone wrong? For sure, our long periods of absence, when only cursory surveillance of the garden by friends or neighbours occurred, was a strong contributory factor. It could never be an adequate substitute for daily scrutiny, when matters of concern can be attended to promptly.

Our decision to 'import' plants from the UK that were not available locally was novel but took no account of the impact of plant breeding over many years to allow these plants to accommodate British conditions. We had foolishly imagined that if common British weeds like nettles, thistles, goosegrass, mallow, deadly nightshade and bindweed thrived in our Greek garden, then some British summer-flowering perennials might do likewise, especially if they had ancestry in mediterranean lands. How wrong that notion turned out to be. We also believed that occasional brief extremes of weather – heat waves during a long summer drought or a bitterly cold northerly airstream following a period of winter rain, neither totally uncommon in southern Greece, were enough to account for some of our plants. One such cold snap had killed off a large, ancient, much-admired but fatally exposed bright purple bougainvillea beside Neohori's mini-market in February 1999.

Watering was another key issue. Living in a part of Greece where summer drought is prolonged and water is a precious resource not to be used indiscriminately, we quickly embraced the concept of water-wise gardening. As well as directing rainwater from roofs and terraces to the garden, we installed time-controlled irrigation systems but, except for those watering pots, they were dismantled once plants had established themselves and we judged them capable of surviving independently. But, with hindsight, I think we deprived some plants of summer watering too soon. But that was only part of the equation. Close examination of a couple of dying plants revealed alarmingly underdeveloped root systems. The shallow recycled soil sitting on very porous sandstone bedrock meant that both rainwater and irrigation water drained away so quickly that plants were deprived of much of its benefit. In fact, surface roots, quickly absorbing irrigation water before it evaporated, had become much more developed than the tap roots, which should have found residual water even in summer, had the soil been deeper and less free-draining. The lesson that taught us was that deep watering for, say, ten minutes per week is much more effective than short daily bursts of watering that barely penetrates the surface layers. 'Little but often', an approach so appropriate in many circumstances, is best avoided.

So, what could we have done differently? Although we thought our research was thorough, it did not focus enough on plants with tried-and-tested mediterranean pedigrees. One big regret is not joining the Mediterranean Garden Society earlier and thereby benefitting from members' experience and advice, which might have made us more grounded and realistic in our planning. What's more, we might have come across Olivier Filippi sooner. A well-respected plantsman from the south of France, he is the author of the acclaimed *A Dry Gardening Handbook*. He first came to our attention at the annual symposium of the MGS in Athens in November 2007. In an inspirational audio-visual presentation, he enthusiastically promoted indigenous Mediterranean plants, lampooned attempts to create temperate gardens and lawns in a mediterranean setting, ridiculed the widespread obsession with irrigation systems, and highlighted the twin importance of soil and root development. Filippi's gardening philosophy is simple: embrace drought, don't fight it. It is a powerful and well-argued theme of his comprehensive and lavishly illustrated book that has become a bible for those mediterranean gardeners who espouse his views. Whether adopting his approach to our situation would have worked any better is open to question. It certainly provided food for thought.

There's little doubt that our plans were too ambitious. Our determination to make our Greek garden different – a British herbaceous border in a Greek setting – was hopelessly optimistic. At the outset we fondly imagined a fusion of Home Counties and Greek garden styles might work but we soon learned otherwise as our botanical and horticultural shortcomings were exposed. With hindsight, we would have been better off dismissing the crazy and somewhat dubious notion of importing plants in hand-luggage – 'phoney imposters', as someone called them – and have searched more widely in Greece for sources of a more interesting and obscure selection of indigenous Mediterranean plants. Our choice of plants could also have taken more account of our pattern of absence.

Then there was the decision to recycle the soil that we found when clearing the site. Might it not have been better to have discarded that and filled all the beds with *terra rossa*, purchased from builders' yards, with its much greater moisture-retaining properties? If we hadn't been so precious about preserving intact the imprint of the former flour mill, some modest amount of dynamite – à la Sparoza – or some energetic activity with a pneumatic drill would have deepened the depressions in the sandstone bedrock and made them more able to accommodate shrubs and bushes. And should we have taken more note of the micro-variations within our small garden – the day-long sunlit super-hot spots in summer and the cold, dank sunless corners in winter – and the way certain plants can be quite choosy? I tried growing a trailing Santolina (cotton lavender) in three different locations (including a pot) before happening on a spot where it finally prospered. In the end, any review of what we might have done differently always returns to the same issue: watering. Given the limitations of soil depth and free drainage, how wise was it to have been water-wise?

Putting it Right

The very nature of pleasure gardens demands that their plants and layout are regularly reviewed as some plants become too big or come to the end of their natural lifespan while others disappoint or fail to survive a cold, wet winter or a hot, dry summer. Sometimes it's simply a matter of refreshing part of a garden when it becomes tired-looking with ageing plants that have passed their best. In more extreme cases, a complete makeover under the auspices of a professional landscape gardener is desirable.

The changes to our Neohori garden since its inception in 2006 have been largely in response to plants dying or disappointing. Otherwise, the overall layout remains much the same. The centrepiece is still the former flour mill that we converted into a pleasure garden. It sits in between a broad terrace containing almond, citrus and eating olive trees that provide a year-round verdant backcloth, and is overlooked by our two-storey stone house and its veranda terrace, clad with bougainvillea and star jasmine and the home of pots containing a raft of different plants from agapanthus to russelia. Our pleasure garden has always been pocket-handkerchief size, square-shaped with stone walls on three sides and the free-standing arch on the other. One stone wall harbours four huge earthenware pots containing flamboyant canna plants; the other two are softened by an ancient gnarled fig tree and by a wisteria, while the solid buttresses of the free-standing arch support two aromatic, pale yellow climbing roses. Essentially, it's a green-clad stone box with the sky as a blue lid – not something that common in southern Greece.

Although they had always been part of our original plan, especially where soil was thin or suspect, we only intended succulents to perform minor roles in a supporting cast. The 'imported' perennials were going to be the stars of the show. Succulents are commonplace in southern Greek gardens and yards and comprised at least half of the plant gifts we had received from friends and neighbours. Prior to our arrival in Greece, we had only a vague knowledge of the amazing range of size, form and flowering habits of succulents and they hadn't featured in our research. The only ones vaguely familiar to us were those in small pots on sale in supermarkets and DIY stores in the UK, and intended as easy-maintenance, trouble-free houseplants.

With more familiar plants failing to flourish as we would have liked in our Neohori garden, we have taken much more notice of succulents. We have discovered that many varieties of agaves, aloes, aeoniums, crassulas and echeverias create a variety of form and interest throughout the gardening year and we have been surprised to find that so many flower. Today, our garden contains succulents that range from ground-hugging creepers like the dewplant, with its blue-green, chunky 'leaves' and fragrant pink flowers, to the bushy aeonium Schwartkopf with its multiple rosettes of purple leaves, to the American agave, often known as the century plant. In its variegated form, this makes an eye-catching pot plant with its upstanding, sharply pointed, cutlass-shaped thorny leaves and surrounded by a host of offspring. These days, the centrepiece of our garden is dominated by succulents, with just two clumps of strelitzias with their palm-like leaves and stunning bird of paradise flowers augmenting their appeal.

Succulents have proved worthy substitutes for the 'imported' perennials that betrayed our misguided trust, but they are complemented by survivors from the original plantings and by a range of other newcomers. Most of them have been obtained from local garden centres, which in recent years have expanded and diversified their range of plants. In the beds where our 'imported' plants prospered and then promptly perished, clivias with their conspicuous orange, multi-flower blooms form an upstanding evergreen backcloth to the more delicate, red-flowered salvias. A persistent summer-flowering lantana shrub, content to grow against a sunny stone wall, is fronted by trios of pink-flowered gaura and the mauve spikes of perovskia, while a row of spider plants in small pots and overhung by the wisteria provide the background to a mix of red-flowered sphaeralcea and the numerous orange spikes of the spring- and autumn-flowering bulbines. It's a far cry from what we originally planned but an interesting potpourri of size, shape, form and colour, and much more sustainable.

We are certainly proud of what we have achieved. Without too much expenditure and largely through our own toil, we have fashioned a hidden garden that generates gasps of surprise and appreciation when visitors first clap eyes upon it. We have not been afraid of experimenting or of failure, taking to heart the late Beth Chatto's advice in her book *The Dry Garden*. We have created a haven for relaxation and engaging in uninterrupted pleasures like reading, listening to music, writing emails, snoozing or just daydreaming. Offering shade from the full force of the sun in summer, yet in winter sheltering us from cooling winds at the same time as admitting the lower sun's rays, the giant arch offers year-round comforts. Eclipsing all else is the tableau of succulents, flowering plants, shrubs and trees that we have planted and nurtured, responding to the passage of the seasons and the ever-changing light and breeze. Only the disturbing presence of mosquitoes and the continual drone of cicadas in summer can diminish a comforting sense of wellbeing. Pottering in this garden in the early morning or evening hours is a gentle, absorbing, pleasurable pastime: no muddy boots, cold hands or wet jumpers here. A garden fashioned from a Greek hillside with indigenous and exotic plants replicating and embellishing nature might be an appealing objective for some, but we had little choice: we inherited a shady 'brownfield' site much modified by humankind before we transformed it into a garden. I sometimes wonder what the women of Sparoza might have made of it.

Gathering storm over the Gulf of Messinia

Chapter 3

EVERY PRECIOUS DROP

First Impressions

Hydra (pronounced 'eedra') was my first experience of a Greek island, in the summer of 1969. Variously described as the most charming, the most laid-back, the most romantic, the most atmospheric tourist destination in Greece, Hydra is a small island on the western fringes of the Aegean Sea, just a fifteen-minute ferry ride from the nearby Peloponnese mainland or up to two hours by sea from Piraeus, the port of Athens. Hydra's bare, rugged limestone profile rises out of the Argo-Saronic Gulf like a whaleback. Despite having few sandy beaches and just one main settlement, it is a quintessential Greek island resort that attracts hundreds of thousands of visitors each year, who consume vast quantities of water.

Considering the name of the island is derived from the Ancient Greek word for 'water', you would think it safe to assume that this demand could be easily satisfied. However, the ancient springs that prompted the adoption of the name were never numerous and often seasonal. Today they are almost all dry. It's as though the first inhabitants of Hydra were just as keen as those early Greenlanders to coin a dubious name to attract other settlers to join them in a fairly inhospitable place. For many centuries, collecting winter rainfall in underground cisterns supplemented the spring supply and provided enough water to satisfy demand in a normal year. But the boom in tourism, which started in the '60s, required a radical new approach.

Many vivid memories of my first visit to Hydra have survived the intervening years. One concerns the regular arrival of water from the mainland, a vital ingredient for locals and tourists alike. In those days, water was transported to the island in a giant black rubber 'sausage' towed by a tug that moored in the outer harbour. From there, the water was pumped to tanks high up above the town and gravity flow through a network of steel pipes did the rest. As tourism on Hydra has flourished, the demand for water has risen exponentially. These days, according to the *hydradirect* website, between three and a half and four million bottles of drinking water are imported to the island every year. The opening of a desalination plant in August 2014 created a large and more reliable supply of water but is unlikely to much diminish the import of bottled water with all its related cost, logistics and recycling implications. It seems that many tourists continue to be wary of consuming drinking water straight from the tap.

The Vikos brand strapline, '*Natural Mineral Water. From the spring and from the heart*', is fairly typical for Greek bottled water, stressing its pure origins and alluding to its health-giving properties. Bottled water is big business in Greece and very competitive. Lots of intense and persistent advertising using a range of conventional media is the norm, with the dominant brands like Avra, Vikos, Loutraki and Zagori all keen to maintain their market share. But now and again an interloper arrives on the scene. A new and relatively unknown company from near Karditsa in western Thessaly has recently been claiming all the quality and taste awards at a number of international competitions. Theony is the brand name of this natural mineral water, which is obtained from the Gouras springs, found on the eastern flanks of the Pindos Mountains. On its website, the company describes the chemical properties of its water, which it claims has a pH value of 8 (7 is neutral), a balanced hardness (113 mg per litre), low content of sodium, nitrates and chlorine, and an absence of heavy metals. But when you're parched and desperate for a drink, the make-up of the water is probably the last thing on your mind. If it's cool and refreshing and quenches your thirst, why concern yourself overmuch with the small print on the label?

Precipitation

For people considering a summer holiday in Greece, the possibility of rain doesn't come into the reckoning. One of Greece's many attractions is the reliability of its weather during the months of June, July and August. Daytime temperatures that consistently soar above 30°C and cloudless blue skies with endless sunshine are the summer norms. It's a sun-worshipper's paradise. Rainfall is definitely a freak occurrence during these long, hot, dry Mediterranean summers. Drought conditions prevail, which pose challenges for authorities entrusted with providing a reliable and good-quality water supply.

Although water is a precious commodity that needs to be carefully conserved and managed, Greece as a whole cannot be described as a dry country. A small country by many standards – its land area is very similar to England's – it nonetheless has a much broader geographical spread due to its many islands dispersed across the three seas that surround the mainland. It is this spread that helps to explain the great variation in rainfall from one part of Greece to another.

The mountain ranges that form the backbone of mainland Greece and extend from the Albanian border in the north all the way south to the island of Crete divide the country into two major rainfall regions: the water-rich west and the semi-arid east. In mountainous areas of western Greece, the mean annual rainfall exceeds 2,000 millimetres, whereas in eastern regions of the mainland and in the Aegean islands it can be as little as 500 millimetres. Surprisingly, these figures roughly correspond with those for high and low rainfall districts in England – the Lake District and East Anglia, for example. The small town of Astros, which overlooks the Argolikos Gulf, lies in the rain shadow of the Peloponnese mountains and is one of the driest places on mainland Greece. On average it experiences just thirty-nine days of rain each year, producing an annual total of 491 millimetres. By contrast, Ioannina, the capital city of the north-west region of Epirus and at a height above sea level of 500 metres, receives double Astros' annual rainfall, and it is spread over 124 days.

Of course, the annual rainfall totals and number of days with rain only form part of the picture; the rainfall season is just as important. In Greece it's the winter months that bring the rain, but as a rule it is less frequent, less prolonged and more intense than winter rainfall regimes in Northern Europe. Snow is not uncommon in Greece in January and February, extending into low altitude locations in northern Greece while normally confined to mountain tops in the Peloponnese and Crete. Mary and I were stopped in our tracks during a day trip to Thessaloniki, the second city of Greece, during a family holiday in Halkidiki in August 1984. Red-faced and perspiring freely, we were astonished to pass a series of small shops near the railway station that specialised in two main products: vehicle batteries and snow chains. The chains were dangling like Christmas decorations from the ceiling of the shop window, creating an incongruous picture at the height of a Greek summer.

Rainfall is the consequence of the interplay of several factors. The topography of the land, distance from the sea, prevailing winds, intense heating of the land surface and changing atmospheric pressure all play their part. In Greece, the sharp contrast between rainfall patterns in summer and winter is largely due to weather systems associated with the forever-changing patterns of atmospheric pressure. In summer, a strong ridge of high pressure commonly establishes itself over the Balkan peninsula, bringing very settled, dry conditions. In winter, the polar jet stream – high velocity, meandering, upper air winds, which are known to strongly influence weather patterns – can curve south into the Mediterranean Basin, creating east-moving centres of low pressure and cyclonic disturbances. These are primarily responsible for Greece's winter rainfall.

Detailed studies of data over the last fifty years have revealed that rainfall norms in Greece are changing, exposing disturbing trends that, if sustained, could prove a barrier to development in some parts of Greece, especially the smaller Aegean islands. It seems that there has been a decline in the annual rainfall across the whole of Greece, which is most pronounced in the west and north of the country. Furthermore, the duration of the winter rainy season has become shorter, especially across the mainland, and rainfall seems to be occurring in less predictable, more intense and more destructive episodes than in the past. These rainfall trends are unlikely to reduce the attraction of Greece for summer tourists yearning for a fortnight of reliable sunshine, but they will create additional pressure on water supply during peak demand periods.

Extreme Phenomena

'Ακραία Φαινομενα' ('Extreme Phenomena') is a phrase beloved of Greek headline writers, especially when news of exceptional weather events makes the front pages. However, more down-to-earth terms confronted readers of Kalamata's daily newspapers *Eleftheria* and *Tharros* as they scanned the headlines on the morning of September 8th 2016. *'We're Drowning'*, *'Cataclysm'*, *'Three Deaths'*, *'Colossal Damage to Houses, Vehicles and Farmland'*, *'Grief and Desperation'*, *'Saved by an Act of God'* were just a selection, summing up the devastating outcome of twelve hours of almost continuous heavy rain, accompanied by violent thunder and lightning, which had crippled Kalamata and the whole of the prefecture of Messinia the previous night.

A wide and deep depression that had tracked south-eastwards across Western Europe on Sunday and Monday, September 4th and 5th, continued across Italy and the Adriatic Sea, and by the night of September 6th was centred on the Ionian Sea, where it remained stationary for two or three more days. At the same time it intensified, with moisture-laden warm air circulating in a clockwise vortex over most of mainland Greece, the Balkans and southern Italy. Greek weather forecasters had anticipated the passage and duration of the depression and predicted heavy rainfall accompanied by thunder and lightning. However, they had underestimated the intensity of the rainfall. Records for the four days reveal that an amazing volume of water fell from the sky, most of it in the twelve hours between 8pm on Tuesday evening and 8am on Wednesday morning. Arfara, a village north of Kalamata, reported 279 millimetres, Kardamyli 186 millimetres, and Kalamata 162 millimetres. John Phipps' hobby weather station in Neohori recorded 252 millimetres of rain – that's over ten inches and in only twelve hours!

We had arranged for North Devon friends Jan and Fred, on holiday in Stoupa, to join us for a meal at home in Neohori on the evening of September 6th. The decision to chance eating outside on our covered terrace turned out to be ill-judged. The distant thunder and lightning that had punctuated the first course quickly gained ground and, in no time, the intensity of the neon flashes and the lung-crunching compression of air accompanying the thunderclaps indicated that the centre of the storm had stationed itself right above our village. A sharp squall of wind and rain sent us scurrying headlong inside clutching plates, cutlery and drinks. The meal resumed with minimal delay but the heavy, relentless rain that hammered down on our roof proved a constant distraction and made conversation difficult; it was like eating in a tent. Between courses we could not resist adjourning to the veranda to witness this spectacular force of nature at work. The haunting, strangely melodic sound of rainwater draining off the roof into the metal guttering contrasted with the persistent, thumping explosions of thunderclaps. It was as if a wind chime and a First World War field gun were vying in their opposing ways for our attention, with a spectacular light show thrown in for good measure.

Fortunately, Jan and Fred had previously accepted our invitation to stay the night. Driving back to their accommodation in Stoupa in these conditions would have been a risky exercise. Although our bedrooms are in the semi-subterranean basement of the house and have thick stone walls and vaulted ceilings, the persistent claps of thunder penetrated my consciousness time and time again, despite my best efforts to get to sleep. As the night wore on the thunderclaps abated, but were replaced by the menacing, tuneless downrush of huge volumes of rainwater in our downpipes. As the rain eased and dawn emerged, I became aware of a disturbing, alien noise that I was unable to comprehend. A squint-eyed reference to my bedside clock persuaded me it was time to investigate.

Exiting our bedroom, I crossed our small yard and tentatively opened the steel gate to the street. In front of my eyes was a raging torrent, deeper, wider and faster flowing than I had ever seen. We are used to our street becoming a temporary stream as a consequence of summer/autumn storms or more prolonged periods of rain in winter. The noise it makes is gentle and familiar; this looked much more threatening. The street dog-legs around our house and this had generated vicious rip currents that instantly reminded me of TV coverage of the kayak course at the Rio Olympics. Despite the fifteen-centimetre stone lip against which our street gate shuts, there were clear signs that the flood water had been deeper earlier in the night and had forced itself under the gate. Fortunately, it had flowed away safely into the garden through a strategically placed drain hole in the base of an outside wall and had left our bedroom high and dry.

It wasn't long before Fred joined me. He was keen to go beyond the house and witness for himself some of the consequences of the night's events. Wearing a rarely used pair of my wellington boots and advised to proceed with extreme caution, he gingerly edged his way out of the gate, avoiding the deepest water and strongest current. Reminding me somewhat of Neil Armstrong's first moonwalk, Fred's progress up our narrow street was understandably ponderous, hindered by the strong oncoming rush of water, which necessitated taking small steps while clinging to the street-side stone walls. An attempt to cross to the other side of the street filled one wellington boot with water and nearly toppled him but eventually he arrived at the small square at the top of the street. Here he found Vangellis, our village shopkeeper and Stoupa restaurateur, re-parking his white van in a less vulnerable spot. With a grim smile and in broken English, he muttered to Fred, "Our village has become like Venice." Thinking Fred was about to drive off in one of the adjacent parked cars he quickly added, "The road to Stoupa is closed – no cars can get through." The full extent of the destruction and damage was yet to become apparent.

Much to the amazement and disbelief of a full contingent of late summer tourists, Stoupa had been badly hit. What had their favourite holiday resort done to deserve such a battering? Many premises, including Vangellis and Dina's Riviera restaurant, suffered rain, silt and floodwater damage, and the beach was badly eroded, with beach beds and umbrellas rudely desecrated. The most serious outcome of the storm was to be found on the 'Laundry Road', a concreted riverbed linking the Kalamata-Areopolis main road and the sea front. Concreting a riverbed to use as a road might seem like asking for trouble but, covering a distance of only 500 metres, it rarely flows with water and even then, it's often just a trickle. But these circumstances were abnormal and extreme.

Some locals declared they hadn't experienced rainfall like it since November 21st 1993. The last twenty years' building boom in the catchment area has diminished nature's ability to absorb rainfall. The proliferation of hard surfaces – roofs, patios, paths and roads – have concentrated and hastened rainwater's run-off to stream and river courses and thence to the sea. In this case, the sheer volume of rainfall and its cumulative power, once channelled, converted the normally placid 'Laundry Road' into a roaring, violent torrent that created havoc. At least seven parked vehicles, including three white vans belonging to

Mani Pools – a swimming pool supplies and maintenance business – were swept up by the fast-moving and powerful waters and deposited in the sea in Stoupa Bay. Even the low concrete bridge that carries the seafront road failed to act as a barrier for long; the erosive power of the turbulent water burrowed away at the riverbed beneath it until the vehicles were released to their saltwater fate.

Amazingly, Stoupa took less than forty-eight hours to recover and by the time the next batch of visitors arrived, there was little remaining evidence of the catastrophe that had befallen the resort just a few days earlier. With some difficulty, the 'drowned' vehicles, some weighed down by quantities of sand, were winched from the sea by heavy lifting gear. Divers searched the seabed for remaining debris while skilfully manoeuvred, pirouetting 'Bobcats' (mini-earthmovers) restored the beach to its normal profile, allowing beach beds and umbrellas to be reinstated. The flooded basement of Riviera restaurant was pumped out and crockery, glassware and other durables recovered. However, significant quantities of fresh fruit and vegetables had become unfit for human consumption and, along with defrosted frozen food and the un-repairable large freezers, were loaded onto lorries and removed to landfill sites. Silt had infiltrated everything; even piles of new plates with paper dividers possessed a thin layer of silt between each one. To everyone's surprise and much to the credit of Vangellis, Dina and their staff, Riviera reopened for the last six weeks of the season. Subsequently, new solid steel shutters with robust rubber seals have been installed to prevent any repeat of this unwelcome and depressing episode. Only time will tell if they are a wise and effective investment. Global warming and climate change are likely to increase the frequency and intensity of such extreme weather episodes.

Water Cycle

Also known as the hydrological cycle, the water cycle represents the continuous and natural movement of moisture from sky to land, from land to sea, from sea to sky and from sky back to land again. It comprises four main processes: precipitation, land drainage, evaporation and condensation, during which water changes state from a liquid to a gas, from a gas to a solid and then back to a liquid again. In some extreme cases it can involve a round trip of several hundred kilometres. In other cases, the cycle is more localised and more vertical than horizontal, the result of intense heating of the land surface. This causes rapid evaporation and evapotranspiration (evaporation from trees, shrubs and plants) and stimulates the kind of conditions that make clothes dry rapidly on a washing line. Sometimes it can generate strong moisture-laden thermals that form towering cumulus clouds, which are capable of delivering short, sharp thunderstorms.

Together, evaporation and evapotranspiration seriously deplete the water volumes provided by precipitation in Greece and throughout the world's subtropical zones. On Milos, a horseshoe-shaped island in the southern Aegean Sea and the original home of the famous Venus de Milo statue in the Louvre gallery in Paris, a staggering 75% of its meagre 411 millimetre annual rainfall is lost through evaporation and evapotranspiration. The net result is an acute water shortage, which is overcome by annually importing 240,000 tonnes of water by tanker and 300,000 tonnes in plastic bottles and by converting seawater into fresh water in a desalination plant that came on stream in 2008. Without these additional sources of water, the 7,000 permanent residents would find their lives unsustainable and the 700,000 tourists who visit the island each year would be compelled to seek alternative, less parched destinations.

The sound of running water, even in the winter rainy season, is uncommon in much of Greece. Many rivers are seasonal, only flowing after a sustained period of heavy rain or when augmented by snowmelt in springtime. In the driest parts of Greece, rivers hardly ever flow, leaving their channels dry and stony for years at a time. When they do flow, they prompt local media reports and excited conversations amongst the populace. The Pamisos and the Evrotas, the two main rivers in the southern Peloponnese, flow all year round but become diminished and sluggish during the summer months. However, they still manage to provide a source of water for irrigation and industry. The situation in northern Greece is different, thanks to higher rainfall. Two rivers, the Aliakmonas and the Achelous, both rising in the Pindos Mountains, have a total of ten dams backed by reservoirs along their courses, providing hydroelectric power as well as water.

Situated in one of the driest parts of mainland Greece, Athens and its surrounding region of Attica are inhabited by almost five million people – nearly half Greece's population – who pose a major challenge for the local water authority, known by its acronym EYDAP. It is one of the largest public corporations in Greece and, with local water sources long depleted or polluted, it has been forced to search far and wide to satisfy demand. A permanently flowing river in central Greece provides the solution. The Mornos River flows south-west from the Oiti Mountains into the Gulf of Corinth. Sitting astride the river, just twenty-five kilometres from the sea, is the Mornos dam, completed in 1972 – at the time, the largest gravity dam in Europe. Behind it is a huge reservoir with a surface area of seventy square kilometres and a capacity of 780 million cubic metres of water. Assisted by two other artificial reservoirs at Erinos and Marathon, and the natural Lake Yliki, it supplies Attica with an average of one and a half million cubic metres of water a day via thirty kilometres of tunnel and 190 kilometres of aqueduct. It is an impressive engineering project and vital to Athens' very existence.

For the drier eastern parts of Central Greece and the Peloponnese, and for some Aegean islands, the main source of water is not on the surface but below ground, where rainwater storage occurs in a natural way in rocks known as aquifers. Fortunately, Greece has an abundance of limestone and sandstone, which are both capable of storing water, albeit in different ways. The primary force acting on this groundwater is gravity but Greece occupies an active seismic zone and over many millions of years, the throughflow of groundwater has been interrupted, hindered, even halted by folding, faulting and other earth movements. Although known to abruptly cause springs to go dry, earth movements sometimes have a positive impact, encouraging spring formation by rearranging rock strata and creating conditions where groundwater is forced to emerge on the surface, in the form of springs or resurgences. However, more often than not, it is the water table – the fluctuating upper limit of the saturated zone of surface rocks – that determines where springs and resurgences occur. Many springs are invisible because they occur underwater in the channel of rivers or on the seabed, not far from the shoreline.

Springs, Wells and Fountains

Place names that reference water supply are common throughout Greece. *Pigi*, meaning 'source' or 'spring'; *Krini*, meaning 'fountain'; *Pigadia,* 'wells'; *Limni,* 'lake'; and *Glyko Nero,* 'fresh water', are but a few examples. Although today we distinguish between springs (which are natural) and wells and fountains (which are human-made), in ancient times, the three terms were interchangeable. Springs have always been a key factor in determining the site of settlements and, although used less often since the arrival of mains water in the 20th century, many still exist today and their water is highly valued.

On the lower slopes of the Taygetos Mountains, at the top of the steep-sided, West Mani village of Kastania, is Krya Vrisi (cold spring). Regardless of the season, it always flows with water. Shaded by majestic old plane trees that have prospered from their roots' easy access to groundwater, Krya Vrisi provides a constant supply of cool, crystal-clear, refreshing water, highly regarded by both villagers and visitors. In the past, the volume and reliability of this spring water prompted the construction of a series of four small flour mills downslope from the spring. Linked by a 750-metre long, stone-built aqueduct constructed to ensure a head of water above each mill, the running water propelled cast iron turbines, which in turn rotated mill stones. It is still possible to identify the dilapidated top and bottom mills, although it is many years since they were in use.

Narrow, shallow concrete channels at the sides of narrow streets that lead downhill from the spring testify to past and present use of Krya Vrisi's water to irrigate the narrow south-facing terraces at the top of Kastania, which are full of healthy-looking vegetables throughout the year. Immediately opposite the spring is a taverna, popular with people during high summer. It sits on a platform of reinforced concrete above a large, deep cistern in which water from the spring is collected. As well as profiting from the cooler temperatures that exist at 600 metres above sea level, the welcome shade of the plane trees and the calming effect of the sound of running water, diners are able to drink cool, pure, fresh mountain water gathered straight from the spring, enjoy refreshing after-dinner slices of watermelon that have bobbed about for hours in the cool spring water and, during one summer in the late '90s, even select fresh trout from the menu. The 'imported' fish were happily swimming around in a spring-side concrete tank, blissfully unaware of their intended fate.

Springs also played a major part in supplying water to the inhabitants of Greek cities in Classical times. Ancient Messini is the archeological site of a city founded in 369 BCE and located twenty-five kilometres north of Kalamata. Overlooked by the imposing Mount Ithome and enclosed on three sides by steep hills forming a natural amphitheatre, it occupies an impressive defensive site. In those times, defence was of paramount importance, but water supply was also an imperative consideration. Fortunately, Ancient Messini had both. Issuing from the base of Mount Ithome, where the pre-existing village of Mavromati was already making use of it, was the Klepsydra Spring. Surging with water in winter, it provided a reliable source of pure, fresh water all year round.

The once-imposing colonnaded Arsinoe Fountain House is one of the first architectural features that greets visitors to Ancient Messini. Situated on the northern fringe of the city directly below the

Klepsydra Spring and conveniently adjacent to the *agora* (market), it received water by conduit from the spring, no more than 500 metres above. This water was stored in three on-site cisterns, one forty metres long. Although modified many times, and now in ruins, the layout of the Fountain House is still easy to discern. Partly covered and partly in the open-air, partly decorative and partly functional, the Arsinoe Fountain House was essentially a public building giving access to clean drinking water. Marble channels and impressive shallow marble basins on pedestals are still visible, as are later additions, like the remains of an adjoining Roman bath house. It comes as no surprise that fountain houses were highly valued by residents. After all, water was a precious commodity. Strong regulations governed their management and use, and the Superintendent of Public Water was a highly regarded public office to which only the most able and trustworthy people were elected.

Ancient Athens was similarly dependent on springs. By the time the Romans had overcome resistance and occupied Athens in 146 BCE, the two streams – the Ilissos and the Eridanos – that had previously provided Athenians with water were becoming unfit for use. Thus, in order to supply the new Roman settlers with clean, fresh water, the emperor Hadrian decreed that an aqueduct be built. Manually constructed through solid rock by slave labour, it ran mostly underground from springs at the foot of Mount Parnes to the Roman quarter of Athens, situated south-east of the Acropolis. Considered one of the engineering achievements of its time, it covered a distance of twenty kilometres with a steady gradient of 0.4% to ensure gentle gravity flow. Its most ingenious feature was the way it 'captured' groundwater *en route*, with spurs tapping into springs wherever they were found. It was undoubtedly a major public works and was still in use until the mid-20th century, with remnants still traceable today – in some cases by listening for the croaking of frogs! No records exist to indicate what the neighbouring Greek Athenians thought of being denied the benefits of this new water supply. They continued to rely on the increasingly sluggish and polluted streams and the springs and wells, which were becoming depleted because of Hadrian's grand project.

In Ancient Greece, people appreciated how vital a water supply was to their existence. Springs were seen as life-giving and many obtained a sacred status, thus becoming an integral part of Greek mythology. The Castalian Spring at Delphi is probably one of the most famous. Here the priests would cleanse themselves before invoking the Oracle, officials would use the sacred water to wash the temple floors, and pilgrims would wash and purify themselves as well as quench their thirst. Even athletes competing in the Pythian Games believed they would profit from its powers.

In more modern times, springs have been dedicated to the Virgin Mary, and rituals connected with purity and healing are still conducted during certain Orthodox Christian festivals. Epiphany on January 6th celebrates the Baptism of Jesus in the River Jordan and is known as the 'Blessing of Waters Day'. As well as the local priest tossing the holy cross in the sea, river or lake for youngsters to vigorously compete to retrieve – the winner obtaining honour and good fortune in the coming year – certain springs are blessed, and thus their waters are valued highly for baptisms.

Thermal Springs

Loutra or *Loutraki*, indicating the presence of thermal springs, are place names found throughout Greece, which the website *greece-is. com* describes as '*a paradise of hot springs and thermal baths*'. There are 800 or so in Greece but most remain undeveloped. Some hot springs are the result of the superheating of groundwater deep in the earth's crust due to the proximity of magma that has escaped from the mantle. These springs have considerable power and often manifest themselves as geysers. Common in Iceland and New Zealand, for example, where this type of spring is harnessed to generate electricity, there are very few in Greece. Most Greek thermal springs are the result of intersecting faults, which allow water to access a depth of 2,500 metres or so, where rock temperatures can be 50°C greater than at the surface. Here the water is heated, and it expands and rises to the surface along a different fault line, emerging as a hot spring that contains dissolved minerals that possess curative properties.

Edipsos, on the island of Evia, just a three-hour road journey from Athens, is the site of numerous hot springs, some free for public use. Reliable historical references indicate that Edipsos flourished as a spa before the beginning of the Christian Era, and in more recent times it has attracted notable world figures like Maria Callas, Winston Churchill, Greta Garbo and Aristotle Onassis. The jewel in the crown of Edipsos is the 5-star, luxury Thermae Sylla Spa Hotel, located on the seafront and established in 1897. It comprises a collection of elegant, Neoclassical style, two- and three-storey buildings, containing 108 rooms and enclosing two pools and a host of other facilities. For most of its life it has catered for an elderly clientele seeking cures for their articulation, gynaecological or circulatory problems over a two- or three-week stay and under the supervision of a doctor. However, due to changing demand this hotel has transformed itself in recent years.

In a bid to attract a younger clientele, the hotel now focuses on wellbeing and relaxation, offering a multitude of therapies such as mud treatments, reflexology, Asian massages and aromatherapy. The aim is to invigorate, revitalise and rejuvenate, with pampering an integral part. On an afternoon visit in May 2017 with friends George and Helen, we eschewed other attractions, such as the jacuzzi, sauna, steam baths and thermal grotto, and confined ourselves to the two pools. One is inside with 100% thermal water, housed underneath an enormous, towering glass dome, and the other, in the open air, is a mixture of thermal and sea water. After being reminded by white-coated staff to avoid lingering in the inside pool for more than twenty minutes, and donning plastic hair protectors, we languished in the relaxing, steamy waters. Occasionally drifting effortlessly on artificially induced currents and experiencing assorted powerful mini-waterfalls, we gradually obtained a state of relaxation and wellbeing. A hushed atmosphere of calm and order prevailed, only mildly tainted by the sulphurous aroma and a far cry from the *adrenalin-pumping flume rides* so popular with youngsters and adults in British waterparks.

Cisterns

In the past, where settlements were established primarily for strategic reasons (for example, hill-top defensive sites or sites controlling movement through mountain passes) and where a natural water supply was absent, water had to be obtained by other means. The standard solution was rainwater capture and the key element was the cistern: an underground, human-made water-storage tank. Cisterns used to be common throughout rural Greece and only fell into disuse with the coming of mains water in the second half of the 20th century. For most of its 250 years, our house in Neohori depended on its cistern for water supply. Winter rainwater captured from its roof and adjoining streets was the sole source of water in a village without springs and wells.

Monemvasia, in the south-east corner of the Peloponnese, provides much evidence of a comprehensive system of both private and public cisterns. Known by some as the 'Gibraltar of the East', while for others it recalls images of Mont St Michel in Normandy, Monemvasia is a small but upstanding rocky island, rising majestically out of the Aegean Sea but so close to the mainland that it is linked by a short causeway. It has endured a chequered history with different masters: Franks, Byzantines, Venetians and Turks. Although neither are visible from the shore, Monemvasia contains two fortified settlements: the Lower Town, where renovation and rebuilding has restored much of the original style and form, and the Upper Town, which is largely derelict and abandoned. Towering above boutique hotels, pricey restaurants, souvenir shops and lavishly restored second homes, the Upper Town contrasts dramatically with its flourishing neighbour below.

A wander through the maze of overgrown former streets and paths that criss-cross the Upper Town reveals an astonishing array of cisterns in varying states of decay. Most were excavated from the underlying rock and lined with impervious plaster before stone houses, mainly two-storey, were built on top. Water was collected by temporary wooden guttering erected during the winter months, by damming paved streets during rainstorms and, in a few cases, by paved miniature catchment areas if house owners possessed sufficient adjacent land. In each case, the captured rainwater was directed into the cistern through clay pipe drains and conduits, and the water extracted at need by rope and bucket.

An aerial view of Monemvasia's Upper Town reveals two outstanding landmarks amidst the jumbled ruins, both communal cisterns. The more impressive is found towards the landward end and comprises stone walls enclosing a sloping area of open ground the size of two soccer pitches. At first glance, it's not easy to comprehend its intended purpose – maybe a compound for livestock or a parade ground? The give-away clue is the 100-metre long vaulted stone building that forms the downslope perimeter. It acted as a cistern for the rainfall captured by the large catchment area above. And just to ensure none of this precious water was lost, the whole enclosed area was surfaced with waterproof plaster, still visible in places but for the most part destroyed by weathering and vegetation growth. The other landmark is the recently restored Byzantine church of Aghia Sophia, which perches impressively on top of high vertiginous cliffs that form the seaward flank of the island. Immediately adjacent to the church is a large double-vaulted underground cistern that collects water from the roofs of the church. Both cisterns were important sources of communal water supply in the past and the rules and regulations governing the water's availabilty and use by inhabitants can only be guessed at. What is certain is that demand during periods of drought or siege – there were several – would have required their strict enforcement.

Seeking Sustainability

Increasing human demand and signs that global warming and climate change are beginning to make water even scarcer have forced water authorities in Greece, especially those in the Aegean islands, to look beyond short-term fixes and adopt a more strategic approach to obtaining water. The sheer cost alone of shipping millions of plastic bottles of drinking water or transporting it in bulk tankers demands they find a more sustainable alternative.

Desalination is the process by which dissolved salts and minerals are extracted from seawater and brackish water, making it fit to drink and to use for other purposes such as irrigation. Experiments were made in Ancient Greece to purify seawater by passing it through soil and sand filters, while ships engaged in long sea voyages obtained drinking water by distillation, whereby seawater was boiled and the steam absorbed by sponges, which were allowed to cool before the 'fresh' water was squeezed out. However, desalination technology then stood still until the mid-20th century, when burgeoning demand required new innovative approaches to water supply. Modern high-tech desalination plants seem to be at least part of the solution.

Although relatively slow to adopt this new technology, by 2016 there were almost 200 desalination plants in Greece, most of them using a process called reverse osmosis, which involves forcing sea or brackish water through sophisticated membrane filters that trap salts and impurities. Most are found in the eastern half of the Greek mainland and on islands in the Aegean Sea and produce water for human consumption. The region of Thessaly is an exception. It is one of the foremost agricultural regions in Greece, accounting for nearly half of the country's output of cereal crops, cotton and tobacco. Here, the supply of crucial irrigation water in the summer months is being augmented by the desalination of brackish water, some of it derived from salty springs.

The costs of desalination are high, twice as expensive as collecting and treating rainwater or waste water. This, allied with a bureaucratic project approval process, high electrical energy requirements to power the plants, and the environmental impact of disposing the saline concentrate waste in the sea help to explain the slow adoption of desalination in Greece, compared with countries like Kuwait and Saudi Arabia. But now costs are coming down with the development of more efficient membrane technologies and the harnessing of renewable energy, especially solar and wind. Thus, the installation of modern, compact desalination units on islands, sometimes under lease with a fixed supply cost to be renegotiated after five years, is accelerating.

A more unconventional source of fresh water has been the subject of offshore research by the Hellenic Centre for Marine Research (HCMR). Many visitors to the Mani seaside resort of Stoupa become quickly aware that the crystal-clear seawater is cooler and more refreshing than expected, even in high summer. It's one of its attractions. The ice-cold freshwater stream that issues from a spring beneath the Potomaki restaurant and flows no more than thirty metres into Stoupa Bay might appear to be responsible, and to a degree it is. But a quick scan of the Bay on a calm day reveals a random scattering of several rings of smooth water, of varying size. They occur above freshwater springs on the seabed, which act as a constant coolant for the seawater around them.

The water in Kalogria Bay, just a kilometre north of Stoupa Bay, is even more refreshing. Two springs are primarily responsible. One, called *Prigkipas* (Prince), issues forth in a deep rockpool at the side of the beach and in summer attracts queues of overheated beachgoers eager to revive themselves in its ice-cold water. The other occurs in deep water, 100 metres beyond the headland on the other side of the Bay. It is the biggest of all the seabed springs in the area and Yiannis Marambeas, the leader of the local municipality, was eager to establish its potential to supply the expanding summer tourist industry.

Thus, during two periods in late 2009 and early summer 2010, the Greek research ship *Aegaeo* undertook a thorough assessment of the viability of tapping fresh water from this spring. The investigation involved scientists, technicians and divers, as well as a host of sophisticated, state-of-the-art electronic and mechanical equipment. Initial findings gave grounds for optimism: the fresh water was very pure and its outflow plentiful and continuous. However, obstacles were also identified. Two in particular were significant: the spring was located at a considerable depth (between twenty-five and thirty metres) and the large, oval-shaped depression in the seabed where the water emerged appeared dangerously unstable. Coupled with these considerations were other issues. Was the technology available to extract this fresh water without contaminating it with seawater and, if so, had it been successfully trialled? Could the necessary engineering be undertaken without threatening the local sea and coastline environments? And, perhaps most importantly, where would the considerable investment come from? Although an outline technical proposal based on the findings of the HCMR research was drawn up and presented to the regional Peloponnese government, it came to nothing. The looming economic crisis saw to that.

West Mani's Water

The geological structure of West Mani has given it a great advantage as far as water supply is concerned. The groundwater slowly flowing through the limestone rock, which is widespread, has provided the main source of water ever since the area was inhabited. Up until the 1960s, water supply was a very local matter and villages were located around reliable springs, wells and fountains, where rudimentary communal washing facilities were constructed and where water was collected for domestic use, often on a daily basis. The villages of Petrovouni, Kastania, Proastio, Kariovouni and Pigi have impressive relics of this past provision. In villages where springs and wells were absent – Neohori, for example – capture and storage of rainwater in cisterns was the main alternative.

Today, the former municipality of Lefktro – now part of

West Mani – needs to tap into multiple sources of water to satisfy burgeoning demand. Since 1990, tourism has boomed and, thanks to the influx of North European settlers, its population has returned to pre-war levels. Because the water supply infrastructure has grown up piecemeal over the last sixty years, the way it works is not easy to fathom. Just one or two employees of the municipality seem to understand it fully. As for local Greeks, a wave of the hand in the general direction of the mountains vaguely attributes all their water to the Taygetos. It seems that Lefktro's water supply operates at three levels, all related to altitude: the mountain villages, the intermediate villages on the narrow, dissected plateau below, and the coastal settlements on the shores of the Gulf of Messinia.

At the highest level, mountain villages have their own independent sources and pipeline networks distribute water from nearby springs. The villages on the plateau below are served by water from Lefktro's primary source – the gushing springs in the bottom of the majestic Viros Gorge. Capable of supplying 2,500 cubic metres a day, this incessant flow of pure mountain water is pumped southwards as far as the village of Langada, over fifteen kilometres away, and serves many other villages *en route*. Maximum water demand in Lefktro's coastal towns and villages coincides with peak-season tourism in the months of July and August. With the exception of Kardamyli, which receives its water by pipeline direct from the Viros Gorge springs, the other coastal resorts depend on boreholes far enough inland to avoid the groundwater being contaminated by the sea. In summer the water from these boreholes is supplemented by water from the Viros Gorge, sometimes leaving higher altitude villages with irregular supply; not a situation that goes down well with the communities affected.

During our twenty-two years living part time in Neohori, Mary and I have had minimal cause for complaint. Living in an old-established village, served mainly by pipelines from the Viros Gorge and populated by many inhabitants who earn their living in the local tourist trade where a reliable water supply is vital, ensures that we are rarely without mains water. Occasionally, due to a power cut disenabling the pumps or repair work on a broken valve or leakage, short interruptions do occur, but Neohori residents expect the supply to be restored as soon as possible. If there are delays, then we can often overhear irate neighbours on the phone to the water department in Kardamyli, demanding to know what's going on and stressing that their patience is running low. It usually does the trick.

Nonetheless, we are glad we invested in a black plastic 2,000-litre reserve water tank not long after the restoration of our house was completed. Located alongside the end of the house and connected to the plumbing, it automatically activates in the event of a loss of supply. Being fully soaped up in the shower when the water suddenly stops for no apparent reason is something to be guarded against. People who live in Neohori also benefit from an additional water bonus. Like Stoupa and Aghios Nikolaos, it has a network of street-side taps that provide drinking water direct from the Viros Gorge springs, and this supply never seems to fail. The freshness, purity and natural taste of this water is highly prized by locals and tourists alike and queues at the taps are not uncommon in summer. Mary and I collect water for drinking and cooking from our nearest tap every other day; usually bright and early in the morning while it is still deliciously cool.

Everyday Issues

Unfortunately, our reliable water supply is not something enjoyed by everyone who lives in West Mani. Water rationing, pump failures, leaks, unapproved links, sabotage and meter tampering are regular matters of concern for some residents whose lives seem to be blighted by their inconsistent water supply. Sometimes they find themselves without mains water for days at a time. A quick scan of the back pages of *parea-sti-mani.com*, a local community website, exposes two recurrent issues, both the responsibility of the local municipality. One is waste disposal and the other is water supply. In an effort to raise awareness within the municipality's water department, residents raise matters of concern online. In summer, when tourism multiplies the local population several times over, water supply is a regular source of comment and complaint.

'*Although we usually get plenty of winter rain, there is little collection and storage, the distribution system is old and full of holes, so a lot of water is wasted. Also, many people use it extravagantly*' was a statement made by the website in June 2016 about the situation in West Mani. Few local residents would find much to disagree with and, inevitably, the municipality takes a large proportion of the blame. Constrained by limited financial resources, equipment and manpower, the municipality only manages to deal with immediate problems and emergencies, patching up, making good and repairing faults and breakdowns. It's a sticking-plaster approach that cannot be sustained in the long run. Some people would say that West Mani's water supply system needs a complete overhaul and, in some places, total replacement. This would require forward planning, disruption and heavy investment and, like Greece's national government, West Mani municipality has been seriously strapped for cash. However, there are ways the West Mani water department could help itself to improve matters; but what is possible without the approval of higher tiers of regional and national government is difficult to judge.

First and foremost, West Mani's water department needs to generate more income. Only then will there be sufficient ongoing financial resources – hopefully matched by investment from elsewhere – to embark on a programme of renewal and upgrading its water supply infrastructure with the appropriate degree of professional guidance and supervision. Currently West Mani's water charges are astonishingly cheap for a region that suffers long summer drought and unpredictable winter rainfall, and relies on groundwater to sustain its water supply. Water is a precious commodity here and a strong argument can be made for judging its value – and therefore its cost to the consumer – according to the law of supply and demand. But it's rarely as simple or straightforward as that. In West Mani, water is sourced and distributed by a department owned and operated by the municipality and is subsidised by central government. It has an obligation to keep water charges low. A privatised water company, where profitability is a primary consideration, might see things very differently.

I would advocate a thorough review and reform of West Mani's water tariff, especially how water charges are applied. As I understand it, there is limited discrimination between water customers. A flat rate is charged to all; the only exceptions being discounts for large families with many children, the old, and the infirm. Otherwise, regardless of whether you are rich or poor, farmer or hotelier, high- or low-level water consumer, you pay the same unit price. Can this be right, or indeed wise? At the very least, it promotes a cavalier attitude to water use and encourages waste and misuse. The introduction of a progressive system of water charges that discriminates between domestic, agricultural and commercial use would help to eliminate this nonsensical equality while at the same time protect low-volume users and those on low incomes. And what about swimming pools? Surely they should attract an additional premium on top of the unit charge, as well as their annual filling and emptying being subjected to more regulation and scrutiny. I have no doubt these proposals would meet with stiff opposition from some quarters, and would give rise to some energetic lobbying of councillors and some fierce debate in the council chamber.

Adoption of a more progressive system of water charges will only have a lasting impact if other measures are introduced at the same time. For example, the collection of water charges must be made more rigorous (meter reading is haphazard, to say the least), oversight of the upkeep and maintenance of the water infrastructure should become the responsibility of a professional water engineer, and local building regulations ought to be upgraded to require the installation of an underground water tank with every new house, to collect rainwater for watering gardens, hosing down patios or cleaning cars. For a modest addition to the overall building cost, precious drinking water would be conserved and savings made on water supply costs. Putting water department financing on a firm footing, minimising interruptions to supply, reducing water misuse and developing sustainability should all be long-term aims. Working with the community can also pay dividends.

Elaine and Tony, a British couple who have retired to West Mani, described to me how they and fellow residents of Polliana, a small group of newly built houses, sought to overcome their ongoing water supply problems by taking matters into their own hands. Fed up with the regular problems associated with a single pipeline bringing their water from the hill-top village of Kotroni, just over a kilometre away, the residents invested in 4,500 metres of plastic pipe and connectors and, in November 2011, laid four parallel pipelines linking each of their properties to the municipal mains at Kotroni. Unfortunately, because the new pipelines were deemed as private, the municipality insisted the water meters be located at the junction with the mains supply, not adjacent to each house as is normal practice. This less than satisfactory outcome became increasingly irritating as time passed.

Thus, after a fresh wave of lobbying the municipality, a public meeting was called in the Stoupa Cultural Centre in December 2014. The outcome was an agreement between householders and the municipality. If €9,851 could be raised by public subscription, then a new pipeline to benefit Polliana and other newly built settlements nearby would be purchased and installed with the municipality providing the expertise and labour, free of charge. With the cost of materials turning out greater than forecast and some householders refusing to pay their contribution of €120, the net result was a shortfall of about €3,000. Magnanimously, the municipality agreed to fund the difference and in early May 2015, the work on a new mains pipeline began. Thanks to their dogged determination and willingness to act together, and the goodwill of the municipality, the residents of these fledgling communities now have a much more reliable water supply with good pressure.

For some people, the solution to Greece's water supply problems would be to privatise all public water utilities. Taking advantage of the Greek government's weak economic position since 2008 and its need for regular bailout loans, the primary lenders insisted on the implementation of a far-reaching programme of privatisation. Nothing was sacred: seaports, airports, railways, power generation and water supply were all part of the mix. The state-owned public utility companies that preside over water supply and sewerage disposal in the metropolitan regions of Athens and Thessaloniki were the first targets. However, the news was greeted with public outrage, and large-scale demonstrations and resistance followed. A reprieve came when the Greek Supreme Court ruled against the proposals, declaring water to be a universal human right that should not be subject to profit-making.

It seems probable that the Supreme Court was aware of the content of the Hippocratic Treatises when it made its judgement. Disseminated nearly 2,500 years ago, the Treatises are a collection of texts by the Asclepiad medical community on the island of Kos, in which Hippocrates – known as the Father of Medicine and author of the Hippocratic Oath – played a leading role. One of these texts deals with 'Airs, Waters and Places' and recognises the strong link between clean water and good health. It discusses, in detail, waters that *are wholesome or unwholesome and what bad and what good effects* can be derived from water. The text warns that the consumption of smelly water from marshy, stagnant lakes can lead to unwelcome ailments that range from bile and phlegm to obstructed spleens, fevers, dropsy and dysenteries. On the other hand, waters flowing from elevated grounds are recommended, especially if they '*run towards the rising sun*'. They were considered clear, fragrant and light, and certain to favour good health.

Hippocrates and his acolytes recognised that water is life and all life on Earth is linked to water; a fundamental truth that eventually led to explicit recognition by the United Nations in July 2010 that water and sanitation is a universal human right. But UN resolutions are one thing; international action to put them into practice is another. According to the World Wildlife Fund, water scarcity remains a serious problem for nearly four billion people worldwide. We still have a long way to go.

Ifigeneia moored in Stoupa harbour.

Chapter 4

FROGS AROUND A POND?

An Absurd Episode

Mary and I could scarcely believe our eyes: the episode we witnessed would not have been out of place in a 1930s' Laurel and Hardy movie. It occurred just a few days after our arrival in Neohori in October 1997, while we were taking a Sunday afternoon stroll alongside the nearby harbour of Aghios Nikolaos, where a strong end-of-season mood prevailed. A large fishing boat was heading serenely under its own power towards a tractor-drawn, semi-submerged wooden cradle idling at the foot of a slipway, ready to convey it to its winter quarters.

Suddenly, the boat's gentle progress was interrupted by a loud shout of alarm from the quayside, which prompted the nonplussed captain to immediately cut the engine. From our vantage point on the harbour wall, it was easy to see the problem. The fishing boat's propeller had become fouled with the ropes of several smaller craft moored on both sides of the harbour, causing them to turn in a beautifully synchronised, almost choreographed way in the direction of the slowly passing fishing boat. Brief but heated discourse between the captain and his quayside assistant quickly concluded that no amount of manoeuvring was going to release the boats. Another solution had to be found.

With barely a moment's delay, the young man on the quayside, firmly gripping a knife in his fist, dived fully clothed into the harbour. Then, in a series of well-executed duck-dives, he proceeded to cut the mooring ropes entangled in the fishing boat's propeller, which released the small craft to resume their normal angle to the quay. His final triumphant emergence on the surface of the harbour, clutching a length of offending rope and seeking to recover his floating flip-flops, was greeted by muted applause from onlookers and the noise of the fishing boat's engine being re-ignited. The rest of the process was a practised formality and the fishing boat was soon edging up the slipway on its four-wheeled cradle.

At the time, neither of us could have imagined that the harbour at Aghios Nikolaos would become the location of some of the most memorable moments – good and bad – of our time in Greece. The thought of purchasing an old wooden boat, restoring it and benefitting from hours of pleasure on the water with family and friends was inconceivable at the time. We had other challenges afoot: renovating our Neohori home and making it liveable was a priority.

Greece and the Sea

It's a common misconception that Greece is made up solely of islands. It's true that there are a lot of them – an estimated 6,000 – but many are too small and inhospitable to be inhabited, and they comprise just 20% of Greece's land area. Only thirty islands have an area greater than 100 square kilometres, the biggest being Crete – only 10% of the size of the island of Ireland – followed by Evia, Rhodes, Lesvos and Kerkyra (Corfu). It's often the names attached to groups of islands that are better known than the islands themselves; the Cyclades and the Dodecanese, both chains of islands in the Aegean Sea, are two good examples. The large number of islands and the deeply indented coastline of the mainland account for the fact that Greece has the tenth longest coastline of any country in the world, estimated at 17,000 kilometres.

'*Frogs around a pond*' was the metaphor Plato used to describe the Greeks in *Phaedo*, a dialogue he composed in 360 BCE. The renowned Greek philosopher recognised that the sea was at the centre of the Ancient Greek world, with land forming the fringes and most people living close to the sea. Remarkably, nothing much has changed. As well as providing a means of transport for travel, trade and migration, the sea retains a strong geopolitical and military significance and remains a natural resource with considerable economic value. Greece's regular spats with Turkey regarding territorial water boundaries in the eastern Aegean are mainly about the potential of the seabed geology to yield supplies of oil or gas.

In Plato's time, the complex and sometimes confusing mythology that was closely woven into the fabric of life and the arts of Ancient Greece embraced many sea characters and legends. Poseidon was king of the sea and lord of all the sea gods. His queen, Amphitrite, was said to have given birth to the seas' rich fauna, while their son Triton could calm the waves with a strong blast on a conch shell. There were also powerful sea spirits and nymphs under Poseidon's command. Best known are the three Sirens, with heads of women and bodies of birds, who lured sailors to their deaths with songs. The three Gorgons were ugly female spirits with wings and hair made of living snakes. Medusa was one. They represented the dangers of the sea, especially reefs and submerged rocks. On the other hand, the protection of sailors against the spiteful actions of sea gods and goddesses was the responsibility of fifty Nereids, often portrayed as beautiful young maidens riding dolphins.

Much before Plato's time, Homer had composed his epic poems *The Iliad* and *The Odyssey*. *The Iliad* recounts the many twists and turns of the Trojan Wars and its sequel, *The Odyssey*, traces the tortuous, ten-year-long return sea journey to his homeland of Ithaca by Odysseus, the hero of the fall of Troy. He travels the length and breadth of the Mediterranean Sea and endures many ordeals and temptations, and captivity in the hands of sea gods and goddesses, before eventually being reunited with his loyal wife Penelope. *The Odyssey* confirms the central role played by the sea and its mythical inhabitants in the minds of Ancient Greeks.

The seas surrounding Greece have also been the stage for many famous naval battles. Two in particular, separated by over 2,300 years, changed the course of Greek history. The Battle of Salamis (or Salaminas) in 480 BCE was a last desperate attempt by an alliance of Greek city states to repel the conquering Persian forces of King Xerzes. After a crushing naval defeat at Artemision (which had coincided with the Greek Army's defeat at the Pass of Thermopylae), the remnants of the Greek fleet were assembled by the Athenian Themistocles in the narrow straits between the Attica mainland and the island of Salaminas. False intelligence was deliberately conveyed to Xerzes that the Greek fleet was disunited and on the point of disbanding. Not wishing to miss the chance to finally destroy Greek naval power and remove one more obstacle to his conquest of Greece, Xerzes ordered his fleet to enter the straits and engage the Greek fleet. The dawn battle that ensued was a disaster for the Persians. Expecting little opposition from the supposedly divided Greeks, the Persian fleet was lured into a confined space, which nullified its numerical advantage and restricted its battle plan. Outmanoeuvred and overpowered, it was soon in retreat, with considerable losses. For Xerzes, this embarrassing defeat persuaded him to give up his dream to subjugate Greece; for the Greeks, the tide had turned and the threat of Persian conquest had subsided.

The second Greek sea battle of note played a decisive role in Greece's struggle for independence from the Ottoman Turks, but surprisingly involved no Greek vessels. It took place in 1827 in the wide, sheltered waters of Navarino Bay, off the southwest coast of the

Peloponnese. A fleet representing the three great powers of the time had been assembled in the Ionian Sea as a show of force to persuade the disintegrating Ottoman Empire to afford Greece some autonomy, as set out in the Treaty of London. An Ottoman fleet composed of Turkish and Egyptian warships was stationed in Navarino Bay and the commander of the Allied fleet, Sir Edward Codrington, began negotiations to try to establish a general armistice in the ongoing Greek War of Independence. Lack of progress persuaded him to ramp up the pressure on his opposite number by entering the Bay and anchoring his ships face to face with the Ottoman fleet. And then the inevitable happened: a nervous quarrel between two opposing ships escalated into a full-blown engagement at close quarters. Although the Ottoman fleet possessed more vessels and more firepower, the battle was hopelessly one-sided, with the Allied fleet superior in every other respect. More advanced ships, higher calibre gunnery and better trained crews proved decisive. Over 4,000 Ottomans were killed or wounded and sixty ships destroyed in just a matter of hours. The Allied victory marked a turning point in Greece's struggle for freedom from Ottoman rule and is celebrated on October 20th each year in the town of Pylos – formerly called Navarino. In and around Three Admirals Square, an assortment of music, dance, military parades and formal speeches entertain large crowds, while representatives from the navies of Britain, Russia and France lay wreaths at memorials on islands enclosing the adjacent bay where the battle was fought.

As well as being the patron saint of Greece, Saint Nicholas is also the protector of seafarers, and Greek ships carry his icon, which all on board treat with great respect and reverence. To do otherwise would be to tempt fate. Tradition has it that Saint Nicholas' clothes were soaked with brine and his beard encrusted with salt as a result of spending his life in a never-ending struggle with the sea to save sinking ships and rescue crews from drowning. Although viewed by some scholars as a latter-day, Christianised version of the sea god Poseidon, religious historians credit Saint Nicholas with a life of great devotion and philanthropy. December 6th is the day when Greeks, especially those living by the sea, commemorate his death in 342 CE, in what is now south-western Turkey. It is also the day when all Greeks called Nikolaos, Nikos or Nikoleta celebrate their name day.

Saint Nicholas also plays a part when the Greek Orthodox Church celebrates Epiphany on January 6th. The seaside resort of Stoupa follows the traditions and customs practised on this day right across Greece, wherever there are settlements by water, fresh or salty. After a service of devotion, the congregation files in procession from Holy Trinity Church to the small harbour, where the priest confers Saint Nicholas' blessing on all the boats. He then precipitates one of the most engaging customs of the Greek Orthodox calendar. The priest hurls a wooden cross into the sea, triggering a mass dive from the harbourside into the icy waters by all the youngsters of the village brave enough to endure the conditions. It is a great honour to be the one who retrieves the cross from the water and the intensity of the final struggle to grasp the cross and raise it triumphantly in the air causes much amusement amongst onlookers. The power and threat of the sea are never far from the minds of coastal peoples, who are never shy of underwriting this respect with a dose of Orthodox blessing.

The sea is a fundamental component of Greek life and yet it represents several paradoxes. It forms its centre and its limits, it acts as a barrier and a link and, while offering many opportunities, it also embodies danger and uncertainty. 80% of Greece is mainland, occupying the southernmost portion of the Balkan peninsula. Its topography is predominantly mountainous, with fertile lowland in short supply. While, on the one hand, this unforgiving landscape provided natural security and some protection from invasion by northern neighbours, on the other, it offered limited opportunities for cultivation, food production and communications, and invariably turned people's attention towards the sea. Hence fishing, sea transport, shipping and migration to lands with more potential became strong elements of Greek life. Modern-day tourism has reinforced this bias towards the sea.

Seafaring

As you sift through your euro change at a Greek supermarket checkout you may notice that the smallest coins bear images of Greece's nautical heritage. The 1-lepta (1-cent) coin displays an Athenian trireme, a wooden warship with three ranks of oars like the ones that engaged Xerzes' fleet in the Battle of Salamis; the 2-lepta coin, a twin-masted sailing ship from the Greek War of Independence; and the 5-lepta coin, a modern oil tanker. The old 1, 2- and 50-drachma coins that went out of circulation on the last day of 2001 bear similar nautical images on both sides, while it is rare that five years pass without Greece's maritime traditions being celebrated on postage stamps.

Shipping is one of the oldest and most enduring of Greek businesses and has been a key element of the Greek economy since Ancient times. It surprises many people to learn that Greece has the largest merchant shipping fleet in the world, both in terms of number of vessels and deadweight tonnage, and that Greek-owned ships account for 16% of world trade. For a country of just eleven million people that is extraordinary. They are mainly huge vessels engaged in long-distance global transport of containers and raw materials like petroleum, natural gas, metal ores and chemicals. In simple terms, Greece's pre-eminence can be explained by its geography at the crossroad of historical routes linking Europe, Africa and Asia, and by its long history as a maritime trading nation.

Some of the wealthiest, most philanthropic and influential families in Greece, like the Latsis, Niarchos and Goulandris families, are ship owners. However, things aren't what they used to be. In his November 2015 article for *Reuters*, Tom Bergin explains: '*Today, instead of Greek-based ships manned by Greek sailors, shipping in Greece is made up of small management offices in Piraeus that collect freight fees on behalf of their tax-haven registered parents. The management firms oversee the movement and maintenance of ships that rarely ever visit Greece. In return they receive a small portion of the shipping fees.*'

Even though successive Greek governments have pandered to Greek ship owners in an effort to maintain shipping as a crucial wealth-creating and employment-sustaining element of the Greek economy, the tentacles of globalisation and company structuring to minimise tax liabilities – already substantially discounted in Greece – seem to be undermining this strategy.

Ferries are the lifelines of Greece. They link Greece with Western Europe and with Turkey, and Greek islands with each other and the mainland. They are the vital arteries that allow the country to function as a unit. Greek ferries comprise a motley crew. Sleek, modern, twin-hulled catamarans zip from island to island in the Aegean Sea, while fast-moving but jolting hydrofoils (the so-called Flying Dolphins) link Piraeus with islands in the Saronic Gulf. Smooth, state-of-the-art Adriatic ferries with huge capacity for freight and passengers link Italian Adriatic ports with Igoumenitsa and Patras, while sluggish coasters of an uncertain age – kept in service by experienced shipboard engineers, many layers of paint and hardworking crews – maintain a year-round service that many islands depend on.

Without a regular ferry service, some of the smaller inhabited islands would not survive. Bursting at the seams with tourists in the summer and hopelessly underused in winter, the ferries supply islands with everything from food and medicine to fuel and machinery parts. Without the ferries, agricultural products would not get to urban markets and patients requiring surgery would struggle to gain access to specialist hospitals on the mainland. Islands with airports and regular, year-round air services fare little better. Although virtually bad weather-proof, aeroplanes have a limited capacity for freight and can rarely accommodate vehicles. Bad weather can produce delays and cancellations, especially in winter, and in recent years there have been periods of strike action by seamen trying to force their employers to cough up months of back pay owed to them. Along with the rest of the country, Greek ferry companies have been enduring difficult times. Many are operating in the red with government subsidies insufficient to maintain loss-making winter services. Some, like the four ferry companies operating in the Ionian Sea, have resorted to mergers and collaboration in an effort to cut costs through less route and timetable duplication.

Maniots & the Sea

The thin and deeply indented Mani peninsula that forms the middle prong of the trident-shaped southern coast of the Peloponnese is almost bereft of flat, low-lying land. Its backbone of the Taygetos Mountains descends rapidly to the sea on both sides, their vertiginous rocky slopes and thin soils offering little reward to inhabitants even where hillsides have been painstakingly terraced. In the past, hardship and self-sufficiency were standard; just feeding a family in such a challenging environment demanded huge effort and resolve. No wonder inter-family conflict and emigration were so common.

In these circumstances, many Maniots turned to the sea. Fishing, especially when shoals of sardines or *kinigos* (hunter fish) entered the Gulfs of Messinia and Lakonia in spring and autumn, provided a welcome and valuable addition to the meagre diet provided by limited cultivation, goat and sheep herding, hunting and gathering. Exceptional catches were preserved by salting and smoking. Sadly, in the last twenty years, overfishing, seawater warming and pollution have dramatically reduced the stocks of fish in local waters. The volume of catches has progressively reduced, the average size of fish landed is diminishing and fewer fishermen can provide for their families through fishing alone. Although fish farms are springing up all around the Greek coast in an effort to compensate, as yet they are conspicuously absent in Maniot waters. Elsewhere, Greek fish farms have become a regular source of sea bream and sea bass in North European supermarkets.

For hundreds of years, land transport in the Mani was by mule or donkey or on foot, using the network of impressively constructed stone paths called *kalderimia*. They linked villages with each other, and some are still useable today. To walk from Stoupa to Kalamata, (the nearest large town) was a day's journey, often involving an overnight stay. The first asphalt road linking Stoupa to its northern neighbours was completed as late as Christmas 1956. Major civil engineering work was necessary to enable it to navigate the deep gorges and steep mountainsides that punctuate the route. Today, the forty-five-kilometre car journey to Kalamata takes less than one hour.

In the days before proper roads, the only sane means of transport was by sea, regardless of the length of journey. Small wooden boats called *kaikes* (caiques) with single masts and Latino sails provided a variety of seaborne services for many hundreds of years. Vangellis from Neohori recalls as a boy witnessing huge earthenware *pitharia* (olive and olive oil storage pots) from Koroni, on the opposite shores of the Messinian Gulf, being unloaded onto the beach at Stoupa in the early 1950s. It had been a calm morning, rendering the Latino sail virtually useless. Thus the crew, who had been required to row the whole twenty-seven kilometres, were taking some well-earned refreshment and recuperation at a waterside *cafeneion* and hoping for some favourable breeze before making the return journey.

Towards the end of the 1930s, the ad hoc concrete jetty at Stoupa was reinforced and extended. By then, bigger, motorised wooden vessels called *venzines* had begun to eclipse the caiques by offering a daily service to Kalamata, a journey of no more than two and a half hours. They provided covered seating for passengers and carried livestock as well as general goods. On Kalamata market days (Wednesday and Saturday), when demand for space on the *venzina* was greatest, a pre-dawn departure from mountain villages was required to secure a seat. Long before the advent of mobile phones, passengers sometimes arrived at the coast only to find the service cancelled due to inclement weather. Even when conditions were calm, some passengers suffered sea-sickness and arrived in Kalamata exhausted and anxious about making the return journey in the early afternoon.

As well as providing a source of food and a means of transport, the sea also provided other, less wholesome, opportunities. With the land so unresponsive to toil and endeavour, coastal communities saw the potential for piracy. Cape Tenairon – also known as Cape Matapan – is a rocky promontory sticking out into the Cretan Sea. It forms the southernmost tip of the Mani peninsula and represents one of the most southerly points of mainland Europe. Before the completion of the Corinth Canal in 1893, east-west sea traffic in the eastern Mediterranean had little alternative but to round this dreaded cape. It concentrated shipping and sometimes provided bold and daring pirates, with local knowledge and surprise on their side, with easy prey. In his book *Mani*, Patrick Leigh Fermor describes how Maniot pirates would '*lie in wait for Turkish and Venetian convoys and, being too small to attack them in bulk, pounce on laggards and strays or force them onto the rocks*'. Vast hoards of goods, some exotic, some commonplace, in well-guarded caves and grottoes testified to their success.

Some of the pirates' most valuable bounty was human. During the four centuries of the Ottoman Empire, there was a burgeoning demand in the eastern Mediterranean and Middle East for slaves; for harems, for household work, and to bolster armed forces. This encouraged rampant piracy and human trafficking. In the book *Deep into Mani*, Peter Greenhalgh recounts the funeral lament sung by the widow of a swashbuckling pirate called Nicholas Sassaris from the Mani fishing village of Mezapos. Rather than portray him as an honourable Robin Hood character, plundering the rich to sustain the poor, she berated him for plundering poverty-stricken, coastal villages; taking able-bodied men and women captive; and leaving the young, the aged and infirm to their uncertain fate. Maniot pirates were ready to deal with anybody as long as the price was right; allegiances were forged and broken at will.

As a desperate measure of last resort, migration offered despairing Maniots the chance of a fresh start. The exodus was especially strong during the late 1940s and '50s, fuelled by the deprivation and extreme austerity following the Second World War and the divisive

Civil War that followed. Sometimes it was to Piraeus, where ship owners were keen to utilise their considerable seafaring skills and experience, and where casual but regular employment as dockers was also available. The district of Maniatika, occupied exclusively by Maniots at one time and barely one kilometre from the Piraeus waterfront, is testament to this migration. Some, eschewing the limited employment opportunities in their homeland, emigrated to Australia, the USA or Canada; a long, sometimes hazardous, and uncomfortable ocean voyage. When debts had been paid – few could afford the cost of the sea passage from their own meagre resources – and sufficient funds had been accumulated, families often followed. Today, Greece is suffering a new surge of emigration, prompted by tough economic conditions and high unemployment following the global financial crisis of 2008. Young Greeks seeking work and salaries commensurate with their university education have little choice but to look beyond their homeland for employment opportunities. A June 2017 newspaper report in *Kathimerini*, bearing the headline *'Little Greece in Great Britain'* declared that 62,000 young Greeks were living and working in the UK. Other countries are equally popular, especially where there are well-established Greek communities, but these days, migrants' passage is by air, not sea.

A Living Organism?

In sharp contrast to the huge super tankers, container ships and bulk carriers that are at the forefront of today's Greek merchant shipping fleet, it is images of small wooden boats that always feature in the web pages, travel brochures and TV advertisements that seek to lure people to spend their holidays in Greece. Sun-drenched, brightly painted boats in picturesque harbours, bobbing idly at their quayside moorings, reflected in crystal-clear water and surrounded by slow-moving shoals of tiny fish are standard images. These boats have evocative names proudly painted on their prows; some with conventional female names like *Aleka*, *Kiki* and *Stella* and some combining male and female – a more recent trend – like *Nikos-Koula* or *Petros-Tonia*. Others conjure up romantic images like *Avra* (Dawn) and *Chrisi Akti* (Golden Coast), while some echo the past with names like *Calypso* – the goddess-nymph who detained Odysseus for many years – and *Argo* (Jason's ship). No one can imagine Greece without wooden boats. It would be like Egypt without the pyramids, Italy without pasta or Japan without its cherry blossom.

For every wooden boat there must be a traditional boatyard, and in Greece, as elsewhere in the world, they are fast disappearing. Building boats from wood has a long and prestigious history in Greece, the decimation of ancient forests a testimony to the millennia of demand for timber. The emergence of Greece in Classical times as a major player in the ancient Mediterranean world can be accounted for in no small part by its sea power. That, in turn, depended on the skill, expertise and invention of its naval architects and its boat builders, who nurtured and developed a long and valuable pedigree that today's diminishing number of boat builders have inherited. Generations of the same family, like the Dardanou of Evia, the Polia of Symi and the Konidari of Lefkada, have constructed the same styles of boat, with the same materials and using the same tools and methods, over hundreds of years. Their intense pride in this heritage and passion for their craft are largely responsible for their continued existence.

The traditional small Greek boatyard is like any other. Tucked away behind a headland to avoid the effects of prevailing winds and storms, with plenty of outside space and a gentle slope into sheltered deep water, is ideal. There are virtually no tides to contend with here. A new boat will emerge from the boat shed shortly before the launch date, only when ready for the mast and rigging to be installed and final adjustments made in the light of sea trials. A 2011 newspaper article by Thymiou Kakou in *Ethnos tis Kyriakis* features Doukas Yiamouyiannis, the last wooden boatbuilder on the island of Lesvos. Illustrated by Klairi Mustafellou's evocative colour photos, it paints a romantic picture of a dying trade. Doukas' boatyard in Ploumari is dominated by a substantial wooden slipway, bearing the scars, grease and eroded paintwork of countless launches. At its head is a securely anchored, cast-iron winch – all cogs, levers and tightly coiled, twisted wire cable – fringed by a miscellany of ropes, props, wedges and tough wooden levering bars. Away from the slipway are horizontal stacks of seasoning sawn timber alongside random piles of giant tree trunks.

The boatshed is the beating heart of the boatyard. It is where the slow, methodical, painstaking process of making and shaping the parts, big and small, and their assembly to form the boat, is undertaken. A small Greek boatyard may take up to eighteen months to construct a single vessel, lovingly crafted and assembled by hand. So much still relies on experience, a good eye and specialist hand tools that seem to come from a different era. The boatshed's only nod to the 21st century are three floor-standing, electrically powered machines: a circular saw, a planer and an upright band saw, aligned in a row along one side. Hanging precariously above is an assortment of wooden patterns, distinguished from each other by roughly painted codes. Opposite, some stretching from floor to ceiling, are stacks of sawn timber of varying dimensions. The selection of boatyard timber is done with great care. Hardwoods like oak, mulberry, elm and eucalyptus are used for the frame of the boat and softer wood, like pine or cypress, for planking the exterior. But hardness is only one factor. The grain determines a wood's natural resistance to impact, its tendency to bend – sometimes a good thing – or shrink, and its resistance to humidity and salt water.

Racks of hand tools and clamps of all sizes are housed above a cluttered, wizened-looking work bench that lines the whole width of the shed opposite the giant folding glazed doors that lead out to the slipway. The dominant smell of timber and sawdust mingles with an aromatic concoction of glues, paints, varnishes, pine tar and sealers. Chisels, mallets, planes, adzes, brace and bits and saws are scattered randomly. Piles of sawdust, curls of planings and discarded crusty paintbrushes surround the half-constructed frame of a new boat occupying centre stage. Standing like the upturned carcass of some large prehistoric creature, its flesh and innards long since devoured by vultures and jackals, its backbone and ribs still intact but seemingly bleached by exposure to the sun, it has a natural form of simple, symmetrical beauty. Judiciously applied red lead primer, a long-lasting and effective wood protector, is the only obvious sign that this is a human-made skeleton.

Posing self-consciously for the camera with hammer in hand, Doukas opines that it will probably be another twelve months before his latest boat is ready for launch. He is eager to justify the time it takes to construct a wooden boat, but instead of describing the labour-intensive, step-by-step process, he waxes lyrical about the strengths and qualities of a perfect wooden boat, about its slender, curved lines, about the choice of materials and how they are joined to enable it to withstand the changing seasons and the impact of waves and currents as it moves through the sea. He could be describing a living organism.

Indulging a Fancy

At the turn of the millennium, I spent a few winters doing casual work for Torrington friends in their gardening and building businesses. By the summer of 2003 I had earned sufficient funds from this activity to fulfil one of my Greek dreams: to own a wooden boat. A new wooden boat would cost way beyond my means and involve a long wait so I contented myself with the thought of a second-hand version. Why a wooden boat rather than a plastic one? Nostalgia and a blissful ignorance of what it might entail had a lot to do with it. With the benefit of hindsight, my choice might have been different. However, I was allowed no time to reflect on my decision. Within days of putting about the word that I was seeking a second-hand boat, friends Alekos and Gerda telephoned to inform me that an elderly neighbour in their coastal village of Trahila had reluctantly decided to retire from fishing and sell his boat. He was eager that we should meet.

So, on the morning of September 15th 2003, Mary and I drove the eight-kilometre scenic coast road from Aghios Nikolaos to Trahila, impatient to find out what awaited us. Alekos had kindly offered his services to translate and advise. All was revealed in the vine-covered back yard of Yiorgos and Maria's waterfront house. Carefully removing a securely fastened, full-length tarpaulin, with a mast acting as ridge pole, Yiorgos exposed a five-metre-long wooden fishing boat, painted in light blue and white and standing on a steel trailer. First impressions were positive. Named *Hariklaki*, it had been built by Yiannis Zaharias on the distant island of Symi in 1972. Although it was already over 30 years old and had been out of the water for two years, it looked in good condition to my inexperienced eye. To prove its seaworthiness, Yiorgos insisted we tow it to the nearby slipway and launch it. A quick circuit of Trahila harbour dispelled any doubts, negotiations began and, in no time, we shook hands on a deal.

Three days later, after several postponements due to bad weather, we gathered at Aghios Nikolaos harbour at mid-morning to greet Yiorgos as he completed his last voyage in *Hariklaki*. It was surely an emotional moment for him as he drew up alongside the quay and secured his mooring ropes. But the tension quickly evaporated as he reached into the bow hold and produced two fine specimens of hunter fish that he had line-caught *en route* from Trahila. With a broad grin on his face, he proudly presented them, one to Mary and the other to Gerda. A half-hour trip out into the Gulf of Messinia was judged sufficient time by Yiorgos to instruct me on the workings of the 6HP German-made Deutz diesel engine and the general handling of the boat. He seemed blindly unaware that I was a complete novice and ignored my look of surprise when he informed me that the engine had no reverse gear. It was something we'd have to get used to!

Moving the boat from the harbour to dry land a couple of days later confirmed my suspicions of a small leak, but did not prompt second thoughts. Thus, early on September 22nd, Mary, Yiorgos and

I journeyed to Kalamata by car. First stop was the Hellenic Coastguard offices, housed in an imposing Neoclassical building fronting onto the commercial harbour. Four hours later, after many forms, fees and official stamps, and much walking from office to office, floor to floor, and back and forth to the photocopy shop and the nearby tax office, the transfer of ownership was completed. Without Yiorgos' determined and masterful dealing with Greek bureaucracy and red tape, the process would surely have taken twice as long.

Just the matter of returning to collect the official documents in two or three days' time remained, and the boat was mine. Well, not exactly; more like ours. During the fortnight it had taken for ownership of the boat to be transferred, two Dutchmen (Pieter and Jaap) had been enlisted and, in 2008, we were joined by John, another Englishman. It was now a 'syndicate' of owners, with all that that implied. All four of us were part-time or permanent residents of Neohori and eager to have a small boat at our disposal. We each brought complementary skills and experience to the project and shared the costs of renovation and annual maintenance and upkeep. Joint ownership seemed to make perfectly good sense.

Yiorgos had insisted the boat's name be changed and eventually we agreed on *Ifigeneia*: the name of King Agamemnon's daughter in Greek mythology. She comes to a premature end when her father is driven to sacrifice her to appease the goddess Artemis, who had interfered with the winds and prevented his fleet sailing to do battle with Troy. We hoped this did not constitute a bad omen. By happy coincidence, *Ifigeneia* was also the name of the Greek teacher who had so motivated and inspired Mary and me to embark on our Greek adventure.

Renovation

The thoroughly renovated *Ifigeneia*, looking like new, was gingerly launched into the harbour at Aghios Nikolaos early on the morning of Thursday August 19th 2004, before too many people were around to witness any embarrassing mishaps. Apparently Jaap had hardly slept overnight but he need not have worried because the exercise was faultless. The boat eased off its trailer effortlessly into the harbour, the engine fired first time, the boat behaved and handled perfectly in a short sea trial, and there appeared to be no ingress of seawater. The only difficulty was finding a spare mooring. A chilled bottle of champagne was on hand to celebrate but smashing it against the bows was judged ill-advised. Instead, we eagerly drank the contents, uttering toasts to many hours of future boating pleasure.

Eleven months had passed since the boat had been purchased. Its renovation had demanded more time and effort than we had imagined. Perhaps we had been naïve to think otherwise. In the early days we learned 'on the job', seeking and taking advice from local Greek boat owners, obtaining instruction from the internet and applying our existing practical knowledge as intelligently as possible. As the only permanent resident and the person with the most relevant experience and skills, Jaap was undoubtedly the guiding force, especially after the boat was moved in June 2004 from the harbour-side car park at Aghios Nikolaos to the lofty carport beside his house. As well as providing shade and easy access to power tools, we escaped the unsolicited interruptions that often impeded progress in the very public car park. Well-meaning they certainly were, but the advice or comments from one person often contradicted that of another. Who were we to believe?

Countless hours were spent scraping and stripping the old paintwork, filling the cracks, sanding and applying red lead primer. Thanks to the services of Sotiris Poulakos, a local builders' merchant with a lorry equipped with lifting gear, the bulky, heavy engine had been removed and the boat turned downside up, making this crucial work easier. Some of the ribs were reinforced, the old gunwales were replaced and the bow-hold was enlarged. A bow mast with a single spar and simple rigging was created and fitted, and a wooden housing for the engine was installed. Visits to specialist hardware stores, steel yards, paint shops, timber merchants and chandlers in Kalamata became a regular occurrence. Paints, assorted timber, stainless steel screws and Bison PU (a miracle adhesive) were regular items on our shopping lists during renovation, while the purchase of steel chain, sinking ropes, pumps, navigation lights, fenders, buoys, emergency flares and life-jackets were essential to properly equip *Ifigeneia* and abide by the Hellenic Coastguard's safety code. The old joke about owning a boat being like standing in the shower tearing up £20 notes – you get wet and dispense lots of money – was coming true.

By the end of July 2004, renovation was nearing completion and we were becoming impatient to launch *Ifigeneia* and spend time on the water. After all, what was the point of all the hard work and investment? The final coats of paint were applied, the name and the registration number were painted on the prow and a new lead anode attached to the keel. The final act was the application of a thick coat of red/brown anti-foul paint below the waterline, after which the boat had to be launched within 24 hours for the protection to be 100% effective. The early morning four-kilometre car journey from Jaap's house to Aghios Nikolaos with the boat in tow on its trailer was the penultimate challenge prior to the launch. The route was winding, steep and badly rutted in places, and we were eager to minimise any damage to the paintwork. Thus progress was slow and deliberate with 'outwalkers' in place, shouting advice to the driver. Not for the first or last time was Jaap's handling of his 4x4 Hyundai Galloper found to be skilful and controlled when put to the test.

Reaping the Rewards

Although we had made a brief sea trial on the day of the launch and ventured the fifty-minute-long trip to Trahila and back as an extended trial three days later, our true maiden voyage had to await our return from a few days at the Athens Olympic Games. At 9.30am on Monday morning, September 6th, with wives Helena and Mary on board, Jaap and I cast off our mooring ropes at Aghios

Nikolaos harbour, manoeuvred *Ifigeneia* gingerly into mid-harbour, turned her ninety degrees and headed out into the calm waters of the Messinian Gulf. Our destination was Kardamyli, a small tourist resort and district capital, some ten kilometres to the north. With our confidence rising, we anchored in the sheltered bay of Kalamitsi for our first experience of swimming from the boat – one we would repeat many times. We eventually moored *Ifigeneia* at the solid concrete breakwater in Kardamyli, understandably pleased with the progress of our first real nautical adventure. The unaccustomed loudness of the two-stroke diesel engine had made conversation on the journey virtually impossible but the calm of Lela's taverna gave us an opportunity to discuss our experience. As well as enjoying an excellent lunch, we were able to reflect on the boat's handling and our performance as novice sailors.

Our departure was hastened by the onset of a blustery south-westerly wind and the rapid generation of waves, which made us somewhat anxious. Although Mary and Helena, who were sitting at the bow, suffered some minor soakings from spray, *Ifigeneia* coped well with the conditions. Her elegant, curved bow enabled her to slice through the waves with ease and she responded admirably to the tiller. Our safe arrival in our 'home port' of Aghios Nikolaos after a seventy-five-minute journey was celebrated with a few bottles of Mythos beer – Jaap's tipple of choice – but not before a quantity of water was pumped out from the bilges. We were unsure whether it had penetrated the boat under the waterline or over the gunwales.

Learning the ropes turned out to be more straightforward than we had anticipated although we were conscious of the potential hazards posed by operating a small boat, especially departing from and returning to an overcrowded Aghios Nikolaos harbour in the busiest months of July and August. On the other hand, many factors served to overcome our early unease when we went out in the boat. Our Hellenic Coastguard permit limited our distance from the coastline to two nautical miles (3.7 kilometres) and thus the Mani coastline and mountains, gorges and villages above – all familiar to us – were always in view. The lack of any appreciable tide, the virtual absence of currents, the crystal-clear water allied to the shallow draught of the boat and the reliable and detailed weather forecasts on the website *meteo.gr* all ensured we were safe without charts and other navigational aids, essential in less benign circumstances.

Mishaps

Whatever precautions are taken and regardless of the attention paid to potential risks, mishaps happen. Sometimes it is the fault of an unforeseen mechanical or electrical failure. Jaap and friends were left stranded off the rocky headland immediately north of Trahila when an engine gasket blew unexpectedly. With oars barely making any impact, they were lucky that a local fishing boat arrived on the scene, quickly assessed their dire situation and towed them to safety. My most embarrassing moment with *Ifigeneia* happened much closer to home.

Friends Bob and Moira were spending a holiday with us in October 2004 and were looking forward to an evening jaunt in the boat. Boarding, casting off and manoeuvring the boat into mid-harbour was accomplished with ease. The engine fired first time and, engaging the clutch, we shot forward rather more rapidly than I intended. This would not have been a problem had the rudder not become instantly entangled in a taut mooring rope just below the surface. *Ifigeneia* shuddered and the rudder was unceremoniously wrenched from its substantial metal hinges. It floated helplessly behind us while our reduced but uncontrolled progress put other vessels at risk. Fortunately, our frantic efforts at the bow with outstretched arms and hands prevented any collateral damage. As Eric, a Dutch friend of Jaap's, succinctly put it at the time, *"Shit happens!"* It was little consolation. Bob and Moira's alarm and disappointment were self-evident and my ego would take some time to recover.

Small boats can sometimes be just as vulnerable on land as they are on water. *Ifigeneia* narrowly escaped destruction on February 19th 2011 when parked on her trailer in the car park adjoining Aghios Nikolaos harbour. Securely wrapped and bound, she was in her usual place, abutting the stone wall opposite Litsa's mini-market. Along with several other boats, this had been her winter quarters for seven years and she had hitherto come to no harm. But a storm had brewed overnight. Fuelled by a strong and persistent southerly wind – the *Ostria*, as the Greeks call it – the noise of the large waves crashing against the sea wall had woken and alarmed the residents of seafront properties. Anticipating the worst, they made frantic efforts in the dark to protect their ground floors, move their vehicles to less vulnerable locations and slacken the mooring lines of boats in the harbour.

No one, however, anticipated the scale of damage caused by one giant wave – 'a tsunami' was how some defined it – which struck at around 4am. Eyewitnesses described how it seemed to appear out of nowhere, a giant, fast-moving wall of water that towered over the sea wall and crashed down on the car park behind. With biblical force and power, it demolished the *Nereides* waterside bar, upended parked vehicles and boats and scattered them indiscriminately. The car park was instantly awash with raging seawater, constantly recharged by every newly breaking wave. The swirling debris, some of considerable size and mass, made immediate human intervention suicidal. That would have to await the onset of daylight and the winds and waves abating.

We feared the worst as we drove to Aghios Nikolaos to inspect the storm damage. The scene that greeted us was one of utter devastation, with bemused and numbed locals at odds to explain the extent of the chaotic havoc the storm had left in its wake. For most, it surpassed anything similar they could recall. We found *Ifigeneia* lurching drunkenly on her trailer, half-on, half-off. Although twenty metres from the sea wall, she had been turned 90° and was wedged lengthways against the stone wall, several metres from her parking place. Good fortune meant that the raging seawater had deposited a large boat trailer in such a way that it formed a strong protective barrier in front of her. Reinforced with substantial debris from the demolished waterside bar, the stranded trailer had resisted all the sea's efforts to remove it and mercifully had safeguarded our boat.

It required the same lorry's lifting gear that had removed the engine prior to renovation seven years earlier – but this time manoeuvred by Dimitris (Sotiris' brother) – to extricate *Ifigeneia*. Firstly, he hoisted the large rogue trailer out of the way, which allowed us to remove the rest of the surrounding debris by hand and drain away the dirty sea water, which had half-filled our boat. He then fastened industrial-strength straps around the hull and gently coaxed *Ifigeneia* into the air. Her trailer was manhandled into a new position and stabilised – a tyre had deflated – and the boat lowered gingerly back into place. The damage it had suffered appeared, at first glance, to be superficial. Closer inspection at a later date revealed more serious problems. Had this incident spelt the beginning of the end for *Ifigeneia*?

An Ignominious End?

Fast forward two and a half years to mid-September 2013. The sight that greeted us when we stopped to chat to Jerry, who was in the process of imaginatively transforming a large Stoupa garden, was breathtaking. There, right in front of us, standing proudly erect in a long shallow pit, her seaworthiness no longer an issue, was *Ifigeneia*. She had become the centrepiece of the garden. Jerry had great plans to surround her with a 'sea' of blue, white and purple flowering plants to mimic the real thing.

The cause of *Ifigeneia's* demise was simple. She was forty-one years old and was coming to the end of her natural lifespan. Wooden boats do not last forever. Maybe with more time, more skill, more experience, more advice, more manpower, we may have managed to resurrect *Ifigeneia* for one or two more seasons on the Messinian Gulf, but her days were definitely numbered. A fortnight of daily toil in early June 2013 had exposed a multitude of frailties under the waterline. Every closer examination revealed more weaknesses and every additional repair eroded confidence and sowed doubts that previous rounds of annual maintenance had not aroused. Nonetheless, we persisted until *Ifigeneia* was deemed fit to launch. Early on Monday 24th June 2013, with no little foreboding, she slipped slowly off her trailer into the waters of Aghios Nikolaos harbour.

The launch went like clockwork, but within forty-five minutes, she was half full of water. My worst fears were realised. A relaunch one week later, after acting on the advice of several local boat owners on how to stem the leakage, proved just as disappointing. In just a few hours, *Ifigeneia* had become so full of water that there was a danger she would capsize and end up on the bottom of the harbour. What an embarrassment that would have been! Frantic bailing rescued the situation before she was towed out of the water for the last time.

Ifigeneia's demise caused us owners much dismay; without some miracle she was unlikely to sail again. At least Jerry's offer to accommodate her on dry land absolved us of the considerable responsibility of disposing of her otherwise. The boat's gear was gladly received by Antonis, an Aghios Nikolaos fisherman who had been a constant source of advice and cheerful encouragement. The days that followed were ones of reflection on the abrupt end of another of life's rich episodes; the teamwork, the skills we had learned, the competencies we'd mastered to maintain, handle and navigate a boat, and those unique experiences a landlubber may never encounter, had all combined to create an unforgettable ten-year adventure. Twinges of regret were inevitable. The most poignant memory for me was an evening jaunt with Mary in September 2012 when we returned to harbour as the sun was setting. The calm sea – *'san ladi'* (like oil), as the Greeks say – became an all-encompassing mirror of orange sunlight. It was on fire. A stunning, magical, unforgettable few minutes unfolded. Eight years on, *Ifigeneia* still resides in the garden in Stoupa, and the sight of randomly scattered, stationary fishing boats in the Gulf of Messinia, illuminated by an early morning sun, still fills me with longing and momentary bouts of nostalgia.

A wildfire wilderness.

Chapter 5

A RECURRING MENACE

A Fiery History

'*Developed on the ashes of forests*' is how geographers from the University of the Aegean on Lesvos explain the emergence of the earliest human communities in Greece. The first fires were almost certainly random events due to lightning strikes or volcanic eruptions. Humankind's ability to make fire, initially by creating heat by friction whereby a flammable material was ignited, followed sometime later. In primeval times, all of mainland Greece and some of the islands were densely forested with a mix of coniferous and deciduous trees. Thus the earliest colonisation of Greece involved a process of 'slash and burn' by migrating groups of people. By this means, the denudation of Greek woodland began as areas of forest were cleared to allow cultivation and grazing. Today, almost 80,000 square kilometres (60% of Greece's land use) is classified as forest, of which less than a third is tall trees, which are state-owned and managed by the Greek Forest Service.

Fire was one of the five elements of Ancient Greece. While the masses persisted with their belief in the powers of mythical gods, philosophers were grappling with attempts to explain the creation of the world that did not rely on mythology for its answers. The notion of five core elements – Earth, Water, Fire, Air and Ether (the gas that was thought to fill the heavens) – emerged from this debate. These elements remained almost unquestioned in Europe until the late Middle Ages and had a fundamental impact on subsequent scientific thought.

Greek mythology contains many references to fire. Works by Homer, Hesiod and Thucydides all mention it. An epic poem – the original attributed to Peisander and dated around 600 BCE, but since lost – tells the story of The Twelve Labours of Heracles, undertaken as atonement for killing his wife and children in a fit of rage. The second of these labours involved confronting the Hydra, a gigantic monster that lived in a lakeside lair near the present-day town of Argos in the northeast Peloponnese. A nastier creature is difficult to imagine. As well as its many heads and its poisonous breath and blood, it possessed an amazing capacity to reproduce itself . . . and with interest. As Heracles' sword hacked off one head, another two sprouted in its place, rendering his task increasingly impossible; that is, until he took advice from his nephew, Iolaus, who suggested they used fire to cauterise the decapitated stumps. And it worked. Despite its increasingly violent resistance, the Hydra's heads were systematically removed and, thanks to fire, no regrowth followed. This dynamic duo, mythological precursors of Batman and Robin, had turned the tables on the supposedly indestructible Hydra, and Heracles was free to proceed to his third challenge.

Zeus was the ruler and most powerful and feared of all the gods. He inhabited Mount Olympus, where he jealously guarded the flaming thunderbolt, his sacred source of fire and most potent and coveted asset. Prometheus, the son of a Titan, was one of Zeus' many protagonists. In Greek mythology he is credited with playing a major part in creating humankind, but he continually despaired of their miserable existence. When he approached Zeus and begged him to release some fire to allow humankind some much-needed comforts, his pleading was summarily dismissed. But Prometheus was not easily rebuffed and returned to Mount Olympus and secretly stole a spark from Zeus' fire. With it, he ignited the soft dry fibre at the centre of a dead wild fennel stalk, which he managed to keep smouldering during his journey back to humankind. When he presented them with the precious gift of fire, they rejoiced that they were now able to warm themselves in winter, lighten the darkness at night, cook food and ward off wild animals. However, for Prometheus there was a price to pay. Zeus was furious that he had been deceived, and as punishment ordered that Prometheus be chained to Mount Caucasus, where he was tormented by an eagle feeding daily on his liver (it miraculously reformed overnight). Zeus eventually spared him this eternal torture and he was released by Heracles. Even today, the story of Prometheus, 'bringer of fire', is well known to every Greek child.

In his contribution to the 2015 publication *Wildland Fires: a worldwide reality*, Gavriil Xanthopoulos, an Athens-based wildfire expert, asserts that *'During Byzantine and Ottoman times forest fires did not occupy a prominent part in the collective memory'*. It seems that fire was not a big issue amongst the general population, except when it became a weapon of war. The Egyptian, Ibrahim Pasha, was a strong perpetrator of 'incendiarism', as Xanthopoulos calls it. His ruthless and revengeful re-conquering of the Peloponnese was a last desperate attempt to put an end to the Greeks' uprising against their Ottoman rulers. The 1825 slaughter of 300 inhabitants of the village of Vrontamas, in western Lakonia, is a telling reminder of Ibrahim's uncompromisingly brutal methods. They had sought refuge from his forces in a nearby monastery, tucked away in caves, high up on the valley-side of a tributary of the Evrotas river. The villagers had naïvely believed that the isolated and inaccessible location of the monastery and their faith in the Virgin Mary would ensure their safety and survival. However, whether by luck or betrayal, they were discovered and issued with an ultimatum to surrender. Their refusal prompted an immediate and merciless reaction: the roof was blown off, the monastery set alight and all those inside burnt alive. There were no survivors. Although the war continued for another four years, Ibrahim's ruthless methods were ultimately unsuccessful, thanks to the intervention on the Greek side by the then-great powers of Britain, France and Russia.

Less than 100 years later, another huge catastrophe involving fire beset the Greek population of Smyrna (now the Turkish city of Izmir), situated on the Aegean coast of Asia Minor. At the beginning of the 20th century, Smyrna was a prosperous, multicultural, cosmopolitan city and seaport of about a quarter of a million inhabitants. Fewer than a half were Turks, more than a third were Greeks and the rest were Armenians, Jews and other nationalities. The Great Fire of Smyrna has left an indelible imprint on the psyche of the Greek nation. It represented the end of thousands of years of Greek settlement in Asia Minor and it confirmed every Greek's worst prejudices about the Turkish people. It also marked the endgame of the ambitious, some would say foolhardy, plans of 'The Great Idea', embraced by Eleftherios Venizelos, a charismatic Greek politician and statesman of the early 20th century who sought to expand Greece's borders to their historical limits.

The March 1921 invasion of Asia Minor – part of the recently established independent Turkey but home to one and a quarter million ethnic Greeks – was an ill-thought-out and high-risk strategy that backfired badly. The Greek Army's advance was eventually repulsed by Kemal Ataturk's revitalised Turkish Army and its disorderly retreat and evacuation from Smyrna led to one of the 20th century's grimmest acts of genocide. Four days after taking control of the city on September 9th 1922, Turkish forces began a systematic programme of incendiarism in the Greek and Armenian quarters, which continued for nine days and caused the displacement of thousands of inhabitants, who crowded the waterfront in the forlorn hope of being rescued.

One eyewitness described a solid mass of terror-filled humanity and baggage that lasted for nearly two weeks until an international rescue operation was implemented. An estimated 150,000 refugees were evacuated but many did not survive the grotesque ordeal. As many as 100,000 people died – incinerated by the flames, asphyxiated by the smoke and heat or perished from panic and chaos, from suicide or from random acts of violence by Turkish troops. A further 100,000 Greek and Armenian men were rounded up and interned. The eventual outcome, brokered by the then-great powers, was an internationally sponsored programme of population exchange between Greece and Turkey of almost two million people.

Sacred Fire

In Ancient Greece, fire was deeply embedded in the religious practices of the day. Sacred flames were not just present in temples; almost every home had a small altar with a continuously burning sacred fire of coals. They were covered by ash at night to prevent the fire extinguishing and revived every morning. The sacred fire was seen as a divine link with the gods, whose beneficence was sought by offering daily prayers to the fire. Once a year, to maintain its purity, the fire was extinguished and relit immediately by a magnification of the sun's rays. A similar process is repeated every four years in the run up to the modern Olympic Games.

Along with the interlocking, multi-coloured Olympic rings representing five continents, the Olympic flame has become a potent symbol of the modern Olympic Games. The first Olympic Games took place in 776 BCE and were part of a religious festival in honour of Zeus. They were held in the pre-existing sanctuary of Olympia in the north-west of the Peloponnese, the heartland of Ancient Greece. Central to the whole site was the sacred precinct of Altis, dominated by the grandiose Temple of Zeus as well as the Temple of Hera and many other altars, shrines and sanctuaries. Surrounding the Altis were the Stadium, the Hippodrome and the Gymnasiums where the Olympic competitions took place. Today's Olympia still retains many distinguishable remains of the ancient site. In her book about the ancient Games, Judith Swaddling describes Olympia as '*a site combining a sports complex and a centre for religious devotion, something like a combination of Wembley Stadium and Westminster Abbey*'.

The lighting of the flame for the 2012 London Olympics, which took place in the heart of Ancient Olympia, was described by Helena Smith in her report for *The Guardian* newspaper: '*It was a majestic moment. The clouds came and then they went, and in between the sun popped out. In that moment, Ino Menegaki, the highest of 'high priestesses', gathered before the great stone altar of the Temple of Hera, took her torch, placed it in a parabolic mirror and lit it from the sun's rays. In a second, it seemed, the Olympic Flame was born.*' This simple ceremony was supposed to replicate the way it had happened, in exactly the same place, nearly 3,000 years before when Hestia, Zeus' sister, performed that important role. She was responsible for maintaining the divine fire of the Olympian hearth throughout the Games to remind competitors that their victories were not just for their own gratification and their homeland's pride, but primarily to honour Zeus.

The lighting of the Olympic Flame in 2012 marked the first step on a 16,000-kilometre journey through Greece and Britain, during which the torch was carried by over 10,000 torchbearers. The journey culminated in the new Olympic Stadium in east London at the opening ceremony of the 30th Olympiad of the modern era. Steve Redgrave, Britain's five-time rowing gold medallist, handed the Olympic Flame over to seven young athletes, who ignited copper petals on the ground, part of a huge, ingenious, gas-fired, mechanical contraption. The fire spread in a wide circle and then proceeded inwards to the centre as hundreds of other copper petals ignited and, as if by magic, rose into the sky and coalesced to form a spectacular flaming cauldron. The London Olympics had kicked off.

Seventeen days later, the closing ceremony was a joyous celebration of dance and song, culminating in the solemn passing over of the Olympic Flag to the organisers of the 2016 Rio Games and the extinguishing of the Olympic Flame. At exactly the same time, on the other side of Europe, fires were breaking out on the Greek island of Chios, just off the coast of Turkey. Far from being the controlled spectacle that had inspired spectators and athletes alike during the course of the Olympics, these fires were out of control, threatening lives, properties and livelihoods and causing fear, panic and despair. Instead of a spectacular firework display illuminating London's night sky, it was a two-kilometre-wide curtain of ten-metre-high flames, accompanied by billowing clouds of brown smoke. This was wildfire.

Wildfires

It is the monotonous, throaty drone of a low-flying pair of small spotter planes heading south that heralds the advent of the wildfire season in the Mani. Stationed at the Greek Air Force base in Kalamata, they are a regular feature in the summer sky, reminding inhabitants and tourists alike of the potential for wildfires. It was a very different sound that confronted us on a Tuesday afternoon in June 2000. By then, Mary and I were familiar with the zestful clanging of Neohori church bells calling people to worship early on a Sunday morning and the doleful, muted tones of a single bell that signalled the death of a villager. This ringing was something different; just as intense as on a Sunday morning, but it continued incessantly and possessed a sense of urgency and alarm. Our neighbours shouting *"Fotia! Fotia!"* dispelled any uncertainty. There was a fire in the village. The anxious scampering of people, armed with an assortment of tools for fire-fighting, along our narrow street prompted us to quickly follow.

The wildfire was on the edge of the village, no more than 250 metres away from our house. Fortunately, because of a strong north westerly wind, it posed no immediate threat to the village itself. It had started in the desiccated wild grasses of a small abandoned field but was heading straight for a large adjoining area of olive trees.

Once ignited, they burn with a fierce intensity, fuelled by their highly flammable constitution. Prompt, concerted action was required.

Our first impression was encouraging. Most of the village had gathered to combat the fire and were busy stamping out the burning grasses and attacking the flames with garden and household implements. We had equipped ourselves with neither and were not prepared to risk our flip-flop-shod feet assisting with the stamping process. So, taking a lead from several others, we resorted to branches ripped from nearby trees, with which we flailed the fire, all the while taking care to tread carefully. A garden hose from a nearby property had only reached so far and an abiding memory of the whole episode is of a young man valiantly trying to unite this hose with another by hand and in doing so, spraying himself continuously with a stream of escaping water.

The fire was contained within half an hour, and people returned to their homes in a relieved and self-congratulatory mood. The few who remained to ensure there was no delayed combustion were soon joined by the belated arrival of a fire engine. But how had it started? It emerged that the village electrician-plumber had been repairing equipment in the children's playground adjacent to the church, a process that had required some welding. It took no more than an unnoticed stray spark for this minor conflagration to begin. In such simple, straightforward ways wildfires erupt and can sometimes lead to unmitigated disaster.

This minor incident remains the only wildfire that Mary and I have experienced first-hand and up close during our twenty-three years living in Greece. We have travelled through areas devastated by wildfires and witnessed the misery and suffering they leave behind, but our other personal experiences of Greek wildfires have thankfully been restricted to distant clouds of barrelling black smoke in an otherwise clear blue sky; to ominous orange skies several hours before sunset; to whirling, abrasive hot winds, unpredictable in their force and direction, and to swimming in a sea densely flecked with black cinders and ash. While people across Greece have been stalked by the fear of approaching wildfire, mild apprehension is the most we have suffered.

Summer wildfires in countries with mediterranean climates are not uncommon. Although their frequency, their intensity and their geographical spread seem to be increasing, they have always been an integral part of the mediterranean environment. Even before the end of June 2017 (early by most northern hemisphere norms), wildfires had raged in Portugal, Spain and California. Long periods without rain and regular daytime maximums in the mid- to high-thirties degrees Celsius create ground conditions that the most innocuous spark can spontaneously ignite. Quick on-the-spot action to tackle the source of the blaze and rapid and effective response from the emergency services are normally enough to contain the fire and prevent it from spreading. If that fails, the wildfire often gains a momentum of its own, which becomes increasingly difficult to arrest.

In the summers of 2006, 2007 and 2009, Greek wildfires were more numerous, more intense and more widespread than ever before and emergency services were stretched well beyond their limits. Many wildfires went unchallenged by trained firefighters, spiralled out of control and caused huge devastation. Greeks were numbed by the newspaper reports and TV pictures of one tragedy after another, of charred and blackened landscapes, of burnt-out churches, of families who had lost everything and of a grim death toll.

Catastrophe

Unquestionably, the summer of 2007 marked the nadir of those three years of Greek wildfires. They were the most devastating for fifty years and lasted, on and off, for three months. An official Fire Alert had been declared as early as May 10th and both the Meteorological and the Forest Services were predicting a high risk of wildfire outbreaks. But no one foresaw the scale and intensity of the wildfires that decimated many parts of Greece, especially the Peloponnese, during the final days of August 2007. Prime Minister Kostas Karamanlis declared a state of emergency and appealed to the EU for help, while media coverage brought the unfolding tragedy to a stunned audience worldwide. *"This is our Tsunami, our 9/11"*, one Greek pronounced; another described it as *"a biblical catastrophe"*. The soul of Greece was being tortured by wildfire.

Helena Smith's September 1st report for *The Guardian* newspaper was a most haunting and harrowing account of people's utter helplessness in the face of wildfire that spirals out of control. Her report focused on the area around the small agricultural and tourist town of Zacharo, on the Ionian Sea coast of the Peloponnese. On one day, Friday 24th August, more people died here than anywhere else during the eight days of wildfires that ravaged Greece. She began her report with two graphic stories. The first one involved two men, Spyros Bilionis and Pandazis Chronopoulos (the then-Mayor of Zacharo). They were in a silver jeep that suddenly encountered a giant wall of flames blocking the road ahead of them. The question that required an instant answer was, what to do? Turn around or drive straight through? They chose the latter. Apparently neither man was sure how long the episode lasted but could recall that '*the fire, white hot and fearless, licked at the windows of the vehicle, buckling them as if they were toffee, searing our feet and burning our lips dry*'. Suddenly, the dense smoke, which had proved an added hazard, cleared to reveal a desolate, blackened, ash-laden landscape, devoid of life. They credited their escape from the clutches of the inferno to their desperate pleas to the Virgin Mary throughout their ordeal.

Tragically, the Virgin Mary could not save an Athens schoolteacher, Athanasia Paraskevopoulou, and her four children. She had encountered the same giant wall of flames on the same road a few moments previously. However, her instincts had told her not to drive through the flames, but to turn back and use a parallel road to try and outflank the wildfire. Her decision proved to be fatal. In the smoke-filled confusion she drove straight into a pile-up of burning vehicles from which few people, if any, escaped. Athanasia was found dead in her burnt-out car clinging to the charred corpses of her children. A more gruesome death is difficult to imagine.

Situated in wooded hill country dissected by steep-sided valleys and not far from the village of Almeida, the site of this carnage is marked by a line of fifteen upstanding marble memorials at the roadside. With their bouquets of artificial flowers and their faded coloured photos, they commemorate the deaths of twenty-three people, including some part-time firefighters. I cannot recall a more sobering and poignant sight; a sombre and gruesome reminder of the destructive force of wildfire. Mary and I found it hard to imagine that this tranquil, rural landscape, dotted with occasional small villages and olive groves, bathed in autumn sunlight and with panoramic views of the nearby Ionian Sea, could have been the setting for so much tragic loss of life. Apart from the memorials, little evidence remained of the impact of the wildfire that had savaged this area ten years before. Nature had bounced back in its usual way, but the human loss would take much longer to erase. We couldn't help wondering what sorrow and pain the memorials invoke in survivors who pass by them every day.

Television and newspaper pictures of firefighters slumped on blackened roadside banks, utterly exhausted by hours of toil in horrendous heat, were a constant reminder of the heroic efforts by members of the Greek Fire Service. Often in difficult terrain, remote from adequate supplies of water and conscious of the unpredictable nature of their foe, the courage and self-sacrifice of the firefighters was recognised by all. Forces on the ground were eventually augmented by 5,000 soldiers and were hugely assisted by aerial support and surveillance. Large numbers of fire-fighting aircraft and helicopters from many European countries assisted the overstretched Greek contingent. Their role was to drop large volumes of water on existing fires and fire retardant on vulnerable adjacent property, and give advice and information to ground forces. The lumbering, yellow-painted Canadairs, able to scoop up six tonnes of water from the sea or lakes, and the Russian-built helicopters with fifteen-tonne capacity buckets slung below became reassuring sights in the turbulent and smoke-filled skies.

Although these superhuman efforts to control and extinguish the wildfires eventually prevailed, the sum of destruction and devastation in Greece during the summer of 2007 became apparent only slowly. Suffering and loss on such a scale had not been experienced since the Second World War and the civil war that followed. The figures are staggering. 3,000 square kilometres of land was burned – equivalent to the English county of Lancashire – and over half the area razed comprised protected nature reserves and forest. More than 750 swarms of bees were lost, 400,000 sheep and goats in the Peloponnese were deprived of pasture, and an estimated 6,000 people were made homeless. Most depressing of all, sixty-seven people lost their lives. It was a death toll that Greeks and the rest of the world found hard to comprehend. How could a relatively rich, developed country with a long history of dealing with summer wildfires suffer such a devastating loss? One of the answers lay in the power and unpredictability of a natural phenomenon unleashed.

Recovery

"*There was so much anger, so much pain, rage and even hatred*", a survivor who lost both her parents in the 2007 wildfires recalls. Recovery from any catastrophe is a long and tortuous journey, especially traumatic if families have been blighted by the death of loved ones, the razing of homes and the shattering of livelihoods. Tormented by images of death and destruction, the emotional toll is immense. The mourning of loved ones, their funerals, the picking over of blackened and burnt belongings, the search for temporary accommodation, all have a profound emotional impact. And all the while, an acute anxiety persists over money and compensation and worries about how things might never get back to normal. Depression becomes commonplace and can consume whole communities. An understandable immediate reaction is to wish to escape the consequences… but how? Without the help and support of relatives and neighbours, Orthodox priests and teams of volunteers, as well as local and national organisations providing welfare, professional advice and counselling, the mental health of stricken individuals and families can quickly deteriorate. Both in the short- and long-term, emergency action and funding are vital components of the recovery process.

Although the 2007 wildfires threatened and even invaded the edges of some suburban communities, it was rural, agricultural communities that bore the brunt of the destruction. In many ways, livestock farmers were worst hit. The wildfires that destroyed large swathes of pasture in the Peloponnese left many sheep and goats dead or injured, despite the heroic efforts of their shepherds and peripatetic veterinarians. Deprived of pasture, surviving animals had to rely on the government's emergency feeding programme. In the *Athens News* of September 14th, Vasillios Sekos summed up his village's predicament, typical of many afflicted by wildfires. "*We have around 1,000 animals in total and we have nothing for them to eat: our village has lost 100% of its grazing land. We have been summoned to the Town Hall to pick up foodstuffs but they only gave us 3–4kg per animal which is expected to last four days*". The government feeding programme was supposed to provide one kilogram of corn and one kilogram of hay and clover per animal per day. However, inadequate funding and logistical supply problems meant that many animals received only half that amount. The scale and duration of the emergency feeding programme would cost the Greek government something in the region of thirty million euros. Those farmers whose livestock were not registered with their local veterinary directorate were forced to rely on animal welfare groups, charities, and corporate and private philanthropists.

Almost exactly one year earlier, John Phipps' report in the *Athens News* had described the consequences for seventy-two-year-old beekeeper Stylianos Theodorakos of a wildfire that devastated a swathe of the Mani peninsula between Areopoli and Gytheio. Sage, thyme and heather grow in abundance here and for years have provided the local beekeepers with excellent crops of high-quality honey. Half of Theodorakos' 140 beehives were completely destroyed by fire, while the inhabitants of the rest all perished in a bid to escape the heat and smoke. A business built up over twenty years, supplying tourists and locals alike from its makeshift premises beside the main road, had been destroyed in less than twenty-four hours. Purchasing replacement hives and breeding new colonies of bees would be a long and expensive business, with no guarantee of financial aid or compensation. At his age, Stylianos could have been forgiven for calling it a day, but fourteen years on, his apiary is flourishing once again, a tribute to his beekeeping passion and dogged determination.

Mother Nature Bouncing Back

Just six weeks after the wildfire had devastated Stylianos' apiary, Mary and I were on our way to Gytheio when something seemed to explode like a firework in the night sky from the blackened ground overlooking the road. I brought the car to a shuddering halt and reversed cautiously to investigate. We were astonished to find a large clump of bright pink autumn cyclamen in flower. Nothing else seemed to have survived the wildfire that had engulfed this valley. Scarcely a trace of groundcover plants remained and the blackened branches of bushes and severely scorched trees all bore witness to the inferno. But the cyclamen had declared its survival in the most dramatic of ways. Just like asphodels, sea squills, orchids and crocuses, its hardy tuber, protected by the soil, was able to withstand the heat and survive to bloom for another season.

Nature's powers of recovery from Mediterranean wildfires are well documented. Some plants have remarkable resilience. The cork oak is a good example. With its thick and resilient bark, it can withstand a fierce fire; its leaves and smaller branches burn but its main branches and trunk survive and re-sprout when time and conditions allow. Several trees and bushes like the olive, the prickly oak, the strawberry tree, myrtle, juniper and some heathers can be severely burned by a wildfire but survive by re-sprouting from the base. In favourable conditions, re-growth can reach one metre within just twelve months.

Other trees and plants are destroyed by wildfire but replicate themselves by seed. The master of this kind of natural regeneration is the cistus, more commonly known as the rock rose. Each plant produces a substantial annual crop of small seeds, most of which remain dormant. It is only the intense heat of a wildfire that ruptures the cistus seeds' hard outer casing and engenders life potential. In favourable conditions germination is prolific, and the cistus can quickly outgrow and overcome all its competitors in just a few years. Whole swathes of low bushes festooned with masses of elegant pink and white flowers in early summer are evidence of the cistus' ability to re-establish itself.

The Aleppo pine, common throughout Greece, also needs fire to trigger the release of its seeds. The heat melts the resin that seals the seeds in the cone, the cone scales open and the winged seeds are scattered by the wind. Studies of regeneration rates of Aleppo pines after wildfires that have eliminated most of the competition show a startling rate of natural regeneration when conditions are ideal. The wildfire leaves in its wake a fresh supply of ash containing plant mineral nutrients, encouraging seedlings to prosper and vegetation to recover after the first rains. Simple practical measures can encourage regeneration of forest. For instance, wooden barriers erected across small gullies and water courses serve to reduce soil erosion, which accelerates once mature vegetation cover has been destroyed. It is also essential for the Forest Service to keep grazing and indiscriminate logging of partially burned timber under control.

A visit to the area around the small coastal town of Kotronas in East Mani in the wake of the August 2017 fires provided much evidence of nature's restorative powers. Subjected to a raging, fast-moving wildfire requiring emergency evacuation of inhabitants by sea, large areas of woodland and Mediterranean shrubland – as well as grazing land – had been comprehensively burned. Only a few random, isolated patches had escaped the devastating consequences that stretched from valley floor to mountain top. The landscape had been profoundly scarred. Speaking to *Reuters*, Greenpeace's Nikos Charalambides' comments were brief but insightful: "*The green used to cool the area and spread humidity. Now there's just a black box which will absorb heat by day and let it out by night.*" Nonetheless, we were able to observe optimistic signs of life and renewal. Kermes oaks were sprouting new branches and leaves from their resilient trunks; the doleful remains of olive and wild almond trees and roadside oleanders were sending out vigorous new shoots from their root crowns; and multitudes of wild grasses and bulbs, triggered by the first autumn rains, were bursting through the blackened soil and declaring their survival. The colour green was once again beginning to re-assert itself.

Wild animals, birds and insects do not possess the same resilience or ability to recover after wildfires. Their chances of survival are governed by their size, speed of movement, stamina and the sophistication of their sensory powers. It's really quite simple: animals unable to flee the flames perish. Slow movers like tortoises and snails have no chance and their whitened shells are a common sight, scattered across recently burned areas. Birds and flying insects have the speed and mobility to escape but they too can perish from the heat, turbulence, smoke and air-borne red-hot cinders generated by wildfires. Larger mammals like boars, jackals, foxes, hares and rabbits are much better equipped to outrun wildfires but exhaustion, exacerbated by inhaling foul air, and the destruction of their food supply can sometimes cause fatalities. Surviving a wildfire is rarely good news for wild animals. They inherit a desolate, sterile habitat where food and water are hard to come by until the ecosystem re-establishes itself. This may take several years.

Accident or Arson?

Research seems to indicate a trend of more frequent wildfires occurring across the lands bordering the Mediterranean Sea. Not only are they becoming more widespread but they are starting to occur outside the normal peak season, and their increasing levels of intensity are proving difficult for fire-fighting agencies to combat. The main reason for this trend is almost certainly climate change. There appears to be solid evidence that the eastern Mediterranean is becoming warmer and drier and experiencing more extreme and often hazardous weather events. At the same time, the duration and frequency of heatwaves and the number of consecutive dry days is increasing. Governments ignore these trends at their peril. Without sufficient planning and investment in personnel and resources, wildfires could have a lasting and widespread detrimental impact on ecosytems, forestry, agriculture, communications and tourism. People's lives, livelihoods and homes will be increasingly at risk without bold and effective action.

What is undeniable is that the natural conditions in the last few days of August 2007 were ripe for wildfires. Three blistering heatwaves with daytime temperatures exceeding 40°C had punctuated a relentlessly long, hot, dry summer. Everywhere was parched. And then, to add to the high-risk situation, the calm air was replaced by a northerly wind that would fan the flames and accelerate their progress. Changes in how the rural economy operates had also played a part. The diminishing number of shepherds and goatherds has reduced the winter grazing of olive groves, leaving the grasses and low undergrowth to grow unchecked. The conscientious olive farmer will strim these dried grasses and burn them, along with the olive tree prunings, before the April 30th deadline arrives; after which, bonfires are banned for six months. On the other hand, absentee olive farmers often spend just a few days harvesting before abandoning their olive groves for another year. In this way, a dangerous build-up of perfect kindling accumulates. Added to this is the poorly resourced and underfunded Greek Forest Service, which strains to manage and protect the 25,000 square kilometres of tall trees under its jurisdiction.

The cause of the wildfires is the subject of prolonged, heated debate in Greece. A few minutes watching the talking heads on morning

TV news programmes distils the many arguments into a single issue: was it accident or arson? Human carelessness and thoughtlessness are at the core of most accidental wildfires. A cigarette stub carelessly discarded from a car window, wayside rubbish dumping – especially if it contains broken glass that can focus the sun's rays – or an indiscriminate firework display to celebrate a wedding or a baptism can all have devastating consequences. Poorly doused, illegal campfires in forest areas, sparks from old or ill-maintained petrol-driven equipment or a short circuit on the national electricity grid have also been responsible for triggering outbreaks.

But in the aftermath of the 2007 wildfires, the focus was on arson, not accident. An embattled prime minister, Kostas Karamanlis, had little doubt when he appeared on national television on August 25th. *"So many fires sparked in so many regions are no coincidence,"* he said. *"We'll get to the bottom of this and punish those responsible."* This statement generated a torrent of criticism from his political opponents, who accused him of trying to deflect attention from his government's mishandling of the crisis. In Helena Smith's opinion, many Greeks believed that the government had done little to prevent the fires and had bungled a rescue operation that went from bad to worse as the scale of the problem escalated. And yet there was a groundswell of opinion amongst ordinary Greek people that arson was a significant cause. Was it misanthropes or political extremists intent on embarrassing the government, or maybe property speculators with the aim of obtaining the release of fire-ravaged, protected land for development? Perhaps it was copycats with a mischievous desire for a brief moment of anonymous fame, or part of a vendetta or a spiteful act of revenge? The debate is far from over.

The Aftermath

The summer 2007 wildfires featured prominently in the hard-fought general election campaign that followed. The outcome of the vote on

September 16th maintained the status quo, with the much-criticised prime minister, Kostas Karamanlis, and his Nea Democratia party securing a reduced majority of seats in the Greek parliament. But the matter of wildfires did not go away. So many claims and counterclaims had littered the election campaign, it was now time to get to the bottom of the matter. A groundswell of public opinion demanded that action be taken so that such a catastrophe would never occur again. *"We are old; we have no future in our lives. But please help our young ones!"* an eighty-year-old villager pleaded.

Transactions that took place so soon after the last of the 2007 Peloponnese wildfires had finally been extinguished seemed to confirm mainstream opinion in Greece that regarded arson as the primary cause. On September 12th, in his town centre office, the Zacharo mayor signed a memorandum of cooperation with the Greek deputy finance minister, acting with the full authority of the government, on behalf of the Hellenic Real Estate Corporation. The memorandum paved the way for the release of sixteen kilometres of virgin Ionian Sea coastline from conservation and building controls and its lease to private companies for unspecified tourism development.

Outrage followed, especially from those in the arson camp, who had predicted all along that fires in sensitive conservation areas were started with the precise aim of reclassifying land for building development. Environmentalists were also up in arms because Zacharo's sandy beaches and coastal pine forests are included in the EU's Natura 2000 programme, which seeks to protect areas of significant ecological value. Even local people in the tourist business had cause to be wary. The suspicion was that the memorandum would favour big tourism, funded and developed by Greek or international corporations based in Athens, at the expense of sustainable, smaller-scale local development, where profits would be channelled back into the community.

In a hard-hitting feature in *The Guardian* newspaper on November 9th 2007, entitled *'After the Inferno'*, Maria Margaronis boldly states that catastrophe means opportunity. She goes on to declare that *'Both*

Zacharo's mayor and the Greek government appear to give priority to corporate investment at the expense of accountability, both pay lip service to conservation while seeing it as an obstacle to economic growth. [...] And both are taking the fires as an opportunity not to restore and build on what has been lost but to push through the rapid capitalisation of the region's natural resources, regardless of human and environmental cost.' In a September 2007 *Athens News* report, the director of the Greek branch of the World Wildlife Fund opined that much of the outcry was skin deep. *'Every Greek says he loves trees, but in reality we have a love of cement'*, Dimitris Karavellas wrote, adding that, *'The problem with fires in Greece is not the fires themselves, it's what happens after the fires. Within months of a forest burning down, you will see a villa, a hotel or even a new town springing up'*. And yet, despite all the post-fire hullabaloo thirteen years ago, there are few signs that Zacharo's virgin coastline is undergoing large-scale tourist development. Maybe the economic crisis has delayed matters?

A Safer Future?

Although a series of reports and conferences highlighted shortcomings and proposed solutions, there was no comprehensive, all-embracing analysis of how the summer wildfires of 2007 were handled. Yet some lessons were learned. Despite its funding remaining static since the onset of the economic crisis, the Greek Fire Service has striven to improve its planning, organisation, training and liaison, and has begun to embrace more sophisticated means of predicting and monitoring fires. While its fleet of fire-fighting aeroplanes and helicopters is showing signs of age, it has adopted GPS and drones as a means of surveillance and developed fast-response ground units, which are ferried by helicopters to outbreaks of fire in an effort to curb them before they enlarge and spread. However, if progress is judged by effectiveness there is still much to do. The reaction of local inhabitants to the Fire Service response to the outbreaks of wildfires on Zakynthos and in East Mani in the summer of 2017 was less than complimentary.

The continued emasculation of the Greek Forest Service is difficult to understand. Entirely responsible for forest fire-fighting up until 1998, when that role was transferred to the Fire Service, it now plays a negligible part in combatting forest fires. According to Gavriil Xanthopoulos, it has become a weak, broken-down, underfunded organisation. Thus, planned forest management and development, maintenance of forest tracks and the promotion of fire prevention measures have all suffered. The considerable expertise, insights and experience of locally based Forest Service personnel have been lost or ignored. One positive step forward, in which the Forest Service has been involved, is the long overdue nationwide compilation of a comprehensive forest register – the so-called Forest Maps. Although controversial and currently subject to an extensive programme of consultation and amendment, the Forest Maps, once rubber-stamped, should establish clear boundaries between private and forest land. Thus, the incentive to commit arson to persuade the government to release burnt forest land for development will be reduced. Or that's the theory.

The widespread unease amongst the Greek people in the months following the 2007 wildfires, and their suspicion that government promises would come to nothing, prompted some communities to embrace self-help as a way forward. Named after the mythical Mother Earth goddess born at the dawn of creation, Gaia (pronounced 'yeah') is a voluntary organisation based in Aghios Nikolaos in West Mani. It was established in the year 2000 by Gregoris Orfanidis, a Greek doctor returning to his homeland after a career in Switzerland, but is now managed by a committee of five elected officials. Initially it concerned itself with environmental matters, especially shoreline and roadside cleaning, but now it embraces a wide range of activities, including cave and mountain rescue, medical emergencies, recycling, animal protection and, most importantly, fire-fighting.

The West Mani tourist resorts of Kardamyli, Stoupa and Aghios

Nikolaos and their hinterland are located an hour's drive from the nearest Greek Fire Service stations in Kalamata and Areopoli, and are thus particularly vulnerable to wildfires spiralling out of control before fire-fighting crews arrive. Gaia's fire-fighting team was established to address this situation. Comprising ten volunteers, all fully trained, it is a most dedicated and professional outfit operating a twenty-four-hour standby system from May to October. The vital role it plays was recognised in November 2017 with the presentation of a special award by the Greek Fire Service in Athens to Christina Constantios, the then-chairperson.

Equipped with three donated second-hand fire engines, a rapid response 4x4 vehicle (also donated) and a motorbike, and working in liaison with the Greek Fire Service and other emergency services, Gaia firefighters are ready to respond to call-outs at a moment's notice. Since 2010, Gaia fire crews have attended over 100 fires each year ranging from small, easily extinguished local outbreaks to assisting with major conflagrations throughout the Mani. In return for the wide-reaching reassurance that Gaia provides for West Mani inhabitants, much of the money needed to fund their operation is raised through membership fees, donations and local fundraising events. With its focus on self-reliance, Gaia provides a model for other areas to aspire to and follow.

There is little doubt that the threat from wildfires across the whole Mediterranean region will continue to rise as the effects of climate change deepen. Mediterranean peoples have always managed to co-exist with occasional outbreaks of wildfires, but the 21st century has brought a change in their frequency and intensity. The vague equilibrium that once existed between wildfires and humanity has been replaced by a greater unease as wildfires have become more of a menace. Progress in the Greek Fire Service's fire-fighting capacity and effectiveness, restoration of the powers and resources of the Forest Service, and promotion of local volunteer fire-fighting units must go hand-in-hand with other measures. Following the devastating summer of 2007, several reassuring developments appeared for all to see. Inadequate water supplies for firefighters had registered as a common problem, so gradually, in more inaccessible areas, huge tanks appeared, some able to hold up to 20,000 cubic metres of water. Located beside roads and dirt tracks, some are made of heavy-duty black plastic while the biggest are stainless steel, creating the disconcerting impression of a stranded UFO on a moonlit night. In addition, dramatic new fire breaks have been forged through thickly forested hillsides, leaving fifty-metre-wide barren scars intended to arrest the spread of forest fire. Hopefully they will be properly maintained, unlike those overgrown breaks that did nothing to stem the rapid spread of the 2007 wildfires near Zacharo. More recently, small, secondary fire-fighting units have been stationed in villages remote from the main fire stations during high-risk periods, and more lookout posts have been established, staffed by both fire service and local authority personnel.

But practical measures need reinforcing with other action, involving a more difficult challenge: changing people's attitudes and behaviour. In an interview for the *news247.gr* website in August 2017, the Pyrgos Fire Chief, Yiannis Petroutsos, praises the valiant contribution of villagers to fire-fighting but bemoans their indifference to fire prevention. He quotes the example of the widespread decline in the late springtime ploughing of fields, which used to enable them to act as fire breaks. His counterpart in Olympia, Vasilis Yiakoumis, urged all villages to specify a safe fire assembly point within the village, like a football pitch or basketball court. He discouraged all attempts to evacuate villages, quoting evidence that indicates that most fire deaths happen to people in flight. With a wildfire fast approaching, simple precautions can also make a big difference. For instance, the removal of a highly combustible butane or propane gas bottle from kitchen to garden – or better still, down a well – can reduce considerably the risk of a house burning down.

Changing attitudes must involve regulation and education, and neither will happen without government commitment and resolve. To persuade Greeks that arson is not the sole cause of wildfires and that many are preventable, mindless acts of carelessness requires the government to take a lead. Investment in updating the Fire Service and improving its effectiveness is wasteful unless it goes hand-in-hand with a fire prevention programme. A public education campaign involving schools, local authorities, conventional and social media, repeated annually at the onset of summer, would surely pay dividends. Emergency alerts via mobile phone by the Civil Protection Secretariat during the 2020 Covid-19 pandemic demonstrate that the means exist to raise levels of vigilance and safeguarding during periods when the risk of wildfires is high.

Learning from other countries' experience and protocols might also prove valuable. 'Hotshots' are local heroes in the forest zones of the Rocky Mountains. They are fire rangers who conduct regular controlled burns to keep down the accumulation of dead undergrowth and fallen branches. Their skilled and masterful work ensures that the ground fuel for forest fires is eliminated and thus the risk of spontaneous combustion reduced. In rural parts of Greece where forest and mountain coincide, there are sufficient people – some ex-Forest Service employees – with fire know-how, augmented by relevant retraining, who would be more than capable of conducting controlled burns.

A commemorative t-shirt bearing the logo 'EVAC 2017' was the reward for three hours of unusual activity on the evening of September 21st for English friends who spend their summers on the Atlantic coast of western France, not far from the town of Royan. Organised by the local prefecture and involving sixty firefighters, twenty-five police and fifty soldiers, it involved a simulated evacuation of a heavily forested area of pine trees much favoured by campers and caravanners. A 7pm siren accompanied by mobile loudspeakers prompted 250 residents and holidaymakers – who had been forewarned – to make their way in an orderly fashion to predetermined muster points, from which they were evacuated by coach. Meanwhile, aerial drones recorded fire hoses being deployed and pretend casualties stretchered away to waiting ambulances. Escorted by police motorcycles – blue flashing lights and all – the 'evacuees' were taken to the Sports Hall in Les Mathes, the nearest town. Lengthy speeches from the mayor and other dignitaries were the price to pay for all this excitement but bags of sandwiches, cakes and drinks were offered as compensation for missing dinner. The exercise was judged a big success with lots of lessons learned and holidaymakers reassured that their safety and security were being taken seriously and not just down to the strict ban on barbeques and fires. Similar simulations in wooded camping zones in Greece would surely have similar positive outcomes.

Sadly, there is a grim postscript to all of this that casts doubt on Greece's ability to prevent future wildfire disasters. In July 2018 a wildfire engulfed the seaside settlements of Mati and Kokkino Limanaki, north of the ferry port of Rafina and just twenty-five kilometres east of Athens. 102 people died, 172 were injured and over 1,000 buildings were destroyed or damaged in the worst Greek natural disaster in living memory. Once again the Greek nation was numbed by the scale of devastation and loss of life. It seems many lessons from the 2007 wildfires remained unheeded; in particular the high risk of fleeing a fire by car, which caused unimaginable chaos and pile-ups on narrow roads that became instant death traps. Furthermore, access to the sea, which would have provided temporary safety and a potential evacuation route, was often denied by heavily fenced properties built illegally too close to the shore.

In the search for answers in the aftermath, blame was widely spread. Inevitably, the government was called to account but sought to deflect it; local authorities were held responsible for underestimating the scale of the tragedy and for a lack of emergency evacuation procedures; the Greek Police were castigated for their inept handling of the traffic chaos; and the Greek Fire Service's tardy initial response was blamed on operational cut-backs due to austerity. Even the Greek Meteorological Service did not escape blame. It was accused of failing to predict the high winds that fanned the flames and grounded aerial fire-fighting units. In March 2019, twenty people – politicians and high-ranking police and fire officials

– were charged for their operational mishandling of the disaster. A report by the prosecutors found that there was a criminal lack of civil protection planning, as well as poor co-ordination and an absence of effective communication between the public services responsible for tackling the fire.

Prosecution of individuals will satisfy some, but a determination to reform and strengthen the systems and organisations that failed the victims of the 2018 fire would be welcomed by all. In fact, it's an undeniable priority. In a world where climate change and its impact are gathering pace and the threat of more frequent, more intense and more devastating wildfires in Greece is beyond reasonable doubt, suppressing and controlling wildfires will become increasingly difficult. On the other hand, developing well-understood and well-rehearsed procedures to minimise losses is within human grasp.

Amid all the gloom of this chapter, there are glimmers of hope, epitomised by letters published in the Kalamata daily newspaper *Tharros* following the wildfires that ravaged Zacharo in August 2007. These were open letters written by pupils from a local *gymnasio* (junior high school) to their peers in Zacharo. One in particular, which echoed the common sentiments expressed in many others, resonated strongly with me:

> *Dear Friends,*
> *Sometimes life becomes so unfair for us that we wonder what we have done to deserve such punishment. Sometimes we are trapped somewhere and realise we cannot escape, whatever we do. At other times we believe that something bad that has befallen us is the worst thing that could possibly happen. But everything, except death, can be put right. However, you young people who have not just lost your house in the fire, but also members of your family, take courage. No matter how difficult or impossible it seems, remember that crying doesn't fix things and consider if the person who passed away would want to see you upset. Take courage and accept that a person only dies if you forget*

them. Take courage, no matter how impossible or how difficult it is for you. Whatever life throws at you and for whatever reason, don't let it undermine you. Stay strong and don't forget you are not on your own. All the young people of Greece are on your side. Tread boldly, take a deep breath and reflect on how life doesn't always make us smile. Whatever happens we must be strong and ready to face anything.

Be strong, take courage!!
Vasiliki

Compassionate and wise words from a thirteen-year-old that surely offered great succour as well as advice and encouragement. All Greeks, whether they are urban dwellers or country folk, have, deeply lodged in their hearts and minds, a profound understanding of what destruction and loss wildfires can cause. There is a strong, enduring empathy with those fellow citizens affected by wildfires and this can manifest itself at an early age, as Vasiliki's letter shows. Yet empathy alone will not be enough to rid Greece of a repeat of the tragedies that cruelly beset the nation in 2007 and 2018.

A rack of Greek newspapers on display outside a kiosk.

Chapter 6

IT'S ALL GREEK TO ME

A Minority Language

Compared with English, which emerged during the 20th century as the world's No.1 language with an estimated 1.3 billion speakers, Greek is very much a minority language. It is spoken by about thirteen million people worldwide, mainly in Greece and Cyprus but also in parts of Albania and in large Greek communities in Australia, the USA and Canada. These communities – in Melbourne, Chicago and Toronto, for example – established themselves in the 20th century as a result of Greeks fleeing from poverty, dictatorship, ethnic cleansing and civil war in their homeland. In more recent years, the global economic crisis that started in 2008 and had serious repercussions in Greece has created a new wave of emigration. Yet this *diaspora* (dispersal) is not something confined to recent times. It has been a common phenomenon throughout Greece's long history.

Greek is part of the Indo-European family of languages that contains several different branches. The Romance branch includes Spanish, French and Italian, and the Germanic branch, English, German and Dutch, for example. The Greek language occupies a branch on its own, called Hellenic. Despite its linguistic uniqueness and its status as a minority language, Greek has played an important role in the early dissemination of pioneering works on subjects as wide-ranging as astronomy, philosophy, mathematics and literature, as well as in the spread of Christianity. Without Greek, Western civilisation might have developed somewhat differently. Furthermore, along with Latin, Greek has had a profound influence on the development of other European languages, and English is no exception.

Writing on the language website *babbel.com*, Natali Lekka claims there are more than 150,000 Greek words that have been adopted by the English language, most of them derived from Ancient rather than Modern Greek. Many have undergone change as they were acquired and modified by Latin, and maybe subsequently by Old Germanic or Old French, before entering English. Most are to do with politics, the legal system, economics, science, education and medicine. Words like 'democracy' from the Greek words *demos* (people) and *kratos* (government/state); 'monopoly' from *monos* (sole/alone) and *poleio* (selling); and 'cardiologist' straight from *kardiologos*. Many words beginning with 'ph', such as philosophy and philanthropy, as well as words with the prefixes anti-, hyper- and infra- are almost certainly derived from Greek. Some suffixes also indicate a Greek origin, for example words ending in -ist, -ology, -gram and -phobe. Other English words have been coined using Greek roots, like isotherm from *isos* (equal) and *thermos* (heat) but they are rarely found in a Greek dictionary unless they have been borrowed back in more recent times. There are also words like 'euphoria', 'phobia' and 'amnesia' that have been adopted from Greek with minimal changes.

As well as words, the English language has also borrowed a great many expressions from Greek. 'She has the Midas touch', 'You've taken on a Herculean task' and 'It's his Achilles heel' are just a few examples still in common use and widely understood, even though the Greek myths they are derived from are maybe less well known. A reference to something being 'a Pandora's box' is no less common even though there's an English equivalent: 'a can of worms'. According to Greek myth, Pandora was the first woman of humankind and was given a box – more probably a jar – by Zeus, the ruler of the gods, to pass on to her new husband with strict instructions not to open it under any circumstances. However, her inquisitiveness eventually got the better of her and one day while her husband slept, she opened the jar and unleashed a multitude of unforeseen evil and misery on the world.

The impact of the Greek language on English was emphasised in a unique manner by Xenophon Zolotas. He was one of the outstanding Greeks of his generation: a polymath, an internationalist, an ardent socialist and an acclaimed economist. He also attained high office as Director of the Bank of Greece for three terms and as Prime Minister for a brief interim period in 1989. Mention of his name to elderly Greeks is almost certain to invoke memories of the two speeches he delivered to delegates at World Bank annual assemblies in the late 1950s. Rather than pontificate on economic theory, the gold standard or international trade, Zolotas chose to indulge his audience with a brief discourse in English, using only words derived from Greek, with the exception of prepositions and articles. The speeches make amusing reading but are barely intelligible even with a dictionary, and were probably incomprehensible to most delegates who were bankers, financiers and economists rather than linguists. Was it merely an episode of self-indulgence or a bold attempt to promote the Greek language on a world stage?

'Gibberish' is a word beloved of old-fashioned teachers in Britain. It's in school where most English speakers get to know and understand its meaning, when it's used to describe a pupil's unintelligible speech or writing. Of course, there are plenty of alternative expressions that can be used in similar circumstances. When exasperated by failing to understand someone's directions to the local post office or the assembly instructions accompanying a furniture flatpack, Brits are equally likely to dismiss them as 'double Dutch' or exclaim in frustrated tones, *"It's all Greek to me!"* And that's a measure of how impenetrable the Greek language is viewed by most English speakers . . . . and by other language speakers too. Many foreigners visiting or settling in Greece take the easy way out and rely on the fact that more and more Greeks, especially in popular tourist hotspots, speak and understand English. Few take learning Greek seriously and most are content to get by with a handful of words and phrases in everyday use. It's unfortunate that the presence of many words and expressions that derive from Greek in the English language does not seem to give more assistance to Brits trying to learn Modern Greek.

A Change of Tack

Neither Mary nor I had given any attention to learning Greek before we holidayed in Greece for the first time in the summer of 1969. With the bravado and self-assurance of youth, we managed with the tried-and-tested combination of pointing, gesticulating and mime, with occasional recourse to pidgin English, always expressed loudly and deliberately as though the waiter, cleaner or shopkeeper was somewhat slow-witted or suffering some hearing impairment. With English-speaking waiters much less common than today, a pale orange, hardback version of Collins Greek Phrasebook, its pages impregnated with splashes of assorted Greek food and oily thumbprints, was put into regular use. Fortunately, back then – before menus in multiple languages became the norm – it was standard practice for tavernas and restaurants in Greece to put their hot dishes on display in the kitchens. Often, before they were ushered to a table, customers were invited to see what food was on offer, thus easing the process of ordering for both diners and waiters.

Nothing had changed a decade or so later during subsequent Greek holidays in Halkidiki and at Valimitika on the Gulf of

Corinth. By this time Mary and I had become parents and moved house from south-east London to North Devon. We encouraged our two young sons to learn and use a few basic Greek words – the only ones we knew – and much to our shame, they soon matched our woefully inadequate levels. We were muddling through just as before, relying overmuch on Greeks who knew some English. Inevitably, mishaps occurred, some mildly embarrassing, but most just oddly entertaining for all parties involved and quickly laughed off. The most humiliating occurred at the end of a day trip from Valimitika to the nearby town of Egion. The excursion had not gone well: it was very hot, the guidebook had exaggerated Egion's attractions, and our sons quickly lost interest. My ineptitude at the bus station, failing to find the return bus, made things worse. Eventually, with tempers fraying, we resorted to a taxi. That would have been the end of the matter if Will, our older son, had not been so observant. As we approached Valimitika, he noticed from a roadside sign that its name in Greek began with a 'B', and I had spent the whole time at the bus station looking for a bus going to a place beginning with 'V'. It took several days before the mockery ceased but I have never forgotten that the English 'V' sound in the Greek alphabet is formed by the letter 'B', a *veeta*.

The turning point came in August 1992 – our second Greek holiday based in Stoupa, a small, seaside resort on the west coast of the Mani Peninsula in the southern Peloponnese. By now our sons were holidaying independently and Mary and I were taking a day off from lazing on the beach and heading south in a hired Fiat Punto towards Cape Tenairon, one of the most southerly points in mainland Europe. Less than half an hour into our journey we decided to stop and explore the village of Thalames.

Our short walking tour through the narrow village streets flanked by stone houses was coming to an end when we were hailed unexpectedly by someone sitting across the street under a thick canopy of grape vine. Although clearly aimed at us, we couldn't fathom why we were being beckoned. Had we inadvertently done something wrong or offended somebody? It turned out to be nothing of the sort. Once she emerged from the deep shade, it dawned on us that it was the old lady in black whom we had overtaken earlier on in our visit. She had been having trouble with her truculent grandson and we had cast a sympathetic glance in her direction as we slipped by. She had obviously recognised us from our previous brief encounter and wished to reward us for our discretion.

She gestured to us to cross the street and follow her. Talking incessantly in Greek, she led us through a courtyard and up some stone steps into her house. It didn't take long for her to realise we didn't understand a word, so we were ushered to sit down before witnessing a master class in how to communicate by gestures. We were clearly being offered coffee, even the choice of hot or cold, which she managed by going first to the stove and then to the fridge and miming the appropriate actions. We both decided on a cold coffee and watched intently as she demonstrated, step by step, how cold Greek coffee (*frappé*) was made.

The penultimate step was to vigorously shake a well-used plastic Tupperware container to thoroughly mix the coffee powder and cold water inside. She did this with the flair and confidence of an accomplished cocktail hostess. Thus, the moment when the top of the container flew off and the contents pebble-dashed the front of Mary's white t-shirt took her, as well as Mary, by complete surprise. Promptly regaining her composure, she proceeded to dab Mary's chest with a handy tea cloth, all the while uttering what we assumed was a litany of apologies in Greek while we watched in stunned silence.

Amazingly, composure was restored on both sides within a matter of minutes and Mary easily communicated her forgiveness before the cold coffee-making routine was repeated, with extra special attention paid to the security of the lid. The well-mixed contents were evenly divided between two glasses, evaporated milk stirred into the mix and ice cubes added. As is the Greek custom, glasses of cold water were also brought to the table. For the first time, we were enjoying a *frappé* with milk, Greek-style. Unfazed by what had gone before, faded photos and dusty envelopes with foreign postage stamps were offered as visual aids as our host attempted to describe her extended family and where they lived in the world. However, despite her undisguised enthusiasm, our muted responses and the one-dimensional nature of the conversation were undermining all her efforts at communication and engagement.

We left with the usual gestures of thanks and farewell, acknowledging to ourselves that we had experienced a rare and special encounter with Greek *filoxenia* (hospitality). But how much better it could have been had we known just a few more words of Greek. *Parakalo* (please) and *Efharisto* (thank you) had been our woeful limit and we hadn't even learnt our host's name! This episode represented a turning point in our approach to the Greek language. Never again were we going to miss such an opportunity to engage in conversation with someone so keen to talk and make us feel at home. So, there and then, we committed to learning the Greek language, and this time we were serious.

A Long History

The origins of the Greek language go back a long, long way, maybe as far as 5,000 years. The common antecedents of Greek were probably brought to the Balkans and Greek Peninsula by peoples who migrated from the region north of the Black and Caspian Seas sometime in the third millennium BCE. This was a spoken language only, expressed in many different but related dialects. It would be another 1,000 years or so before the first written forms of Greek emerged: the so-called Linear A and Linear B scripts. They were discovered on clay tablets at archaeological sites such as Knossos in Crete and Nestor's Palace in the southwest Peloponnese, and are associated with the Minoan and Mycenaean civilisations.

Homer's two epic accounts of the Trojan Wars and Odysseus' subsequent return to his homeland – *The Iliad* and *The Odyssey* –

date from the late 8th or early 7th century BCE. They are the earliest known Greek literary works to survive and were written in a mix of two Greek dialects, Aeolic and Ionic, using the first Greek alphabet, which had recently emerged. Curiously, this alphabet bore little resemblance to the hieroglyphics of Linear A and B and was based on the Phoenician alphabet, which had been developed in the region that now comprises Lebanon, Syria and Israel. It was this alphabet that allowed the flourishing of Classical Greek literature and the emergence of a host of scholarly treatises. By this time, Attic – a form of the Ionic dialect used in Athens, which was the centre of learning and the arts – had become the pre-eminent form of spoken and written Greek. Famous Classical poets like Sappho and Pindar, dramatists like Sophocles, Euripides and Aristophanes, historians like Herodotus and Thucydides, and philosophers like Socrates, Plato and Aristotle composed their great works in this form of Ancient Greek.

Eventually, Attic Greek superceded all other dialects and became known as Koine (pronounced 'kee-nee') or Common Greek. It survives to this day as the liturgical language of the Greek Orthodox Church and is the language in which the New Testament of the bible was originally written. It became the lingua franca of the East Roman Empire, which evolved into the Byzantine Empire, and remained its official language until its final demise in 1453, when Constantinople – now Istanbul – was overrun by the Ottoman Turks. At its height, Koine Greek was the common language for an estimated twenty-six million people. From medieval times onwards, it slowly evolved into Modern Greek while Ancient Greek remained almost intact, creating a rare contemporary situation where two closely related forms of a language co-exist, one vernacular and the other historical.

Ancient Greek was revived in the nineteenth century when Greece gained its independence from the Turks after nearly 400 years of Ottoman occupation. It was renamed *Katharevusa* (pure Greek) and became the language of government, newspapers, schools, universities and some literature. In its written, printed and spoken forms, it remained in use by the professional classes until the 1970s. At the same time, the majority of Greeks contented themselves with a spoken form of Greek that was not much different to the Koine Greek used by their forebears 1,500 years earlier. Not surprisingly, it has been supplemented by several strata of words pilfered from other languages over a period of 2,000 years or more. These other languages included Italian (from the Venetian and Genoese occupations of Greek territory after 1200 CE), Turkish (from the Ottoman occupation 1453–1830 CE), and in the 20th century, French and then English.

Examples of words adopted from other languages abound. Some are translated into Greek (e.g. the French *chemin de fer* – iron way, railway – became *siderodromos* from *sideros* – iron – and *dromos* – road). Others have their foreign letters substituted by Greek letters in order to sound the same (e.g. *ascenseur*, the French word meaning 'lift', which becomes *asanser*). The Greek word for race or breed, *ratsa*, comes from the Italian *razza*, while the Turkish word *manav* provided the origin of the Greek word *manavis*, meaning greengrocer. It is not surprising that in 21st-century Greece you increasingly see and hear English words, sometimes in their original form. A football commentary on Greek TV is punctuated with words like 'goal', 'corner', 'foul' and 'offside', even though in some cases there are Greek equivalents.

After the fall of the military dictatorship in 1974, Modern Greek – by now also known as Demotic Greek – was defined by legislation as the official language of Greece and has subsequently superceded *Katharevusa* in all walks of life. However, many remnants of Ancient Greek remain in everyday use. For example, the modern Greek word for 'fish' is *ipsari* and for 'shop' is *magazi*, but the Greek word for fish shop is not 'ipsaromagazi' as you might expect. It is *icthopoleio*, from two Ancient Greek words: *icthys* (fish) and *poleio* (selling). Little seems simple or straightforward for those embarking on learning Greek. That's why Greeks appreciate and respect the efforts made by foreigners to learn and use their language.

Greeks Learning Greek

Learning a language, even a native language, is a complicated process. With babies, toddlers and young children, the process is natural and progressive but profoundly influenced by the levels of interaction and communication with parents, grandparents, siblings, carers and neighbours. Our Neohori neighbour, Angelo, who possesses a well-used, penetrating voice that travels with great clarity, was determined to teach all her grandchildren, at an early age, the difference between *mama, papa, yiayia* (granny) and *papou* (grandad). She did this by a process of regular repetition, which the whole neighbourhood was party to. Thankfully, this repetition never lasted for more than a few weeks, suggesting that her grandchildren were quick learners and that Angelo's approach worked. By the time they are four years old, 90% of what children say is grammatically correct but it takes another eight years or so before their language truly resembles adult language. Becoming proficient at all four components of language – listening, speaking, reading and writing – can take much longer.

The curriculum of Greek state schools places strong emphasis on teaching and learning Greek in both its forms: Ancient and Modern. Of the standard thirty hours a week that pupils spend in primary school (*Demotiko*), nine hours at the start, reducing to seven by the time they are ready to leave, are devoted to learning Modern Greek. When they move to junior high school (*Gymnasio*), aged twelve, they begin to study Ancient Greek as well, and the timetable differentiates Language from Literature. A quarter of overall curriculum time is still occupied by studying Greek in some form or other, known as *Filologika*. Senior high school (*Lykeio*) is not compulsory but most pupils continue their education there at the age of fifteen. At Lykeio, students have the opportunity to choose groups of subjects they wish to specialise in, but they have no choice about continuing with Ancient and Modern Greek, although the hours of study are reduced. Even for pupils opting for a trade-based course, such as plumbing or electrics, in a technical Lykeio, there is still a requirement to continue studying Greek each week. For pupils who choose to follow the humanities group of subjects in a standard Lykeio, the study of Greek in all its forms can occupy over one-third of the thirty-five-hour school week.

It's hard to judge the overall reaction of Greek children to the overloading of their school curriculum with the language and literature of both Ancient and Modern Greek. No one disputes that there are good and bad teachers and many in between. The same also applies to pupils. But for those I know who have gone through the system in the recent past, there is agreement that both the time spent on learning Greek and how they learn it, leave a lot to be desired. Teaching remains very formal, is whole-class based, and closely follows the textbook issued for free by the Greek Ministry of Education to each pupil every year. Teachers have limited flexibility with syllabuses and teaching and learning styles, in schools that are often underfunded and under-resourced. Many pupils declare that they are bored during Greek lessons and many fail to see the relevance of spending so much time studying Greek, especially the Ancient version.

Second- or third-generation Greeks who formed part of the 20th-century *diaspora* and are now living in well-established communities in Australia, the USA and Canada are keen for their children and grandchildren to be fluent in the language of their forebears as well as in the language of their adopted country. They recognise that mastering the Greek language is an essential first step in promoting a strong sense of identity and preserving the culture, history and traditions of their origins.

Melbourne contains a large Greek community of over 350,000 people, situated thousands of kilometres from their homeland, making it the third largest Greek community in the world, after Athens and Thessaloniki. As well as many Orthodox churches and Greek restaurants, there is a dense network of organisations – youth, welfare, philanthropic, social, cultural and sporting – that underpin the Greek community. There is a twenty-four-hour Greek radio station

(3XY Radio Hellas) and a long-established daily Greek newspaper called *Neos Kosmos* (New World). What is most impressive, however, is the existence of nearly 100 Greek language schools, including three bilingual colleges; a sure sign of the importance Greek-Australians attach to preserving their mother tongue.

Sometimes, close-knit communities with foreign origins that have a strong determination to preserve the language and traditions of the home country can result in an inward-looking perspective that is counterproductive. New arrivals can exist without the need to learn the native language of their adopted country and thus integration with the broader community remains slow and difficult. Maria, our next-door neighbour in Greece for ten years, had spent twelve years in Melbourne in the 1970s and '80s and had only one English word to show for it; "Alright?" expressed with a strong Australian twang was a regular greeting.

It goes without saying that Albanians don't strictly qualify as Greeks, but they comprise the biggest ethnic minority in Greece and represent 5% of Greece's total population of eleven million. Since the collapse and dissolution of the former Yugoslavia in the early 1990s, many Albanians have migrated south to seek work in Greece. Most are young male labourers seeking jobs on building sites, harvesting olives or manual work of any kind. They have temporary work permits, travel overland by coach (regular weekly services operate from all the main Albanian cities), live in cheap, often crowded accommodation and rarely stay for extended periods of time. Those arriving in Greece for the first time and searching for work often have no alternative but to assemble early in the morning at predetermined places at road junctions where, if they are lucky, a building contractor or farmer needing extra hands will employ them as casual day labour.

Some Albanians already have a limited grasp of Greek because they come from Epirus, which spans the Albanian-Greek border. This region has, from time to time, been part of Greece and thus has a legacy of Greek language and customs. However, for those migrating from other parts of Albania, an immediate imperative is to learn the language. Even if time, money and opportunity allowed, there is little alternative but to 'pick up' Greek as they go along. Fortunately for most, it's only the spoken word that is crucial and often it is job-specific, acquired by hearing key phrases and sentences repeated again and again at the workplace and getting to know the range of responses expected. Without some command of the Greek language, job prospects are limited to working with teams of other Albanians, where a Greek-speaking team leader liaises with the farmer, developer or client. This is probably the norm for first-time migrant workers.

For other Albanians who have been working for the same employer in the same locality for several years and have come to value the higher income and better prospects and opportunities in Greece, the next step is a big one: to move their family and establish a permanent home in Greece. This involves a lot of red tape and bureaucracy that demands more than a basic mastery of Greek in order to acquire a residency permit and allow access to education and healthcare. Often their younger children speak Albanian at home and learn Greek at school; a bilingual ability that can be a considerable asset to the family, as well as to themselves. Sometimes, second-generation Albanians who have benefitted from an upbringing and schooling in Greece are the most determined to take full advantage of the opportunities available and add English to their portfolio of languages. Over a period of ten years or so, they can evolve from being casual labourers to seasonal waiters or bar staff and, in rare but significant cases, to owning and running a successful restaurant or taverna. In addition to their single-minded determination and their entrepreneurial spirit, their mastery of the Greek language is a key factor in accounting for their achievement.

Getting Started

When Mary and I committed to learning Greek after our humbling experience in Thalames in the summer of 1992, we gave little thought to how we were going to do it. Furthermore, our return to the UK and resumption of work and a normal routine meant that our Greek holiday soon became just a pleasant memory, which the arrival of a bundle of photos from Truprint resurrected only momentarily. Our resolve to do more than just muddle along with a smattering of Greek words when we next holidayed in Greece was already weakening.

In the end, it was late November and a Christmas shopping trip to Exeter that prompted us to take the first step. Scanning the non-fiction shelves in Waterstones, hoping for some inspiration for presents, we stumbled across the Language & Reference corner and there, in amongst a wide choice of French, German, Spanish and Italian study manuals, were just a couple featuring the Greek language. It turned out to be a pivotal moment and, with little hesitation, we chose to buy *Greek Language and People* published by the BBC. This was a coursebook designed to accompany a TV series first broadcast in October 1983 on BBC2. Although we had missed the TV series – and have never managed to see it since – we found the book and audiotapes an indispensable adjunct to our early efforts to get to grips with Greek. Even today, nearly thirty years later, we still occasionally make reference to the book, which, despite its grainy black and white photos and corny cartoons, introduces Modern Greek in an accessible, systematic and engaging manner.

Today there are many more ways of learning a second language, many taking advantage of the internet, but using a coursebook and systematically working through the chapters in an ordered and progressive manner suited us perfectly. We had both studied French and Latin at school and thus we were familiar with the formal, old-school approach to foreign language learning, with the emphasis on reading and writing and correct spelling, grammar and syntax. We set aside an evening a week during the remaining winter months and worked through the coursebook conscientiously, doing all the written exercises and listening and responding to the audiotapes. We had successfully prepared the ground for the future development of our

Greek language but we needed a Greek teacher to help us focus on our speaking and listening skills, which were already lagging behind. After all, they were the primary purpose of us deciding to learn Greek in the first place.

Even today, North Devon is hardly cosmopolitan, and we were surprised to learn that a Greek woman was running weekly evening classes in our neighbouring town as part of Bideford College's adult education programme. We managed to persuade her to conduct weekly hour-long tutorials at her home especially for us, and thus began a long and fulfilling relationship with Iphigeneia White. Iphigeneia was the daughter of a Greek Orthodox priest on Poros, an island in the Saronic Gulf, just three hours by ferry from Piraeus. She had come to Britain in the 1950s with her sister and had married and settled in North Devon, where she had brought up two daughters. As well as teaching us the Greek language, we learned so much else about Greece and its history, culture, traditions and people, and on special occasions she even cooked us Greek food; locally caught *kalamarakia* (squid) was a speciality.

The dominant memory of our lessons with Iphigeneia involves the part of each lesson when, with our mini-dictaphone in record mode, she guided us through our first unsteady attempts at Greek conversation. She would articulate the sentences loudly and clearly for us to repeat parrot-fashion and to record them for practice at home. Her unforgettable words in English preceding each pair of simple sentences were *"You will say..."* and then *"And they will say..."* It was a fun way to learn and some of the sentences are so ingrained we are still using them today. However, as we began to spend more time in Greece, it soon became clear that the *"And they will say..."* bit rarely followed the same script in real life. Iphigenia was delighted that we were so eager to learn her native language and to appreciate all the insights and incidental information that came with it. She gave us the desire and confidence to persevere with learning Greek. Without her enthusiasm and passion for her roots, we might have quickly lost momentum.

A Fresh Impetus

The opportunity to begin restoring our recently-purchased Greek home came much quicker than we expected. In the summer of 1997, due to falls in projected pupil numbers, Mary and I were both granted redundancy from our respective North Devon schools. For some people at our age, this would have been a tragic coincidence at a time in their working lives when finding commensurate employment would be difficult. For us, it provided a great opportunity. Our sole surviving parent – my ninety-year-old mother – was in good shape and living in an Abbeyfield Home with its healthy balance of independence and care, while both our sons had left home and completed their higher education and were in employment. Furthermore, the financial compensation was sufficient to allow us to pursue our dream, providing we kept tight control of our budget. It was a no-brainer, and a new chapter in our lives began.

We downsized to a small terraced house in Torrington – the same North Devon town where we had lived and worked for twenty years – and on October 2nd 1997 we set off for Greece on the first of many 3,000-kilometre road trips across Europe, in a recently purchased white Leyland-DAF van, packed to its 'highloader' limits. Although we planned to do a lot of building work ourselves, we accepted we would need to employ local builders and tradesmen to do the bigger, more technical jobs beyond our capabilities. Thus, we put our formal learning of Greek on hold as we gave priority to renovating our house and making it habitable for family and friends who were eager to visit and find out why our lives had suddenly gone off at a tangent.

Contrary to our expectations, this period turned out to be particularly fruitful for our Greek language development. Being faced with builders, electricians, plumbers, building suppliers etc., none of whom spoke much English, gave us little alternative but to use and improve our Greek. In those days, brothers Dimitris and Sotiris

Poulakos ran a builders' yard and emporium in the nearby fishing village of Aghios Nikolaos. There were periods when I visited their premises two or three times a week. Dimitris spoke competent English but was always content to allow Kostas, his Albanian assistant, to deal with me. Kostas (surely not his Albanian name?) spoke no English but our joint searches through the giant hangar, which must have represented the largest, most well-stocked hardware store in southern mainland Greece, were conducted entirely in Greek: a genuine case of 'learning on the job'.

On some occasions, when it was clear that our comments or opinions had not been fully understood by our builders or tradesmen, we resorted to pen, paper and an English-Greek dictionary. Aided by roughly drawn diagrams – common currency on building sites worldwide – and a notebook of key words we had compiled in English and Greek under various headings like 'Roof', 'Fireplace', 'Stairs' etc., we managed to communicate our preferences without too much difficulty. That notebook, its dog-eared state testifying to its almost constant use during that period, might yet become a family heirloom. As a last resort, we could always enlist the invaluable help of one or other of two local bilingual women: Susan Shimmin, who had found the house for us and was acting as project manager, and Shelley, formerly a ward sister in a Chicago hospital, who had settled in our village, the home of her Greek husband. At the same time we continued to practise our less specialist Greek by dealing with enquiries from inquisitive neighbours, often keen to offer advice and opinion. Regular shopping trips to Kardamyli and Kalamata also demanded that we put our Greek into practice. In those days, big, foreign-owned, self-service DIY stores like Praktiker were nowhere to be seen. So, buying building materials, wall and floor tiles, paint and varnishes, and kitchen and bathroom equipment all required going to small specialist shops, builders' merchants and timber and marble yards. Speaking Greek, with a crib sheet of key vocabulary to hand, was often the only option.

Consolidation

Once the house and terrace were usable and the builders and tradesmen gone, and before we embarked on another project, Mary and I sought more help to enable us to consolidate our Greek. We were recommended Marina Vlassi, a thirty-six-year-old teacher who runs a foreign language *frontistirio* in Stoupa. *Frontistiria* are common adjuncts to the Greek education system. For a modest fee, they offer supplementary lessons in the afternoons and evenings to top up what youngsters have learned at school. During the mornings and at weekends, Marina's *frontistirio* also offers Greek and English lessons for adults.

Mary and I have developed a great respect for Marina. She is thoroughly professional and has a single-minded sense of purpose, she can modify her approach and teaching style to suit all manner of backgrounds, abilities and needs, and, above all, she is always positive, encouraging and reassuring. As well as being our Greek teacher she has become a good friend and over the years our lessons have become social occasions as well as learning sessions. After all, we share news of our families, our ups and downs, our activities and our socialising in a friendly and relaxed manner every week, so how could it be otherwise?

Our first ever Greek lesson with Marina was in June 2000 and I estimate she has provided us with nearly 400 lessons in the twenty years since. Whenever we are staying in our Greek home, we engage in weekly Greek language sessions with her. It has become a regular part of our Greek routine. The format of our lessons has changed little over the years. True to the message on the sign above the entrance to her *frontistirio* – English Lessons, *Tailor Made* – Marina was keen to accommodate our needs and after brief negotiation we agreed on a pattern that, give or take occasional adjustments and experiments, we have stuck with ever since. The focus is squarely on speaking and listening. We sit around a small table in one of Marina's small, cluttered teaching rooms that overlook Kalogria Beach and all conversation is conducted in Greek, from the moment we arrive to when we depart. Our friend Allan, another of Marina's students, recalls one occasion when after a lesson had ended, he rose awkwardly from the chair he had been sitting in for an hour and exclaimed in English while rubbing his thigh, "I'm a bit stiff!" Marina was quick to politely suggest he repeat the phrase in Greek!

We prefer to begin the lesson with Marina speaking to us because that requires careful listening, which quickly attunes us to the sounds, flow and rhythms of the Greek language. Almost always, the conversation that follows covers a wide range of personal, local, national and international news. American presidents, Greek wildfires, Brexit, Greek university entrance, extreme weather, Classical Greek drama, earthquakes, water supply and organic farming are examples of how wide-ranging discussion has been. Sometimes we bring Greek newspaper cuttings with us, other times we talk about photos on our phones – maybe of our grandchildren or of places we have visited – but mostly it's about day-to-day things such as work we have been doing in the garden, places we have visited or news of mutual friends. We have also learned, recited, translated and even sung the words of Greek popular songs, including the National Anthem.

There are several moments every lesson when we are stuck in mid-sentence, unable to recall a key bit of vocabulary. Marina usually allows us time to find an alternative to the word we don't know by substituting a short phrase – one of the elements of successfully speaking a foreign language – before interceding with the word she intuitively knows we are searching for. She can also quickly tell if we have not understood something she has said, solely by the puzzled look on our faces. In both cases, she tries her hardest not to interrupt the flow of the conversation, preferring to record the error or omission on paper and wait until we have finished what we are trying to say. It's only then that she corrects us or points out how we could have expressed ourselves in a better, more conventional way.

Sometimes, after a particularly error-strewn lesson, Marina's record of our mistakes and their corrections can aggregate to as much as eight or nine sides of A4 paper. But this is not wasted paper, consigned to the bin at the end of the lesson. These sheets are the basis of our homework. Much like many schoolchildren worldwide who leave it to the last minute, Mary and I rarely get to do our homework before the eve of our next lesson. We sit down side by side at a table at home and, assisted by an assortment of dictionaries and verb compendia, our errors come back to haunt us as we go through everything that Marina noted down the previous lesson. We read out loud and then translate into English all the words, phrases and occasional whole sentences that we had expressed incorrectly and conjugate any verbs we had mangled, in their four main tenses.

Designed to reinforce our learning, more often than not our homework simply confirms our sluggish progress. We just don't seem to learn from our mistakes; it's embarrassing and frustrating in equal measure. We've tried several ways of improving matters, such as taping a short weekly list of new Greek words on a kitchen cabinet and reciting them out loud, along with their English meaning, every time we pass by. It works, but only in the short term. Three or four weeks later, after we have done the same with another fifteen or twenty Greek words, we've already forgotten the meaning of most of the ones we learnt earlier.

On the other hand, our lessons with Marina have nurtured in us a profound respect for and love of the Greek language with all its intricacies. They have also engendered a confidence to keep on using the Greek language whenever and wherever possible, and, at least, they ensure that our modest levels of proficiency are maintained. Marina's Greek lessons may not have converted us into fluent Greek speakers – how could they on their own? – but that is much more to do with our age, our aptitude and our part-time residency than with her ability to teach Greek. I had always wanted my spoken Greek to reach the standard of my spoken French – not exactly fluent, but competent enough to be effective in most everyday situations. Sadly, I am convinced neither of us have attained that level, despite Marina's assurances otherwise. I sometimes wonder if the moment will ever arrive when we can play Greek Scrabble, or one of us will dream in Greek. Either would be a milestone.

No matter how much stuttering progress we make during our lengthy stays in Greece, when, as well as our weekly lessons and homework, we are surrounded by the Greek language on a daily basis, there is always a rapid realisation when we return to our UK home that unless we do something about it, our Greek will deteriorate through lack of use. We were lucky to start with, finding a Greek language coursebook and a Greek teacher that suited us perfectly at our beginners' stage. But the completion of the coursebook and Ifigeneia's retirement forced us to search once more for ways of sustaining our progress with the Greek language.

We tried several different ways, such as a new, more advanced coursework book, a Greek evening class at our local tertiary college, an informal Greek conversation group – made up of students who had abandoned the unsatisfactory evening class – and an assortment of one-to-one teachers, none of whom lasted long for a variety of reasons. We were disappointed that none worked half as well as we would have liked and by the time we again returned to Greece, there was always some catching up to do. In more recent years, matters have improved with weekly hour-long online conversation sessions on the *italki.com* platform with an assortment of native Greek speakers while we are resident in the UK. Available now are also a host of foreign language websites, such as Babbel, Mondly and Duolingo, that all exaggerate the ease and pace of foreign language learning. If only it was as simple and straightforward as they make out.

A Challenging Language

Learning Greek is patently not for those without commitment and determination. Elizabeth, a well-respected tourist guide and English Language teacher made just that point in Athena's *cafeneion* in Aghios Nikolaos in 1998. We had joined a morning gathering of Brits partaking of coffee and conversation while awaiting the arrival of the day's mail in the post office across the tiny, harbour-side square. Elizabeth was complimented on her fluent Greek by one of our number, who then proceeded to enquire how she had 'picked it up'. This generated a robust, if brief, riposte: "Most of us don't pick up another language. It takes a lot of hard work. Osmosis is for plants, not humans!" A pregnant silence ensued for a few brief moments while we all digested Elizabeth's comment before someone obligingly sought to change the subject.

I had never been in any doubt that Greek is a difficult language to learn but I was reassured by the findings of the website *effectivelanguagelearning.com*. It has assessed the levels of difficulty of learning foreign languages for native English speakers and classified them into five groups. The least difficult are in Group 1 and include French, Spanish, Italian, Dutch and Portuguese, while at the other extreme, Group 5 contains Arabic, Cantonese, Mandarin, Japanese and Korean, which are judged to be exceptionally difficult. Greek is in Group 4, along with Bengali, Hebrew, Polish, Vietnamese and many others that are classified as difficult. And how could it be otherwise when even the simplest of Greek words is so counterintuitive? For most Europeans, expressing a negative involves a single syllable word beginning with the letter 'n': the French say *non*, the Russians say *nyet*, the Germans *nein* and the Portuguese *nao*. So, it's understandable if foreigners in the early stages of acquiring some basic Greek vocabulary inevitably choose the word *nai* (pronounced 'neh') to express a negative. It's an instinctive, almost subconscious thing, but it has the opposite meaning to that intended: it's the Greek word for 'yes'. *Ochi* is the Greek word for 'no'. To add to the confusion is the customary gesture Greeks use to accompany saying *ochi*. Instead of shaking their head in British fashion, they tilt it backwards or simply raise their eyebrows.

Louis de Bernières' 1994 novel *Captain Corelli's Mandolin* captures the challenge posed by the Greek alphabet when the author describes the confusion Italian occupying forces experienced with Greek language graffiti on the Ionian island of Cephalonia during the Second World War. The Greek alphabet puzzle de Bernières sets his readers on page 163 is perplexing, even for fluent bilinguists, and a measure of the pitfalls it poses for novice students of Greek. Although the English word 'alphabet' derives from the names of the first two letters of the Greek alphabet, the Greek version is somewhat different to the English. For a start, it contains only twenty-four letters and they are in a different order; for instance, 'z' (*zeeta*) is the sixth letter, not the last. Then, as with many alphabets, each letter takes a different shape and form depending on whether it is written or printed, or in lower or upper case.

The biggest challenge is the confusing divergence from some letters of the English alphabet. Fourteen capital letters look the same as their English counterparts, but four sound different: 'B' is pronounced *veeta*, 'H' has an 'eee' sound, 'P' is the equivalent of the English letter 'R' and 'X' has a guttural 'H' sound. Not all the other ten capital letters are completely unknown to English speakers and some can be guessed at, like Γ, Δ and Π. But for the rest, their shapes and form are strange and their sounds unfamiliar: Θ (*theeta*), Ξ (*ksee*), and Ψ (*psee*), for example, while Φ (*fee* = F), Σ (*sigma* = S) and Ω (*omega* = O) are different letter forms but with familiar English sounds. An added complication is that some common speech sounds are only obtained by combining two letters. The Greek word for beer, ΜΠΗΡΑ (pronounced *beera*), where the ΜΠ represents the 'b' sound, is a good example that can take some getting used to on the labels of beer bottles.

Young Greek children learning to read their native language do not have the comfort of simple sentences composed of single-syllable words, such as 'the cat sat on the mat', to ease their progress. There are very few single-syllable words in the Greek language but it is renowned for having an abundance of long words with many syllables that pose yet another hurdle for learners. The existence of these multisyllable words is the primary reason why 'tonos' marks are used in written and printed Greek. If you have ever quickly scanned the front pages of newspapers on display outside a *periptero* (a kind of mini corner shop found on pavements in Greek towns and cities), you may have noticed that most words have a little mark over one letter. This indicates which syllable to emphasise when speaking. Stressing the wrong syllable can render a word incomprehensible to most Greeks. What makes things especially difficult for English speakers are those Greek words that have passed directly into the English language but with the stress on a different syllable. The word 'panorama', which in English has the stress on the third syllable, has it on the second syllable in Greek. Try speaking both and see how different that makes them sound.

Word order in a sentence, called syntax, is another difficulty for any English speaker who is predisposed to putting the subject at the beginning, the object at the end and the verb in the middle. In Greek there is no such convention, even though most sentences do conform to the English norm. A sub-headline in the Kalamata daily newspaper, *Eleftheria* in October 2015 illustrates this perfectly. It's an English translation with its original Greek word order intact: *'A rural house in Messinia when will to them be provided a visa to come whenever they want to a European country are dreaming many rich Russians'*. And how does the Greek language get away with it? The answer is simple: the subject and object in a Greek sentence are identified by the form and sound of their word endings and their pronouns. It's just another complication.

Coping with a different alphabet, multisyllable words, stress marks and unpredictable word order may pose problems for many people learning Greek, but its most difficult aspect is its grammar. For native English speakers, whose grammar is uncomplicated by comparison, this is especially so. Whether it's nouns, which all have a gender – masculine, feminine or neuter – and multiple sets of word-endings; or adjectives, which have to agree with the nouns; or verbs, which are either active or passive, Greek language grammar is a minefield. What's more, verbs are mainly used without personal pronouns ('I', 'we', you' etc.), which means that the verb ending and the location of the stress are the sole indicators of who the speaker is referring to and whether the action is taking place in the past, present or future. It certainly remains mentally challenging for Mary and me and yet, in the same timespan as we've been learning Greek and achieving only a very modest level of competence, thousands of Greek children have been born and, with the aid of their parents, teachers and community, have achieved a high level of proficiency in listening, speaking, reading and writing their native tongue. Where have we been going wrong?

It's inconceivable to blame our teachers. Marina and Ifigeneia have provided us with all the motivation, encouragement and learning we could possibly have wished for. Neither can we blame ourselves for a lack of diligence or commitment. Yet we have to take some responsibility. One fundamental problem is that, with the passage of time, our mental capacity to learn and retain vocabulary, the different genders of words, where the stress lies and the conjugation of verbs is diminishing. When we were younger, it used to be so effortless! Then there's the choice we made to divide our time between the UK and Greece. Our efforts to mitigate the deterioration in our Greek while in the UK only partially compensate for our absence. Probably most significant of all is the failure to integrate ourselves in our local Greek community in the way we had hoped. Right from the start of our Greek adventure, I heard myself saying to family, work colleagues, neighbours and friends in England that knowing the Greek language was "the key to the door" if we were really going to feel at home in Greece. As it turned out, the door has remained only slightly ajar despite our efforts learning the language. Probably it's a catch-22 situation in which the door would open wider quite rapidly if we became much more fluent in Greek . . . but achieving that would require more integration. Perhaps we should endeavour to spend more time with locals – say, in the *cafeneion* or in winter Greek dancing classes; maybe we could seek some seasonal work in a travel agent or hotel or, in the most inconceivable of circumstances, Mary and I could agree on a trial separation – after fifty-two years of contented marriage – and seek Greek partners. But that would amount to an extreme sacrifice simply to improve our Greek. And anyway, who'd be prepared to take us on at our age?

Worth the Effort?

I would find it shameful to know just a handful of Greek words, used sparingly in the local shop, *cafeneion* or taverna; neither could I accept communicating almost exclusively in English while domiciled in Greece. Of course, there are occasions when acting the 'dumb foreigner' might be appropriate. At a road traffic accident, an emergency hospital admission or a visit to the regional tax office, for example, it might be advisable to swallow your pride, forget your hard-earned Greek and proceed with your native tongue. This minimises the risk of misunderstanding – crucial in some instances – and improves the chance of obtaining the desired and correct outcome. However, in most situations, I consider using Greek with Greeks as a sign of respect and a measure of my desire to be more than simply an expat taking advantage of the sun, sea and sand, a laid-back lifestyle, and the lower cost of living.

There are many examples of the access to little, everyday things that knowing some Greek affords me. The mobile vans, endlessly touring the network of villages with their recorded loudspeaker messages alerting potential customers, would be a mystery were it not for some basic Greek. Visitors always want to know what they are selling. Is it fruit and veg? live poultry? earthenware pots? footwear? bagged manure? clothing? fresh fish? My favourite is *O Paliatzis*, who is not selling anything. He's the Greek equivalent of a scrap metal dealer and has a call that recalls the days of "Any Old Iron?", which echoed along British city streets in the past.

Graffiti has a long history in Greece, with examples dating back to Classical times. Since the advent of the economic crisis in 2008 it has become increasingly commonplace, especially in towns and cities. A few are large, colourful and artistic with a subtle message and no need for words, some are extravagant 'names', but most Greek graffiti comprises hurriedly sprayed political and football slogans. Most of the football graffiti relates to the four main Greek teams and is mundane, repetitive and designed to be provocative. Political graffiti is more interesting, especially during a period of austerity or in the run-up to elections. The discredited neo-Nazi party in Greece calls itself *Chrisi Avgi* (Golden Dawn). How sad that an evocative name, often adopted by small Greek fishing boats, has been so purloined and found daubed in big black letters throughout Greece. Fortunately, with a little adjustment, making the 'i's into 'a's, it becomes *Chrisa Avga*, which means 'Golden Eggs'. What better way to mock a far-right political movement you don't agree with? Without any Greek, how would we grasp the subtle change in this graffiti, which turns this name on its head?

Being able to read some Greek adds interest to most days. With the aid of a Greek-English dictionary I try to read a copy of Kalamata's local newspapers *Eleftheria* or *Tharros* two or three times a week. It's never from cover to cover – that would take days at a time – but just the reports and features that interest me and keep me abreast of local news and opinion from a Greek perspective. Some foreigners claim that watching Greek TV has helped them acquire Greek but that approach has never worked with me. The news programmes, weather forecasts and sports commentaries are all spoken too fast and the TV soaps, which some people credit with much of their Greek, just leave me cold. High-level banners slung across roads to advertise an event or performance, giant advertising hoardings beside urban and suburban motorways, and posters in shop and supermarket windows alerting customers to sales and cut-price offers would go unheeded without a little Greek. How boring life would be without a little eavesdropping while sitting next to a Greek family on the beach, and how frustrating, while travelling in Greece, to be unable to unravel the origins of a village or town from the meaning of its name. *Rizomilos* ('rice mill'), *Chrysokellaria* (meaning 'golden cellar', denoting a very productive farming region) and *Kokkinorachi* ('red ridge') would just remain anonymous.

There are few things more satisfying than engaging with a Greek stranger in their native language and maintaining a coherent and meaningful conversation. Without some grasp of Greek, that would never happen, and the opportunity for assistance, local knowledge or simply a fleeting exchange of goodwill would be lost. Over the years I have discussed many different subjects in these situations, ranging from Winston Churchill, David Beckham, the British Royal Family and Brexit to the comparative value of state pensions and the workings of our respective national health services. Even more satisfying is a positive outcome to the battle of wills that sometimes occurs when the Greek person knows some English. If Greek, not English, prevails as the conversation proceeds, then it is a small victory for all the hours spent learning Greek. The difficult bit is not being smug afterwards.

Even with errors of pronunciation, vocabulary and syntax, most Greeks try hard to understand what you are trying to say and appreciate the efforts you make to learn and use what they themselves acknowledge is a difficult language. We would have missed out on so many things if we had no Greek. In themselves, they may be minor, insignificant little things, but added together they help to make up our Greek experience. They differentiate between us living in Greece or somewhere else in Southern Europe. They help form the backcloth to our existence there.

A coastal walk to Arfikia, an isolated rocky cove not far from the small town of Itylo, in September 2009 provided a perfect example of how our Greek transformed a chance encounter into a memorable experience. The stunning, panoramic view of the cove from the rim of the ravine above normally beckons us onwards without delay. But on this occasion, something unusual attracted our attention: there were human beings down there! In the past, we had occasionally come across farmers in pick-up trucks tending their livestock or beehives, but this was always on the early part of the walk. The bay at Arfikia had always been free of human beings; it's one of its attractions.

Our hesitation and disappointment were only momentary however, and we quickly descended down the rocky, twisting stone path into the ravine and thence onto the foreshore. It appeared that there were three people, all engaged in some activity by the two makeshift stone shacks situated close to the shoreline. They seemed totally unaware that strangers were approaching. Not knowing what to expect and prepared to be rebuffed, we decided to introduce ourselves in Greek and ask if they could recommend a good spot to swim. Although curious, and not a little surprised, they responded warmly to our greeting, directed us to the best place to swim and invited us to join them for coffee when we had finished. A case of instant *filoxenia*, and typically Greek.

Keen to experience whatever awaited us, we quickly concluded our swim and returned to our hosts' shack. Additional plastic chairs had been assembled in the shade of the veranda and, after some cordial introductions, there followed an intriguing two hours in the company of Antonis, his wife Maria, and her sister, Voula. They live in Areopoli but spend some of the summer living *al fresco* at Arfikia, collecting sea salt from the rock pools owned by their family. We consumed freshly prepared fish soup with potatoes and drank Greek coffee and some Tsipouro spirit together, before Antonis took us on a boat tour of his salt pools, all the while explaining the history, the processes and the modern problems associated with this ancient occupation.

We were in high spirits as we walked back from Arfikia, carrying two heavy bags of salt and a string of garlic. What a richly rewarding experience it had been and yet, without our Greek, it would surely have swiftly terminated. Not only had we conversed in Greek for an extended period, but we had also done some translation back into English for the benefit of Keith, our walking companion. Our Greek lessons had once again paid dividends.

We were only aware of one difficult moment. I had introduced Keith as an old school friend and former PE teacher who had been a gifted footballer in his younger days, as well as a lifelong Manchester United supporter. Hugely impressed, Antonis responded by enquiring if Keith had ever played with Bobby Charlton and George Best! This was greeted by scarcely concealed amusement on our part, which understandably unsettled our host. Fortunately, a follow-up explanation quickly corrected the misunderstanding, and with the situation defused, the potential for our visit ending awkwardly evaporated.

Traditional Mani olive harvest.

Chapter 7

LIQUID GOLD

Initiation

The sun had yet to emerge from behind the backdrop of mountain peaks above us, their dark profiles contrasting sharply with the brightly illuminated, cobalt blue waters of the Gulf of Messinia far below. The air was crisp and fresh, a joy to inhale, the grasses and undergrowth varnished in dew, and coats and jackets were a necessary protection against the morning chill. The plaintive screech of invisible buzzards, smoke from a nearby bonfire slowly drifting skywards, and the honky-tonk bells of goats engaged in their never-ending search for nourishment all combined to create a sense of timeless rural idyll. And all this contained in an apparently endless, uniform green forest of olive trees.

It was just after eight o'clock on a November morning in 1997, barely a month after we had moved to Greece. Mary and I were being initiated into the age-old activity of olive picking by Allan, a new friend and prospective mentor. He and his wife Celia, long-time residents of West Mani and fiercely grecophile, own nearly 100 olive trees, not far from where they live in the village of Tseria, perched at about 600 metres above sea level on the steep, west-facing lower slopes of the Taygetos Mountains. For several consecutive Novembers in the late 1990s and early 2000s, we volunteered to assist with their annual olive harvest. The basic process is simple and straightforward: stretch out a large plastic sheet or net under the tree, prune the fully-laden branches onto the ground, and then employ small plastic rakes to comb off the olives. Once the olives remaining on the tree are stripped, the whole process is repeated, again and again, until the plastic sheet is too full of olives to drag easily to the next tree. Then, on hands and knees, the unwanted debris (leaves, twigs, spoilt olives etc.) is removed before the olives are transferred into large hessian sacks, ready for heaving to the nearest roadside at the end of the day's harvesting, for transport to a local olive press.

The memories of those olive-picking days are vivid. Allan gladly shared with us much of what he had learned about olive farming from his Greek neighbours and from his own experience. We were greatly influenced by his enthusiasm and passion and quickly became dedicated students. These pleasurable early experiences of olive picking made a considerable impact on us. In some ways they represented a step back in time as we harvested olives by hand in a way that had barely changed in thousands of years. By mid-morning the sun had normally taken charge and harvesting was in full swing with the prospect of a hearty lunch prepared by Celia urging us on. Enthusiasm and energy levels often waned by mid-afternoon, by which time Allan would have assessed the day's productivity. After consulting with his fellow pickers, he would decide on how many more trees to harvest before 'calling it a day'. With clothes and hands impregnated with oil, and joints and muscles yearning for reprieve, we were always glad to return home and linger in a rejuvenating shower.

Origins & Dispersal

Olives and olive oil are etched deep into the common psyche of the Greek people. It doesn't matter if they are country folk or city dwellers, or if their status, background and way of life are markedly different. The influence of olives and olive oil is wide-ranging. Many references are found in Greek mythology, religion and history, and there is no denying the considerable impact they have had on Greece's landscape, culture and rural way of life.

Homer is credited with coining the term 'liquid gold' and makes more than twenty references to olives and olive oil in his epic poems *The Iliad* and *The Odyssey*. Hippocrates (460–377 BCE), known as the Father of Medicine, referred to olive oil as 'the great healer'. He advocated its use to treat a variety of complaints from soothing burns and abrasions, to curing infections of ears, nose and throat; from easing stiffness and aches in muscles and joints, to relieving stomach upsets and acute indigestion. As well as healing, olive oil also played a crucial part in everyday life in Ancient Greece. It nourished, protected, cleaned and beautified, it stimulated and it provided light. Its significance came to the fore during great festivals – like those at Olympia, Delphi and Athens – that combined religious, cultural and athletic activities. Contrary to modern practice, there were no gold, silver and bronze medals awarded to the winners of sporting events. Maybe some victors were content with a crown of olive or laurel leaves, some prize money or the promise of a future statue in a public place, but most preferred a supply of olive oil.

The olive tree flourishes in the scriptures, teachings and rituals of the three Abrahamic faiths: Judaism, Christianity and Islam. As well as being used to perform ecclesiastical rituals, olive oil is the prescribed source of light that acts as a powerful metaphor for believers who perceive their God as the Light of the World. It was one of the four most important symbols of early Christianity, along with bread, wine and water. Modern-day Holy Baptism in the Greek Orthodox Church retains a strong link with past rites. Before being immersed three times in a font of holy water – one each in the name of the Father, the Son and the Holy Spirit – the naked baby is anointed with olive oil by the priest and godparent. In this case it is not just the head and feet but the whole body, the purpose being to help the baby elude the grip of sin and the devil.

The story of the first olive tree is one of the pillars of Greek mythology. It concerns a dispute between Poseidon and Athena, the god of the sea versus the goddess of wisdom. They were engaged in a struggle to determine who was pre-eminent in Attica, a leading region of Ancient Greece. Poseidon established his claim by driving his trident into the upstanding rocky outcrop of the Acropolis and creating a saltwater pool. Athena responded by using her powers to make an olive tree spring from the soil. But the King of Attica, Kekrops, could not decide which god had prevailed and invited Zeus to appoint a panel of twelve gods to adjudicate. They decided in favour of Athena because she had given Attica 'its greatest gift'. Henceforth, the olive tree became one of Athena's most recognised symbols; she gave her name to the city that grew up around the Acropolis and the newly built temple on its top, the Parthenon, was dedicated to her.

Scientific research since those times suggests that the olive tree as we know it originated in Asia Minor as much as 5,000 years before Athena's much acclaimed mythical magic. It was probably derived from the wild version, a hardy evergreen shrub that thrives in hot, arid conditions and is part of a family of flowering plants that also includes jasmine, lilac, forsythia and privet. All varieties of olive tree stem from the original domesticated tree, Olea europaea. Through a very elementary and experimental process of plant breeding, based on trial and error and without the benefit of scientific research, early farmers gathered promising looking olive shoots in the wild and grafted them onto rootstock. This required huge amounts of patience and several generations of incremental progress. The aim was to select the best outcomes and repeat the process again and again until eventually the unrewarding wild olive shrub was transformed into a tree with a valuable crop that could be put to a variety of uses.

Despite its value and versatility, dispersal of the domesticated olive tree throughout the Middle East and eastern Mediterranean was surprisingly slow and largely on the back of trade, migration, re-settlement and colonisation. Several thousand years elapsed before the olive tree reached the Lazio countryside around Rome in about 580 BCE, establishing itself throughout the Aegean islands, Crete and the Peloponnese on the way. Despite their reputation for old age, few olive trees have survived from ancient times. The oldest in Greece is the famous olive tree of Vouves in north-western Crete, which was declared a national monument in 1997. It is reckoned to be over 2,000 years old, has a trunk with a diameter of five metres and a girth of twelve and a half metres . . . and it still produces olives!

Plant breeding using modern, scientific techniques has expanded the number of traditional varieties of Olea europaea so that now there are hundreds of different cultivars suited to a variety of conditions. Some are farmed solely for their oil, some solely for their eating olives and some are dual-purpose. The original domesticated wild olive has come a long way in 8,000 years, allowing the spread of olive farming well beyond the confines of the lands surrounding the Mediterranean Sea. Although nearly 90% of olive trees are still found there, in the last fifty years olive farming has spread to other parts of the world with a Mediterranean-type climate, such as California, Chile, and parts of Australia and New Zealand, to name but a few.

Changing Tastes

In the overall scheme of things, olive oil's significance in everyday life in Britain is somewhere near the bottom of the scale. That was certainly the case in 1941 when, in an article entitled *'England, Your England'*, the writer George Orwell described the English taste for food. He declared that: *'As a rule they will refuse even a simple foreign dish, they regard things [such] as garlic and olive oil with disgust. Life is unbearable to them unless they have tea and puddings.'* Fortunately, things have moved on in the intervening eighty years. Thanks to the impact of foreign travel, the healthy eating trend and the popularity of TV food programmes, olive oil has attained a status in the British culinary world that would have amazed Orwell and his generation.

My first encounter with olive oil was as a seven-year-old in the early 1950s, lying flat on my side on the living room floor of our platform-side, station master's house at Holsworthy Railway Station, North Devon. I had been suffering a prolonged bout of earache and my mother had purchased, at great expense, a small brown bottle of olive oil from 'Boots the Chemist', where it had been lurking with other '50s' staples such as syrup of figs, calamine lotion and alum powder. With the aid of a warmed teaspoon, she was carefully dripping a small quantity into my ear and strongly advising me to resist the temptation to move until the olive oil had worked its magic. My first experience of tasting olive oil had to wait another ten years.

In that post-war period of austerity, food shortages and rationing, the priority in Britain was getting by with whatever was available and with whatever you could afford. Improvisation was encouraged and waste was frowned upon. Based on hundreds of years of North European culinary tradition, frying, baking and roasting relied almost exclusively on animal fats (dripping, lard, suet etc.), dairy produce (butter) and synthetic substitutes (margarine). The only alternatives were bland cooking oils, often blended from a variety of vegetable oils from ill-defined sources and used almost exclusively for frying potatoes – although beef dripping was the medium of choice for most fish and chip shops. As for dressing salads, one product reigned supreme: Heinz Salad Cream, a unique British version of mayonnaise. Food culture and culinary styles in Britain – and elsewhere in Northern Europe – contrasted sharply with the Mediterranean lands, where olive oil was king.

It was only in the 1960s that British people began to shake off the post-war blues and look forward with greater confidence. Whether they were responding to Prime Minister Harold Macmillan's declaration that they 'had never had it so good' is questionable, but people found they had more disposable income and they looked for ways to spend it. Exhausted by austerity, the more prosperous, well-travelled middle classes began to seek alternatives to the bland, restricted and predictable food they had endured for twenty years or more. They found an inspiration in Elizabeth David.

One of three sisters, Elizabeth David (1913–1992) was from a privileged, well-heeled background. Unconventional, well-travelled and impulsive, she was dismayed by the gloom and bad food that greeted her when she returned to London in 1945 from war service in Cairo. Thus, she began writing culinary articles for magazines based on her experiences in Southern Europe and North Africa. These were compiled to form her first publication: *A Book of Mediterranean Cookery*, published in 1950. She boldly called for ingredients such as aubergines, basil, garlic, olive oil and saffron, and introduced dishes such as paella, ratatouille and moussaka. Although her publisher was pessimistic about the book's prospects, it had a powerful effect on the British middle classes, who were 'longing for a taste of sunshine'. The age of olive oil as simply an earache therapy had passed, but it would take several more decades before olive oil became a universal ingredient in British kitchens.

My first experiences of tasting olive oil must have come as a student and then as a newly qualified teacher, during holidays in the south of France, Corsica and on the Greek islands during the 1960s and '70s, but curiously, they have left no impression. My recall of some wines and food we consumed are so vivid – although not always for the best of reasons – so it is particularly strange that my recollections of olive oil remain so obscure. I guess in those days, the oil I was most interested in was Ambre Solaire. My youthful take on food was primarily for sustenance; a fuel to ensure all the other, more interesting, active aspects of life could be sampled and enjoyed to the full. Good flavours were appreciated but how they were obtained was of little interest. Thus, early opportunities to learn about and appreciate the qualities of olive oil had been unwittingly spurned. At home in south-east London, the well-stocked shelves of Florian's delicatessen in Blackheath Village tempted Mary and me to try to replicate Mediterranean dishes enjoyed on holidays. But we rarely got further than making vinaigrette to dress our salads, and then we used sunflower or corn oil instead of expensive olive oil. For me, olive oil remained a culinary bit-part player. Very little changed with our move to North Devon in 1979. In fact, some fresh food items – aubergines and green peppers, for example – that we had taken for granted in London were nowhere to be found.

Much has changed in the average British kitchen since Elizabeth David's heyday. In the period 2014–19, Britain imported about thirty million litres of olive oil per year – more than double the volume in 2002 and worth an eye-watering £200 million annually. In a May 2007 *Guardian* magazine feature, TV chef and real food activist Hugh Fearnley-Whittingstall described olive oil in Britain as *'a magic elixir in the kitchens of millions – instant Mediterranean sunshine… It's the brown sauce, tomato ketchup and salad cream of the middle classes, all in one bottle'.* The UK ranks sixth in the world table of olive oil importers, with Greece only supplying a mere 3%, lagging well behind Spain (54%) and Italy (35%). But it's worth noting that neither of these two restrict their exports solely to home-produced olive oil. Some of it originates in other Mediterranean countries like Tunisia and Morocco – and Greece! – and is blended with sub-premium home-produced olive oil and rebranded before being legitimately re-exported as Spanish or Italian oil. A lawful but questionable practice.

Much of the appeal of olive oil that has driven the rise in UK consumption has been its well-publicised health benefits. It is widely acknowledged that the Mediterranean diet, in which olive oil plays a significant role, is one of the world's healthiest. Olive oil, whatever its grade, is 100% fat, but 75% is mono-unsaturated fat called oleic acid or omega-9 and is rich in antioxidants. Mono-unsaturated fats are known to support the normal functioning of the body's immune system, to maintain and uphold cardiovascular health and efficiency, and reduce inflammation. Other more outlandish medical claims that suggest olive oil consumption can slow down the onset of Alzheimer's disease or reduce the likelihood of depression are less convincing.

Even so, the recommendation by one website that a daily dose of two teaspoons of extra virgin olive oil should become standard practice represents sound advice to me.

Terroir

Greece is ranked as the third most important producer of olive oil behind Spain and Italy, accounting for 13% of world production. It is acclaimed for 80% of its output being of the highest quality, making it the world's largest exporter of extra virgin olive oil, most of which goes to other European countries, especially Italy. Equally notable is the fact that Greeks consume more olive oil than any other nationality – an impressive twenty-four litres per person per year! No wonder they seem so healthy and have impressive longevity.

Greece has been granted eighteen olive oil PDOs (a Protected Designation of Origin) by the EU. Ten can be found on the island of Crete, seven in the Peloponnese and one in the north on the Halkidiki peninsula. A PDO is an accreditation system designed to help consumers identify authentic European food and drink products with a guaranteed provenance. It also ensures farmers receive a fair reward for their endeavours. Kalamata is arguably the most noteworthy of the PDO-accredited olive oil producing regions in the Peloponnese but its production is easily eclipsed by tens of other non-designated areas, many of which produce olive oils of comparable quality. The absence of the distinctive PDO emblem on a label does not necessarily mean that the olive oil is inferior, especially if it has a known and reliable provenance.

Extra virgin olive oil from the prefectures of Lakonia and Messinia, which occupy the southernmost reaches of the Peloponnese, has a longstanding and enviable reputation for exceptional quality and taste, not just in Greece but worldwide. The Mani peninsula, with its backbone of the Taygetos Mountains, is at the geographical heart of this region. The natural environment in which the olive tree is cultivated is a primary factor in determining the quality of olive oil. Thus, the industry has borrowed the term 'terroir' from the world of wine and uses it in much the same way – to describe the climate, terrain and soil representative of the region of production.

Olive trees flourish in the typical Mediterranean climate of the Mani Peninsula with its long, hot, sunny summers and mild, wet winters. The old Maniot saying *'Kalokairi afvroko, ladi afthono'* – 'Dry summer, oil aplenty' – is still heard. However, output and yield can be threatened by a prolonged summer drought and by unpredictable bouts of extreme weather. The two most common are heatwaves and high winds in spring when the fruit is setting, and hailstorms in late summer that not only bruise and bring down the ripening olives but also damage the olive tree branches, which encourages the onset of canker, a destructive fungal disease.

The terrain varies hugely in the Mani Peninsula, ranging from undulating coastal lowland to mid-altitude plateaus to high mountain peaks reaching over 2,000 metres. Flat land is at a premium. Olive trees are rarely found at altitudes above 600 metres because of the risk of frost damage, while steeply sloping ground with sparse soil is terraced to maximise the soil depth, reduce soil erosion and ease harvesting. As a rule, olive trees can tolerate most soils, providing they are free draining, but they have a preference for the red clayey soils called *terra rossa* that are found in areas where limestone is the underlying rock.

The variety of olive tree is another significant factor. In Greece there are seven common varieties of olive trees but in the Peloponnese two varieties dominate: the *Koroneiki* for olive oil and the *Kalamon* for eating olives. They are both local Messinian varieties. *Koroneiki* means 'of Koroni', a historic small port at the end of the Messinian Peninsula. The olive farms of the Mani are almost exclusively planted with *Koroneiki* trees, thus its behaviour is familiar and its few idiosyncrasies well known. It is a small, compact tree which can be planted relatively close to its neighbours, it gives high yields, the olives ripen early, and the oil has a reputation for low acidity, exceptional health benefits and longevity. As with all olive trees, it only crops well every other year.

Unlikely Entrepreneurs

'Tried & Tasted' was the name we gave to the boutique olive oil business Mary and I set up in 2005. It all started in a spontaneous kind of way. No great forethought, no master plan and no ambition to do anything other than bring some of the best olive oil in the world from southern Greece to the UK, share it with friends and family and perhaps sell any surplus. Our first experience of premium quality Greek extra virgin olive oil had been the five-litre cans we earned each November for helping Allan and Celia harvest their olives. The exceptional taste and flavour of that oil convinced us that we should make space for olive oil in the boot of our car when we returned to North Devon each winter. We were sure there would be plenty of takers.

Unfortunately, Allan and Celia's trees rarely produced a volume of oil surplus to their needs and thus it was necessary to find another source. We didn't have to look far. Socrates, the husband of our Greek teacher, Marina, was an olive farmer from whom we had already purchased a small volume of olive oil, and it seemed to tick all the boxes. It was premium quality, fresh, pure, single estate, extra virgin olive oil with a known provenance, and negotiations quickly led to a mutually beneficial working relationship that lasted twelve years. It was a straightforward arrangement: Socrates supplied the olive oil while we arranged its packaging, shipment across Europe and sale in the UK. In 2015–16, Tried & Tasted's final year of trading, we imported 1,750 litres of Socrates' olive oil; a far cry from the first purchase of thirty litres and testimony to the high regard with which it was held by us and our UK customers. We were all winners.

The transformation from small scale 'olive oil running' in the boot of our car to a fully-fledged business goes back to a phone call in late January 2005. It was from a friend of a friend, enquiring if we could sell her some olive oil. The caller had experienced Socrates' olive oil at a local dinner party a few days earlier and was eager to obtain some for her own use. Much to her disappointment, we were unable to oblige; in the space of just eight weeks, our limited stocks had dwindled to a precious residue we intended on keeping for our own use. But this enquiry got us thinking. It seemed we had a choice: keep things small-scale, simple and informal, or convert ourselves into unlikely entrepreneurs. We chose the latter and Tried & Tasted was born.

Everyone we consulted at the outset recommended that we should decide how we were going to distinguish Tried & Tasted from its rivals and competitors. This meant establishing our USPs, or Unique Selling Points. In the back of our minds, we had the lingering notion that we were somehow in debt to Greece and the Greek people for the smooth way we had been assimilated into their country. Thus, we quickly determined that our products would be exclusively Greek, be solely foodstuffs that possessed a known provenance and be as fresh, pure and natural as possible . . . . just like Socrates' olive oil. We also decided to adopt a personal, hands-on approach with our customers, allowing them to sample and taste our products. Following our instincts as former teachers, we were also determined to provide them with as much background information as possible. After all, we had a story to tell and we were keen to tell it.

The Socrates Way

Right from the outset, Socrates' extra virgin olive oil formed the cornerstone of Tried & Tasted's activity. The only son of a family of four, Socrates was born and brought up in the West Mani village of Exohori, which is perched on the edge of the Viros gorge at some 600 metres above sea level. He took over farming his family's 2,500 Koroneiki olive trees from his father when he returned from living and working in Athens in 1998. Tall, lean and strong, with thinning blond hair, a taciturn manner and a deep love and respect for nature, Socrates would not be out of place working a farm in North Devon. But he's got olive oil, not cow's milk, in his veins. He is a knowledgeable, hardworking farmer, dedicated to sustainable production and traditional, environmentally friendly farming. He is rightly proud of the pure, unfiltered extra virgin olive oil he produces. Socrates' olive trees occupy the undulating plateau between Exohori and Kardamyli, which is backed by the Taygetos Mountains and looks down on the Gulf of Messinia. This area is full of olive trees, some of them two or three hundred years old. Scattered in fragmented plots, some on broad, flat terraces, others on narrow, rocky ones, his trees produce exceptional yields of high-quality olive oil – if pests, diseases and inclement weather don't intervene.

The work of a Mani olive farmer involves a range of tasks that vary throughout the year. The only really intensive period is harvesting, which takes place during the winter months. At the other extreme, there are periods in the summer when regular but infrequent inspection of the developing fruit is all that is required. In between times, there is pruning, fertilising, spraying, strimming and repairing terrace walls to do. Pruning is a critical task. It takes place twice each year, during harvesting and again in late spring and early summer. Socrates' knowledge, skill and experience are particularly important in this respect. As well as preserving the desired habit of the olive tree, pruning also aids harvesting, promotes the future yield of olives and encourages the growth and maturation of a healthy crop. Mani farmers favour olive trees that are no more than four metres tall, with five main branches reaching skywards from the trunk, in the form of an upturned hand with fingers and thumb splayed. In other parts of Greece, olive-pruning customs and traditions can be quite different.

Harvest time in the Mani Peninsula begins in mid-November and can last until the beginning of March. For some, it's a long haul only interrupted by occasional days of bad weather. It is heralded by the whine of strimmers in the olive groves and cleaning and maintenance activity in the olive presses. Early season Koroneiki olives are a mixture of green, mauve and dark purple in colour. They produce a strong-flavoured, green olive oil with a grassy aroma, a peppery taste and high levels of polyphenols, which are the key constituent of olive oil's health properties. The last olives to be picked at the end of the harvest are uniformly dark purple and produce a much more mellow, yellow olive oil with a more buttery flavour.

The quality of olive oil depends on a host of factors. Two significant ones are the condition of the olives when they are harvested and the method of harvesting. Olives that are blemished, infected by pests (e.g. the olive fruit fly), or are bruised or wounded during harvest will harm the quality and longevity of the oil. Thus, Socrates favours the old-fashioned but time-consuming way of manual harvesting with the minimum of mechanical aids. In a good year when the crop is plentiful, he is assisted by his mother Angeliki, and sometimes has to resort to hiring casual labour. Harvesting olives in this time-honoured way is a pleasurable, if tiring, business, but is not without its risks and dangers, and minor accidents are common. People fall off ladders, trip over exposed rocks, twist ankles in obscured fox or badger holes, and strain backs and shoulders through too much awkward stretching. Injuries dealt with by local health centres and hospitals during harvest time often involve eyes and fingers; the former the result of whippy, young branches, the latter due to an ill-judged moment with a saw.

In stark contrast are the modern techniques of mechanical harvesting employed in parts of southern Spain which have gone in for mass production of olive oil. Huge, recently established olive tree plantations, comprising rows and rows of uniform-size trees stretching as far as the eye can see, have been created. They are harvested by expensive, specialist machines that grab the trunk of each tree and shake off the olives, which are automatically gathered in a large hopper and delivered by conveyor directly to an accompanying trailer. Burdened by tradition and an unhelpful terrain, Mani olive farmers are in no position to embrace these modern methods, and

Socrates clings to the hope that his well-established, environmentally friendly methods will continue to produce exceptional olive oil, unsurpassed by new intensive olive farming elsewhere.

The Mani olive farmer has little choice but to make the most of the trees he or she inherits and the terrain they occupy. Even though olive farming there remains much as it was 100 years ago, some choices are available to the olive farmer. The most important is whether to be organic or not. Socrates would argue that the old-fashioned way is organic anyway, but these days more precise testing and evidence is required to obtain accreditation from organisations like Bio Hellas and DIO, Greek equivalents of the Soil Association in Britain. A few Messinian oil packaging and export businesses, like Mani Organic (formerly Bläuel Greek Organic Products) in Pyrgos Lefktrou, have led the way in encouraging farmers to become organic by guaranteeing them an outlet for their olive oil if it meets organic standards. This has led to a fundamental change in farming attitudes in parts of the Mani and a revival of the local ecosystem, which had been damaged by indiscriminate aerial spraying of pesticides during the late 1980s and early 1990s.

However, being organic has its additional costs, some of which olive farmers are unwilling or unable to bear. These costs involve joining an organisation empowered to grant organic accreditation – and in addition, paying an annual fee – and buying more expensive organic fertilisers and pest controls. Although organic olive oil can demand a higher price, the growth in demand for organic produce in Europe has not been as rapid as many experts were forecasting at the turn of the millennium, and thus olive farmers can find they are no better off for choosing the organic way. The winners are clearly consumers, who desire a pure, natural, uncontaminated and healthy product, the environment, and an agricultural economy that is sustainable.

Socrates, like all Mani olive farmers, is reassured by a wet winter and encouraged by early autumn rains (provided they are not accompanied by hail and high winds), but dismayed by a summer drought that extends into September. Prolonged summer drought, especially after a relatively dry winter, can have a significant negative impact on yield and output and increases the risk of wildfires. Thus, the prudent olive farmer will weigh up the pros and cons of installing an irrigation system to counteract the effects of a drought. Socrates prefers not to water his trees. He endorses the view expressed by many experts that some water stress has a beneficial effect on the quality of the oil. He is confident that 'dry' olive farming enhances the flavour of the oil and increases its health properties.

Extracting the Oil

The time lapse between olives being harvested and pressed is arguably the most important element in ensuring good-quality oil. The shorter the better; within twenty-four hours is ideal. Delays are best avoided but are sometimes inevitable at the height of the picking season, when all farmers are actively harvesting and keen to have their olives processed promptly. That is why recently constructed, state-of-the-art olive presses in southern Spain have several production lines operating simultaneously. Almost every Mani village has at least one olive press owned and run either by the local olive farmers' co-operative or by a village family, but they operate with just one line and farmers have to wait their turn.

Wandering around a Mani village as a tourist in summer, you could be forgiven for overlooking the local olive press. They are characterised as large, anonymous, apparently neglected buildings with assorted conveyors and augers protruding from them, surrounded by large, empty yards. But during harvest season they come alive, casting noise and an acrid aroma across the village. They operate from midday, sometimes right through the night, only pausing when days of inclement weather interrupt harvesting, and generate abnormal levels of light, evening traffic and enhanced trade in local *cafeneions*, bakeries and tavernas. Workers are often employed on a casual basis and return year after year for three months of exhausting and energy-sapping toil. They need to be fit and strong with ample reserves of stamina. It's a truly physical job.

Both Neohori's olive presses – like those in most Greek villages – have been modernised in recent years, and traditional olive presses are becoming increasingly hard to find. However, the impressive Museum of the Olive and Greek Olive Oil in the city of Sparti provides visitors with an evocative glimpse of how olive oil used to be produced in the past and, in a more intimate way, Mitso and Ioanna's taverna in the West Mani village of Kariovouni does much the same. In the winter months their taverna moves inside to the former village olive press, where much of the original equipment and machinery remains intact and in situ. Surrounded by these imposing relics from a bygone age when olive oil played such a vital role in the subsistence economy of the village, it is not difficult to imagine this small olive press operating at full capacity at the height of the harvest season in the early 1960s. The vivid stories our first Greek teacher, Ifigeneia, had told us of her olive press experiences as a callow teenager during the Second World War on Poros island always helps to stimulate our imagination.

Within the limited confines of the congested press – scarcely more than eighty square metres in size – it would have been the constant noise that dominated proceedings. The thumping steam-powered generator, the rattling overhead gear wheels linked by loudly flapping belts that transmitted power to the rotating granite millstones would have combined to make an ear-splitting racket. And the smell would have been no better. The steam, the pungent smells emanating from the olive processing and the fetid body odour of industrious workers would have added to the gloomy, claustrophobic atmosphere. A well-earned break under the adjacent pair of huge plane trees would have seemed like passing from hell to heaven – breathing in fresh mountain air, relishing the relative peace and quiet and quenching thirst with cool spring water.

The traditional process of extracting oil from olives was

straightforward enough but required skill and experience to ensure the throughput of olives generated an acceptable quantity of decent oil. The millstones pulverised the olives – crushed stones and all – into a pulp looking somewhat like dull green porridge, which was then fed into circular, woven reed mats. They were stacked high on a giant, floor-to-ceiling, cast iron screw press and slowly squeezed manually until all the oil was extracted. A few days of patience was then required for the sediment to sink to the bottom of the galvanised steel collecting tank before the time-consuming process of decanting the oil by hand into storage vessels could commence. In the 1960s, some villagers would still have kept their oil in large earthenware pots (*pitharia*), which were the standard means of oil storage for centuries. Olive oil produced in this way was the purest of pure fruit juice, albeit a good deal thicker than the average supermarket orange or apple juice.

The ultra-fresh olive oil that emerges directly from the press is a magical elixir. If it is made from the earliest pickings, it's a kind of 'olive oil nouveau'. Mary and I were first introduced to this unique, early season oil one early November evening while eating at the homely Nostimies taverna in the fishing village of Aghios Nikolaos, just a few kilometres from Neohori. A tired-looking and disheveled farmer entered the taverna, clutching a plastic Coca Cola bottle that contained a cloudy, lime green liquid that turned out to be olive oil. He had come directly from the nearby Poulakos family olive press, where his first batch of freshly harvested olives had been milled. Before sitting down and ordering his food, he made a slow tour of all the tables, gently pouring a sample of his still-warm olive oil on every spare plate and urging people to taste. The communal slurping was quickly followed by a chorus of approval, sufficient to prompt the olive farmer to slump into a chair with a proud grin on his unshaven face and consider what he might eat and drink to reward himself. It didn't take us long to grasp that this ultra-fresh olive oil with its grassy aroma, strong taste and limited ten-week lifespan in its virginal form, was a product Tried & Tasted could not afford to ignore. Virtually unknown in Britain, we were confident it would be an instant hit with UK foodies and borrowed the Greek word for 'fresh' to christen it 'Fresko!' olive oil.

Over the last sixty years, Mani olive presses have undergone a transformation. Wood, stone and cast iron have given way to stainless steel; and human, animal and steam power have been replaced, first by diesel engines and then electricity. The 21st-century installation of Italian-made, modern machinery and more sophisticated operating systems have combined to make processing more efficient. They have also helped to make the quality of the oil more reliable and maintain competitiveness with international rivals, such as Spain and Italy. Village presses have replaced granite millstones with powerful grinding-crushers, while malaxers and centrifuges have taken the place of the traditional screw presses. The term 'olive press' has become a misnomer but olive *mill* – the more correct modern term – is struggling to take its place. Malaxing is the churning and mixing of the olive pulp by slowly rotating blades in giant horizontal stainless steel tanks for up to forty-five minutes. Warm water is added to increase the yield of oil but its temperature must never exceed 28°C to claim the designation 'cold-pressed' or 'cold-extracted'. This is hardly cold by most standards, but it is cold enough to ensure the quality of the olive oil is not compromised. The powerful centrifuges separate the oil from the remaining pulp and vegetal water before it is piped to a storage tank. No refining is necessary, no chemicals are added; this oil is immediately consumable in its raw state and is designated 'first pressing'. The dried pulp by-product is augered to an outside yard from where it is transported to Kalamata factories for re-pressing to produce inferior second- and third-pressing oils, and ultimately for processing into by-products like animal feeding stuffs and briquettes for barbeques and stoves. Nothing is wasted.

Olive farmers always keep a close eye on the processing of their olives, and some are much fussier than others, making sure there have been no short cuts or dubious practices. Their olive oil is likely to be their sole source of income and so getting it right is crucial. Once the processing has been overseen, there are other important matters to address. Some preliminary testing of the oil is carried out at this stage to give the farmer some idea of its quality. He is keen to learn that acidity is below 0.8% – ensuring extra virgin status – and that levels of peroxides are below twelve, indicating a desirable lifespan for the oil. But he is understandably interested in quantity too. By comparing the weight of olives in kilograms and the volume of the oil they have produced in litres, the farmer can calculate a ratio that gives him a fair idea of the yield. A 1:7 ratio (that is, one litre of oil from seven kilograms of olives) at the start of harvest would be considered good. Later on, yields normally improve and can reach 1:4 in a good year.

Then there is the question of paying the press for its services. This is normally in the form of 8% of the yield of oil, which the press retains and sells in bulk at a later time. There is also the matter of storage, especially if the olive farmer has a large number of trees producing a considerable volume of oil. Small-scale farmers will store their oil in tin cans, while others prefer storing it in traditional, metre-tall, round wooden vats lined with galvanised steel, or in their modern equivalents – versatile, 1,000-litre opaque-plastic cubes, which sit on wooden pallets and are contained in steel or aluminium frames. Where accommodation allows, olive presses will store their oil in large, stainless steel vats, or silos. An ideal storage temperature is between 10°C and 18°C and yet indoor temperatures at the height of summer can regularly exceed 30°C, and in winter, at higher altitudes, temperatures can hover around zero during night time. Neither extremes favour the quality of the olive oil and thus, unless fresh olive oil is packaged and sold quickly or costly temperature-controlled warehouses are constructed, some deterioration is inevitable.

Packaging is normally the prerogative of bigger enterprises that specialise in marketing and exporting olive oil. Examples are Mani Organic in Pyrgos Lefktrou and, in Kalamata, the Union of Messinian Cooperatives, Papadimitriou, Mani Foods and Agrovim. In an ideal world, packaging would follow as soon as the olive oil has cleared, but logistically this is not always possible. There is disagreement about whether filtering prior to packaging is desirable or not. Supporters of filtering claim it gives olive oil a longer life, whereas those who oppose filtering believe the 'pure and natural' state of unfiltered oil retains more of its flavour and health-giving properties.

By the spring of 2010, Tried & Tasted planned to purchase 700 litres of extra virgin olive oil from Socrates, a greater volume than ever before. We also wanted all of it packaged in Greece before shipment to the UK. The time for packaging by hand in North Devon had passed; the volumes were just too great. Packaging in bottles, cans and boxes is not normally undertaken by the individual farmer, or indeed by the farmers' co-operatives that operate most olive presses. Fortunately, our local Neohori Farmers' Co-operative is an exception. Paraskevas, the then-manager of the co-operative press and bottling plant, is a neighbour of ours and we came to rely on him each February to collect Socrates' olive oil from the Exohori olive press and to oversee its canning and bottling. A burly, outgoing and affable character, Paraskevas possesses an intuitive approach to solving mechanical problems. He never failed to cope with the idiosyncrasies of the Italian-made, automatic, stainless steel bottling and canning lines and always managed to meet our deadlines. Two able assistants contributed much to the process; Mario, a lumbering, taciturn seasonal worker from Poland, did a lot of the dirty and heavy work, while Marianna, a chirpy middle-aged Romanian woman living locally, applied self-adhesive labels by hand with amazing dexterity and hand-eye co-ordination. She consistently demonstrated why her labelling was preferred to that of the nearby machine.

Making the Right Choice

It's not difficult to appreciate that the interplay of many different factors, some arising from nature, some from human decision-making, and others derived from the quality of processing and storage, determine whether an olive oil is any good or not. But how do you recognise an exceptional olive oil? It's a difficult task; even experts and connoisseurs can fail to agree.

The International Olive Council, based in Madrid, plays a major role in regulating the production, packaging, marketing and trade in olive oil. It is the FIFA of the olive oil world and its members, representing many diverse countries, businesses and interests, are subject to the same kind of lobbying and pressures. Labels contain much valuable information, some prescribed by the IOC; the most important is the grade of olive oil. This should be printed in a large font size that dominates the front label. In descending order of quality, they are EXTRA VIRGIN OLIVE OIL, VIRGIN OLIVE OIL, REFINED OLIVE OIL and just plain OLIVE OIL. Each is quite different in taste, texture, style and price. Discerning consumers may choose extra virgin for dressing salads, drizzling, marinating and dipping, while plain olive oil is sometimes preferred for frying, baking and roasting. On the other hand, Greeks, with a plentiful and relatively inexpensive supply on their doorstep, use extra virgin for every culinary purpose.

These days, in order to broaden appeal, the range of olive oil products is being widened to attract new customers, address new health fads and, of course, increase sales. This development does not necessarily make selection any easier. Olive oil sprays, where only 53% of the content is actual olive oil, are intended to help consumers who are slimming; light and mild olive oils are a mixture of refined and virgin oils and have the same target consumer in mind, while flavoured oils – infused with chilli or basil, lime, truffle, mint etc. – are aimed at consumers constantly seeking new tastes and flavours. No Greek would even consider this option. And why would they, when the taste of good-quality extra virgin olive oil has so many nuances, depending on the food you are eating and how it has been cooked and prepared?

But choosing your olive oil solely on the basis of the limited information on a bottle's front label is not recommended. It's the details in small print on the back label that confirm if the oil is genuine, of good quality and with a desirable provenance. Olive oil deteriorates with age; the fresher it is, the more flavour and health-giving properties remain. Thus, close scrutiny of the date of harvesting, date of bottling and best before date is strongly advisable. Olive oil is well past its best eighteen months after extraction. Nutritional value tables and logos indicating quality – like a PDO or a recognised international award – are also worth looking for, as is information from artisan producers that makes reference to 'single estate', locates the farm, states the olive oil cultivar and declares its essential properties. But beware of fakes. Thomas Mueller's entertaining and controversial examination of the global olive oil business in his 2011 book *Extra Virginity: the sublime and scandalous world of olive oil* exposes the fraud and fakery that exists, something the authorities are eager to stamp out before trust and confidence is significantly eroded.

The way olive oil is packaged is also critical in retaining its quality. Olive oil suffers if exposed to light and air. Both these common enemies can be resisted by using appropriate packaging. A 'BIB' (Bag in a Box) is ideal. It's a style of packaging pioneered by wine producers, whereby a sealed polythene or foil bag with a tap is filled with olive oil and placed in a cardboard box. A BIB excludes the light, a vacuum forms behind the oil in the bag as it is decanted, it is clean to use and is compact enough in shape and size to be accommodated in any kitchen. A perfect culinary adjunct! Clear glass or plastic bottles are best avoided.

An Uncertain Future

Olive farming in Greece has never been a lucrative business, even for those farmers with thousands of trees. The margins are low and a poor harvest can be devastating. Few Mani olive farmers can rely solely on the income from their olives to sustain their families, so many have other jobs, often in tourism during summer, when olive farming is less demanding. EU subsidies are being systematically reduced and wholesale prices continue to fluctuate wildly. At the same time, international competition is widening and intensifying, and the rising popularity of alternative niche oils – like coconut, grapeseed, avocado and rapeseed oil – are gaining favour and eating into olive oil's market share. Employing seasonal labour at harvest time is costly, and new generations seem to be less inclined to carry on farming olives as their forebears have done for centuries. And then there's Xylella fastidiosa, a deadly bacterium that has recently caused severe dieback in southern Italy, which threatens the health and even the very existence of Mani olive trees. Its impact could possibly be more far-reaching than anything else. An uncertain future beckons.

The much-maligned Common Agricultural Policy (CAP), with its worthy aims, has always formed a major part of the EU's budget. Olive farming has been one of the sectors that has benefited most, with EU subsidies in Greece accounting for 40% of an olive farmer's income. But things are changing as CAP is reformed and expenditure reduced. Payments vary from region to region, but an average Greek olive farmer who was receiving subsidies of €640 per hectare in 2014 found them reduced to €530 per hectare by 2019 – a swingeing cut of nearly 20%. For several decades, these subsidies have ensured the survival of olive farming in many parts of rural Greece. Their reduction is sure to lead to hardship, unemployment and maybe social unrest, accompanied by more rural depopulation and the unwelcome prospect of the abandonment of swathes of countryside to the wild.

The international olive oil market is a fickle one. Fluctuations of supply and demand and their impact on wholesale prices have a significant impact on the Greek olive farmer's income. A bumper harvest in Spain can diminish it, a disease-ravaged crop in Italy can bolster it. Fortunately, CAP mechanisms are still in place to financially support olive farmers if the drop in price becomes extreme. The spread of olive farming beyond the traditional Mediterranean lands has meant increased competition, not just in existing markets but also in emerging markets, like India and China. This has added to Mani olive farmers' uncertainty. More enterprising farmers seek ways to reduce the risk. Some are contracted to packaging/exporting firms with a fixed price agreed in advance, some ship their oil in large cans directly to regular customers in Northern Europe, while others rely on selling to local restaurants or to tourists. The rest have little option but to eventually sell their oil back to the press, at an unrewarding price. This oil often ends up in Italy; nearly 70% of Greek extra virgin olive oil is exported there.

If olive farming in the Mani Peninsula is going to survive, some concerted action is needed. The default mode for Greek farmers is to take to the streets in protest. Huge convoys of slow-moving tractors with black flags can bring city centres and motorways to a standstill. However, the developing crisis confronting Greek olive farmers needs more than protest. It needs a strategic review, followed by effective action at national, regional and local levels. After all, olive oil is Greece's signature product.

The main lesson of the recent crisis-ridden years is that Greece must change and adapt. In an interview with the Kalamata daily newspaper *Eleftheria* in February 2014, Yiorgos Yoniotakis, President of the Greek National Organisation of Olive Oil & Olives, was adamant that the government had a vital role to play. Authenticity was a crucial issue. He highlighted the need to establish, and promote worldwide, a strong national identity for Greek olive and olive oil products. Weak export branding for Greek olive oil products has long been a problem. How is it that Italian brands like Filippo Berio, Carapelli and Bertolli – the latter two now owned by Spanish multinationals, by the way – are more instantly recognisable on supermarket shelves than comparable Greek brands like Iliada and Gaea?

At the same time, in order to safeguard Greece's monopoly of quality olive oil production, Yoniotakis advocated stricter quality controls, more rigorous testing and more robust measures to tackle olive oil fraud and fakery. In his book *Extra Virginity*, Thomas Mueller contrasts the fortunes of the honest hardworking olive farmers with the corrupt and unscrupulous merchants and businesspeople who trade in the product of the farmers' toil. In what Alex Renton in *The Guardian* newspaper described as an 'eye-watering investigation', Mueller exposes the fakery and fraud that has become endemic in the international olive oil market, threatening to undermine the consumers' trust in what the label on the bottle declares. It appears there is no business more slippery than olive oil. International olive oil organisations have been forewarned, but more effective monitoring and enforcement of protocols seem slow to materialise.

Following the examples being set in California and Australia, Yoniotakis called on the Greek government to sponsor an enhanced system of advice, support and re-education, whereby olive farmers are actively informed of contemporary research and developments in their sector and encouraged to refine existing methods and adopt new ones. Olive farmers must also learn to help themselves. Although often conservative by nature, Mani olive farmers have to embrace reform and change, or eventually go out of business. Farmers' co-operatives, properly constituted and managed, with the right kind of professional advice and support and with some access to development funds, could become important agents for change and diversification. Livestock farmers in North Devon have done it by converting surplus barns into holiday cottages, converting pasture to camping and caravan sites during the summer months, and setting up farm shops. Ways forward for the Mani olive farmer might involve raising the profile of Mani olive oil through annual olive oil festivals and a Mani 'Olive Oil of the Year' award. Other options might include agro-tourism, co-operating with travel firms to offer olive picking days for end-of-season tourists, olive oil tasting sessions at local hotels, or online olive tree adoption schemes whereby, in return for an annual fee, subscribers receive their adopted trees' annual output of oil.

Increased investment in processing, packaging and storing olive oil would make a significant impact, but where would the money come from? The EU is reining in its spending, the finances of the

Greek government are still recovering from the recent economic crisis and Greek banks have recoiled from the uninhibited lending of the early 2000s. Looking for promising investment opportunities at the turn of the millennium, the Messinian-born shipping magnate Vassilis Constantakopoulos chose not to invest his wealth in the olive oil business. Instead, he chose tourism and founded the Costa Navarino luxury hotel and golfing complex just north of Pylos in 2010. However, he didn't totally ignore the mainstay of the local economy. As part of this development, he sanctioned the successful relocation of over 1,900 mature olive trees and the establishment of the Costa Navarino brand, which promotes and markets local Messinian olive oil, olives and related products worldwide.

In his *Eleftheria* interview, Yiorgos Yoniotakis declared that '*olive oil is the flagship of the Greek food and drink sector. They depend on us to steer the ship correctly and not end up on the rocks.*' Let's hope the lighthouses, navigation buoys and sonar are all in good working order and the captain is a competent and experienced navigator. To make a sustainable future for themselves, the next generation of Mani olive farmers will need direction, support and up-to-date know-how, allied to that fierce determination and pride for which the Maniots are renowned.

Mary slitting Kalamata olives.

Chapter 8

A NOBLE FRUIT

Diversifying

It is surely bizarre that one of the most often-quoted judgements of the olive was uttered by the third president of the USA, Thomas Jefferson, in a presentation to the South Carolina Society for the Promotion of Agriculture in 1787. Jefferson extolled the virtues of the olive tree by declaring it *'the richest gift of Heaven'*. He had been American ambassador to France in the years preceding the French Revolution and had travelled extensively. He was hugely impressed with the versatility and utility of olive trees in Provence and was eager to promote their adoption by farmers in the American South. His efforts at the time came to nothing, but today, although American output of olives and olive oil trails well behind other leading world producers, olive farms have emerged in several states where conditions allow, with California being the leading US producer.

It was another American, albeit 200 years later, who introduced me to one of the seminal books about olives. Daniel was an emigré living in the Mani with whom Mary and I regularly harvested olives in our first winters there. A picking session would rarely pass without Daniel making reference to *Olives, the life and lore of a noble fruit* by a fellow American, Mort Rosenblum. At the time, I little imagined that I would buy my own copy, which I would consult on many occasions. It is eminently readable, not just because of the comprehensive information it contains but also because it is written in an engaging style. Californian food and wine writer, Caroline Beck, describes it as *'part history book, travelogue, culinary journal and farming manual'.* Rosenblum hops from vast modern plantations on the plains of Andalusia to small ancient groves in the hills of Palestine, from traditional methods of harvesting and processing to large-scale, modern-day equivalents – and all illustrated with lively conversations with colourful characters, amusing anecdotes and vivid descriptions. It's a masterpiece born out of Rosenblum's fifty years' experience as a well-travelled journalist, newspaper editor and author, and of tending his small, olive tree-filled property in Provence.

But not everyone sees the olive as a noble fruit. As soon as Mary and I included eating olives in Tried & Tasted's range of Greek products, we began to realise how they tend to polarise opinion more than most foods. Olives definitely have what Brits call a 'Marmite effect' on people. Virtually unknown except in the UK and British Commonwealth countries, Marmite is a dark brown savoury spread made from yeast extract with a strong distinctive flavour. In 1996, its manufacturers adopted the marketing slogan *'Love it or Hate it'* and this soon led to Marmite becoming a well-known and often-quoted metaphor for something that divides opinion. The 'Marmite effect' manifested itself many times while Mary and I were trading as Tried & Tasted, especially at food fairs and agricultural shows. Customers passing our stall, especially those with no interest in making a purchase, normally kept their opinions about our products to themselves. But our delicious Greek olives often prompted the 'we hate olives' faction to openly express their dislike, without even troubling to sample their taste. Nothing aggressive; just a screwing up of the face accompanied by a retching sound and followed by an apologetic smile. Olives have that effect on people: you either love 'em or hate 'em.

In the olive world, eating olives commonly play second fiddle to olive oil, and Tried & Tasted proved no exception. With early sales of Socrates' oil yet to achieve the levels obtained in later years, we soon realised that we needed to expand our range of products. Maybe when the business had grown to match our dreams we could focus solely on a single product, but in the meantime, adding other Greek food products would make the whole operation more time- and cost-effective. The obvious first choice was Kalamata olives, which we had half-heartedly trialled in 2004. Our next year's purchase of a paltry twenty kilograms – we were still unsure of ourselves – came from a farmer near Messini whom a Greek friend had put us in touch with. His Kalamata olives were a big disappointment. They had been picked several days before we received them, many were bruised and they were past their best . . . . if they ever had a best. With hindsight, we should have rejected them out of hand, but we were still novices and had failed to recognise the tell-tale signs of a substandard product. We were learning the hard way and the only consolation was that we had not purchased a greater quantity. Determined to stick to the Kalamata variety, we committed ourselves to improving our background knowledge of this popular olive before seeking an alternative supplier in 2006.

There are hundreds of different kinds of eating olives, each possessing a distinctive colour, size, shape, texture and flavour. A journey through the countries bordering the Mediterranean Sea reveals a lexicon of familiar eating olive names; Portugal's fine-skinned Carrasquenhas, large rich-tasting Manzanillas and spicy sharp Hojiblancas from Spain, large green Lucques from France, Italy's vibrant green Nocellaras, and large mild Cerignolas and black meaty Gemliks from Turkey are but a few examples. In Greece, three kinds of eating olive dominate: Kalamatas, Konservolias and Halkidikis. As well as their official or botanical names, olives often have regional names, depending on the local language and dialect. In 2019–20 the world produced three million tonnes of eating olives, of which EU countries contributed over a quarter. Spain and Greece dominate EU production, almost a third of which is exported to the USA. Other leading Mediterranean producers include Morocco, Turkey and Egypt.

The Kalamata olive is widely recognised as the king – or is it the queen? – of eating olives. Like Champagne, Parmesan cheese and Cornish clotted cream, its uniqueness is protected and its authenticity guaranteed by the award of a PDO (a Protected Designation of Origin) by the EU. Kalamata olives come from the *Kalamon* (meaning 'of Kalamata') variety of olive tree. Although greatly outnumbered by the *Koroneiki* variety that is farmed for its oil, *Kalamon* trees are nonetheless common in the southern Peloponnese, especially in the prefecture of Messinia. They are easy to distinguish from their oil-producing cousins, possessing a silvery sheen to their new bark, a more rangey, less compact habit, and bearing longer, slender leaves and bigger fruit. The dark purple colour of the Kalamata olive's skin, the above average size, the oval shape with a pronounced nipple and the plump, firm flesh that comes away easily from the stone are other distinctive features. Attempts have been made by unscrupulous businesspeople to muscle in on the Kalamata olive's popularity. A brief report in Kalamata's *Eleftheria* newspaper in June 2017 describes an unsuccessful attempt to pass off Turkish Kalamata-type olives as the real thing. It went on to urge stricter controls to maintain the international reputation of authentic Kalamata olives and to prevent the wholesale selling price diminishing if the market is infiltrated by rogue versions of the real thing.

In a world where producers are constantly striving to reinvent their product in ways that attract new customers or revitalise the interest of existing ones, it seems that the straight olive, in its most natural form, is becoming less common. Just cast your eyes over the display on any market stall or deli counter – what a choice! Competing with straight olives are pitted olives with their stones removed, sometimes halved or sliced, or olives stuffed with something tasty, like pimento, anchovy, garlic or almonds. There are also olives marinaded in herbs like rosemary or thyme or flavoured with slices of lemon or garlic. Mouth-watering cocktails of green and black olives mixed with other tasty Mediterranean morsels, like chilli peppers, sun-dried tomatoes, cornichons and artichoke hearts, also compete for your attention and the contents of your purse or pocket.

Unlocking the Potential

'*A taste older than meat, older than wine. A taste as old as cold water*' was how Laurence Durrell described olives in his book *Prospero's Cell*. The olive has been a fundamental part of the Mediterranean diet for millennia and today its popularity has spread far beyond its original homeland. Its success lies in its versatility. The olive is equally at home as part of a pizza topping, tossed with salads or simmering in a casserole. It tickles the taste buds as a tapenade spread on wafer-thin toast, as part of a mezzé or tapas, or as an appetising accompaniment to pre-dinner aperitifs.

In their raw state, even when ripe, olives are hard and intensely tart, with a strong bitterness. A bite into a raw olive leaves your taste buds recoiling and promotes an instant urge to spit out the offending matter. My only comparable experience was as an innocent child tasting a sloe from a North Devon blackthorn hedgerow – definitely not to be recommended. The flavour of an eating olive is not something intrinsic; it is something that is added after harvest. It's a mystery how humankind, sometime in the distant past, discovered that olives could be transformed into an edible fruit. Two conditions in juxtaposition were surely necessary: a wild olive tree and shallow water, preferably salty. If ripe olives were to fall into the water and rest there undisturbed for several weeks, the colour of their skin would fade, their flesh would soften, and their bitterness would be gradually absorbed by the water, rendering them palatable but hardly tasty. The poorest and hungriest inhabitants of the ancient world were, by necessity, great foragers and always on the lookout for additional sources of food. The eating olive, discovered by chance – and perhaps a little intuition – in a shallow rockpool, was one such.

The first time Mary and I harvested eating olives was from a tree belonging to Dutch neighbours Jan and Joey in Neohori. The tree overhangs a steep, narrow street and required me to gamble on my powers of balance while, with the aid of a wedge or two, Mary held the ladder steady. During what can have been no more than thirty minutes picking by hand, three or four villagers passed by and stopped to ask us what we were doing. We thought it pretty obvious but replied courteously, only to be confronted with a follow-up question that enquired if we knew what to do with the olives once they were picked. Naturally we had done some research on the subject, but nonetheless we were interested in what advice they might offer. We knew it was common practice to slit the skin of eating olives to accelerate the essential de-bittering process but hadn't realised there were subtle differences of approach from family to family. Only one passer-by didn't slit the olive skin at all; she claimed that patience was rewarded and that unslit olives resting in brine for three months or so turned out to be the best. For the rest: one pricked holes in the skin with a pin, one made a single slit and the other two slits, both with a razor blade. We opted for two slits.

Every October for more than ten years, on the terrace of our Greek home, we slit Kalamata olives. A *North Devon Journal* report in December 2010 that featured our fledgling business described how we had mastered the technique: '*5 kilos of Kalamata Olives razor-slit twice by hand in just 21 minutes 45 seconds is their record. That's about 42 olives per minute between the two of them and not a drop of blood spilled! These harvest-fresh, jumbo size olives are delivered in batches of 50 kilos, every Monday in October. Each kilo contains roughly 175 olives, so every week John and Mary slit nearly 9000 olives, making a total over four weeks of 35,000… and nearly 70,000 slits!*' And slitting the olive's skin is all that is required; any deeper and the quality and firmness of the flesh can be compromised in the processing that follows. A deft touch is essential.

The return journey by car to the UK in the late autumn of 2004 was one we are unlikely to forget. It illustrates, albeit in unusual circumstances, what happens next, once the olives have been slit. At the last minute, without sufficient forethought, we had decided to add ten kilos of Kalamata olives – a gift from friends Alekos and Gerda – to our cargo of olive oil. With the help of Keith, an old school friend who was holidaying with us, the olives were hastily slit and deposited in a large bucket of fresh water for the crucial next stage of processing to begin: de-bittering. The aim is for the water to slowly absorb the bitterness from the olive, a process accelerated by slitting the skin and by changing the water every day. This normally takes from ten to fourteen days, but we only had two days left before our departure. An emergency plan was necessary.

Just before we set out from Neohori for the Minoan Lines ferry from Patras to Venice, we transferred the de-bittering olives into a plastic tub, refreshed the water, closed the lid securely and squeezed the tub into the last remaining space in the boot of our car. Our 3,000 kilometre trans-European journey back to North Devon would take five days and we were determined to find somewhere each day to change the water. As usual, access to the car deck was prohibited during the twenty-two-hour ferry journey northwards through the Adriatic Sea. Thus, it was imperative to find somewhere to change the water as soon as possible after we disembarked. The opportunity came in less than a couple of hours. Keith and I must have presented a curious spectacle in the men's washroom of the Autogrill service station on the A4 autostrada just west of Padova. The emptying of red-coloured water into a sink posed no problems but refilling the tub with fresh water was made impossible by shallow sinks that prevented us fitting the tub under the taps. An alternative had to be found and three large plastic bottles of Aquafina mineral water purchased from the adjoining shop did the trick. Never had Kalamata olives enjoyed such luxurious treatment!

Twenty-five hours later, after an overnight stop in Freiburg, south-west Germany, we were eager to find somewhere to change the water before we crossed the nearby River Rhine at Breisach and entered France. The village of Wasenweiler provided the opportunity we were looking for. On a wide grassy verge, we came across a sturdy stone trough, not unlike those historical relics still found throughout Britain bearing the name of the nineteenth-century Metropolitan Drinking Fountain and Cattle Trough Association. It was gently overflowing with spring water provided by an ancient brass tap suspended high enough for us to easily fit the olive tub underneath. The narrow road persuaded us to park on an adjoining private driveway while Keith gingerly emptied the 'old' water onto the grass, carefully restraining the olives with his outstretched fingers.

A be-capped, elderly villager was momentarily bemused by the unusual activity he witnessed as he cycled by. Whether he noticed the British number plates and phoned his neighbour whose drive we were occupying, we will never know. But as Keith returned the refreshed tub of olives to the boot of the car and Mary restarted the engine, the solid wooden gates of the drive opened and a perplexed old man emerged. Half in, half out of the front passenger seat, I yelled four words from my woefully limited German vocabulary – *"Danke schön"* and *"Auf wiedersehen"* – and off we sped. In celebratory mood, Keith and I jokingly urged Mary to 'put her foot down' to ensure we crossed the border into France before the local police were alerted. We also speculated about what the old man might have made of this episode and how he would explain it to his wife and neighbours. It would have surely made an intriguing tale.

By now, a plan had emerged to make our de-bittering olives unique by renewing their water in every European country we crossed. Having spurned the chance to change the water during our overnight stay in Arras, north-eastern France, we had high hopes when we spotted an unexpected campervan recharging facility in the giant Auchan supermarket car park at Boulogne. Keith, now a master of the emptying procedure, had discharged the old water before it became evident that the adjacent water tap was not functioning. The coin feed had jammed. Yet again another solution had to be found, and quickly. Embarkation time for our Cross-Channel ferry was fast approaching.

The barman at the Bar du Terminal, adjacent to the ferry loading queues, came up trumps. Although bemused by my request, he willingly filled several jugs of water from his bar-side tap until our olive tub was full. On the very shores of the English Channel, France had been added to our list of water-refill countries and the UK was added the following day. Just three more days remained before de-bittering was completed and curing the olives in our Torrington home could begin. The lesson learned from our trans-European de-bittering escapade was never to attempt it on the move again. The range of waters had neither improved nor damaged the taste of the olives, but there was surely an easier, less stressful and more reliable way.

Tempering the Taste

Tasting is the only reliable way to judge whether the water treatment has achieved the correct level of bitterness in a Kalamata olive. The softer texture and dull flavour at this stage are a world away from the acute tartness of an olive picked straight from the tree, but there's still a way to go before obtaining a palatable end product with its trademark hints of bitterness, salt and vinegar. After ten days of daily water changing, a small sample of Kalamata olives is examined. This involves prising open each olive with thumbs and releasing it from its stone. If the flesh is still yellow, not beige, and the taste too bitter, then a day or two more soaking is needed before embarking on curing, the final process which preserves the olives and tempers their taste.

The practice of curing varies hugely, depending on the variety of olive, local custom and the scale of operation. A mix of brine and red wine vinegar is the norm for our Neohori village neighbours, although the strength of the brine and the ratio of the mix varies from family to family. Contained in small plastic barrels or large tin cans and housed in a cool dark place, it takes Kalamata olives a minimum of six weeks to cure, by which time they are at their very best – firm, juicy and tasty. The longer they remain in the curing mixture, the softer they become and the more impregnated with the flavour of the mix.

Inevitably, with huge volumes of olives to process, factories adopt a different approach, combining the de-bittering and curing into one operation. Large slitting machines make short shrift of thousands of raw olives per hour, which are then processed more quickly and cost-effectively by immersing them in tanks containing a solution of sodium hydroxide for twenty-four hours. Better known as caustic soda and commonly used for cleaning domestic drains, it is a surprisingly familiar chemical agent in the food industry worldwide. Called the 'Spanish method' in California and the 'Californian method' in Spain, the use of caustic soda to de-bitter and cure olives is widespread, but they then require months of soaking in vats of brine to rid them of any unwanted taste – enough to make you think twice about ever eating another olive, and prompting an amusing headline in a food trade journal: *'Waiter, I've got an olive in my caustic soda!'*

Reassuringly, alternative ways of processing olives on such a scale do exist and others are being researched and trialled. The Blauel family-owned Mani Organic factory, just up the road from Neohori, operates differently. It manages a large throughput of Kalamata olives in a manner not far removed from the traditional village way. The freshly picked, organically farmed olives are not slit but are placed in large barrels or tanks containing high-salinity brine for up to six months. In this way, de-bittering and curing take place gently and unhurriedly and progress is checked and analysed periodically. When an order is received, samples from a batch are tasted by two senior and experienced personnel and, if approved, are further processed according to the customer's wishes. Now they can be slit or pitted, sliced, marinated or flavoured with herbs, and placed in brine or olive oil. No caustic soda is used here, which results in a purer, more natural, wholesome product with a perfect taste and texture.

Finding a Supplier

By the end of September 2006, with the start of the eating olive harvest less than a few days away, we were eager to find a more reliable supplier of Kalamata olives. With only two eating olive trees of our own and neighbours whose focus is on growing olives for oil, we had little choice but to look further afield. Our first stop was at the giant Wednesday and Saturday markets in Kalamata, where from early October onwards there are many farmers with crates of freshly picked eating olives for sale. The difficult bit is selecting which represents the best quality and value. We eventually chose to buy from Chrysoula, a short, plump, elderly woman with an engaging smile and friendly manner who, it turned out, had been trading at the market for over forty years. To our novice eyes, her Kalamata olives looked the best on offer and, with the previous year's disappointments in mind, we purchased an underwhelming thirty kilograms. Closer inspection during the painstaking slitting process revealed that Chrysoula's olives were indeed first-class, restoring our confidence and leading us to regret that a fast-approaching departure date did not allow us enough time to buy and prepare a few more kilos.

Sales of Tried & Tasted Kalamata olives in the UK that winter left us without any stock to satisfy customers who wanted more. Our Kalamata olives had turned out to be more popular than we'd anticipated. We planned to rectify that shortfall by doubling the volume of raw olives we purchased from Chrysoula the following October, but she was unable to oblige without referring us to her suppliers: her daughter and son-in-law, Elektra and Yiorgos. Thus began a very rewarding working relationship with these olive farmers from Vournazi, a small village twenty kilometres north-west of Kalamata. Yiorgos and Elektra are a friendly, engaging, middle-aged couple with a strong work ethic, a pragmatic down-to-earth outlook on life and ambitions for their talented three sons. They farm fertile land on the gentle, east-facing, lower slopes of the Pamisos valley that possess panoramic views of the Taygetos Mountains and the Gulf of Messinia.

In recent years, in order to profit from a better return, Yiorgos has successfully converted many of their olive trees from oil to eating olive production through a systematic process of grafting. They work as a team and are rightly proud of what they have achieved. Thanks to their careful, eco-friendly husbandry, their 500 or so *Kalamon* olive trees consistently produce excellent yields of high-quality Kalamata olives. Yiorgos keeps their trees well-pruned with the intention of maximising each year's output, keeping the crown open to encourage ripening and minimising the need for ladders during harvesting. He fertilises his trees with an annual dose of manure and, to ensure the crop is not compromised by water stress in the event of a summer drought, he has installed a drip irrigation network of black plastic pipes using water pumped from a deep well.

The olives are harvested every day, weather permitting, from the beginning of October to the year end. Deciding when to start harvesting is a matter of judgement: the temptation to start early when the market price is more attractive is always alluring but must be resisted. A Kalamata olive in a perfect state for picking must be firm and fleshy, but without the distinctive dark purple colour all over, they are not fully ripe. Eating olives and olives for oil are harvested differently. As with apples, pears, plums and soft fruit, eating olive trees must be revisited several times to ensure only the ripe fruit is picked. Neither under-ripe nor over-ripe will do and careful picking by hand is the only way to avoid bruising.

Harvesting eating olives is a repetitive and time-consuming occupation for Yiorgos and Elektra, even when they receive assistance from their sons at peak times. An additional pressure is satisfying the demand of customers who want immediate delivery, as soon after harvesting as possible when the olives are at their freshest and best. Mary and I fell into that bracket. Picked directly into plastic buckets strapped to their waists, the olives are transferred to crates for transport back home in a pick-up truck at the end of the working day. There, in an outbuilding especially equipped for the purpose, the olives are examined and sorted into sizes by a simple machine. This grading is important because the bigger the olive, the higher price it can command. Officially there are ten different Kalamata olive sizes, ranging from Colossals (121 to 140 per kilogram), through Jumbo and Large in the medium size bracket, to the smallest, which are known as Bullets (351 to 380 per kilogram). We always purchased a mix of Jumbo and Large, which we judged were best value.

Scaling Up

Right from the start, Yiorgos and Elektra proved to be reliable and obliging suppliers, willing to share much of their know-how about eating olive farming and processing. We were keen to learn as much as we could and before long, we were being taken on regular guided tours of their olive groves and encouraged to assist with the harvesting. In the first few years, we collected freshly picked olives direct from the farm but as the years passed, Yiorgos and Elektra would also deliver to our Neohori home. A key factor was always timing; we needed to obtain the Kalamata olives early enough to allow us to de-bitter and begin curing them before returning to the UK for the Christmas food fairs and markets. Thus, with Yiorgos and Elektra's co-operation, Mary and I developed a routine in Greece during six weeks in October and early November that saw our throughput of Kalamata olives rise over tenfold from twenty kilograms in 2005 to 240 kilograms ten years later. It curtailed our social life and rendered much of our covered terrace unusable for anything else, but it worked.

By the autumn of 2014, we were receiving eighty kilograms

of Kalamata olives on four successive Mondays in October. This tight timetable ensured the first pickings were truly ripe and all the olives were ready for shipping to the UK before our planned departure in mid-November. Once slit, each five kilograms of olives were immediately poured into net sacks and submerged in slightly salted cold water contained in a plastic bucket. At the height of de-bittering, there would be anything up to thirty-five buckets on our covered terrace. To enable us to navigate our way to our marble sink, garden and washing line, the numbered buckets were arranged in neat rows, and as a precaution, covered by a fly net to exclude insects, cats and assorted wildlife. The worst job was the daily changing of water and cleaning the natural scum from the inside of every bucket. Over a period of ten days, the discarded water changed slowly from a burgundy to a light rosé colour, the latter indicating that the de-bittering process was nearly complete.

Even before we resorted to pallets shipped across Europe by international hauliers, our Kalamata olives were transported back to the UK in big tin cans, each lid secured with tensioned blue plastic strapping. Without strapping, the lids could easily 'pop' during transit, creating an unbelievable mess and contaminating other goods. Each full can weighs twenty kilograms and contains thirteen kilograms of olives in their brine and red wine vinegar curing mix. In 2004 we had de-bittered our first consignment of olives on the road; now they were being cured in transit. We often wondered if the continual vibration of the moving lorry aided or hindered the process. Delays on the road, ferry crossings cancelled due to bad weather, and the tight timetable we set ourselves were always a cause of anxiety, so the arrival of the November pallet on our Torrington doorstep was greeted with great relief. A late arrival meant an even more intense period of bottling and jarring before the imminent period of Christmas food fairs and markets kicked off.

Our earliest attempts at packaging Kalamata olives had been little short of comical. Friends and neighbours willingly donated recycled coffee, jam and pickle jars but inevitably they were all different shapes and sizes and with an assortment of lids. This proved to be a headache, with every jar having a unique appearance, weight and price. Individual hand-written tags took the place of standard labels. By the time we were repeating this procedure the following year we had adopted a more systematic approach. We had tracked down a wholesale glassware supplier that allowed us to standardise our range of jars, and had also procured larger plastic tubs to satisfy the demands of olive addicts and wholesale customers. At the same time, our younger son Peter devised a Tried & Tasted logo and designed new labels to enable us to have them properly printed on self-adhesive laminated paper.

We also streamlined our packaging procedures, even though they were still located in our cramped Torrington kitchen. Mary sterilised the jars in the oven while I washed and refreshed the olives in cold running water. They had not seen the light of day since de-bittering had finished six weeks or so before, and in the meantime had been transported from one corner of Europe to the other. Filling the jars followed, first with olives, then with a freshly prepared brine/red wine vinegar mix, topped off with a seal of olive oil – the part of the process that bemused a Food Safety inspector who had not encountered it before. Mary then applied the labels and tamper strips and packed the jars in plastic trays, ready for storage. If no interruptions occurred, a four-hour-long morning session of jarring would normally account for all the olives in two twenty-kilogram cans, which filled eighty medium-size jars and forty-five large jars. Just the not-so-straightforward matter of promoting, marketing and selling the olives remained.

The Marmite effect, whereby people either love 'em or hate 'em, not only relates to olives in general but also seems to apply to lovers of olives and their strong preference for either green or 'black'. Thus, it didn't take us long to figure out that if a customer only ever ate green olives, Tried & Tasted had nothing to offer and a potential sale was spurned. The search was on. Knowing that the southern Peloponnese did not produce green olives of any note, we began searching for suppliers elsewhere and a springtime road trip to central Greece in 2009 with friends Kevin and Judy yielded the solution. The *Konservolia* olive tree, widely grown in central and northern Greece, is capable of producing three versions of eating olive, depending on how long they are left on the tree. The first pickings in late September yield a round, green, nutty olive, which is the most popular. Later pickings from the same tree can produce a softer, more mellow, pinkish version, known as rosé, while if olives are not picked until late February or early March, they have turned black, shrunk and become wrinkled. This version, known as *Zaromeni*, looks a bit like a miniature prune and has a kind of liquorice flavour – definitely one for the connoisseur.

After a disappointingly unrewarding meeting with a pair of olive farmers from Chrysso near Delphi, we accidentally came across the Union of Agricultural Co-operatives in the town of Amfissas, just a few kilometres away. Housed in an undistinguished concrete box of a building on the main street into town, we found Yiorgos, the marketing manager, in a large open-plan office above the factory. Despite our unannounced arrival, Yiorgos greeted us warmly and quickly convinced us that the Union could satisfy our needs. Not only could he supply top-quality, green Konservolia olives but he would reduce the salt levels in the preserving liquid to suit British tastes and package them as we required. He also reassured us that he could arrange for each load to be trucked to Aspropyrgo near Athens and amalgamated with the main consignment sent from Neohori before departure for the UK. These Amfissas olives always played second fiddle to the Kalamatas but quickly became the default choice of our customers who preferred green olives that were firm and fleshy with a hint of salt.

Calling It a Day

Tried & Tasted was formally laid to rest on December 31st 2015 after a short but active life. By that time, Mary and I had been operating with increasing intensity for more than ten years and had diversified further by adding balsamic vinegar, saffron threads, various mustards, capers, dried tomatoes and garlic (all in oil) and assorted olive pastes (tapenades) to our Greek product range. Like our olive oil and olives, they were all sourced from reputable suppliers who we had got to know personally, who all took quality and sustainability very seriously. For us, Tried & Tasted's demise brought no tears or regrets, just great relief that something that had begun to dominate our lives, consume our every thought, demand more and more of our diminishing levels of energy and overrun our Torrington home was finished. It had started in 2004 as a casual hobby but had evolved into something akin to a full-time occupation. From the moment we began to operate seriously, we foolishly claimed that we would manage the business, rather than the business manage us. How innocent we had been.

Our wild dreams of an instantly recognisable white van emblazoned with our black Tried & Tasted logo, leased premises in a local trading estate full of floor-to-ceiling racks crammed with cartons of Greek food products, and a nationwide network of customers had not materialised, but we had achieved more than we had ever imagined. In fact, we reckoned we had reached a plateau and that to grow the business further needed new impetus and an injection of cash. That's why, after ten years of trading, we considered Tried & Tasted was ripe for sale. Sadly, its modest profitability and our very hands-on approach proved a disincentive and, despite several meetings with potential buyers, a sale did not materialise. It was that moment when buyers realised there were easier ways of making money and a glazed look appeared on their faces that we knew we had lost their interest. With hindsight, employing an agency to arrange the sale might have produced a more rewarding outcome.

So, disappointed but not dejected, we abandoned the idea of selling the business and focused instead on selling all our remaining stock before the end of the year. As well as creating some dismay among our loyal customers, we knew our decision would have an unwelcome impact on the Greek farmers and small producers who supplied us. But the time had come to either sell, which wasn't happening, or quit. After all, our seventieth birthdays were fast approaching. The six-week run-up to Christmas always proved the busiest trading period of the year for us, and November–December 2015 proved the most demanding of all. We had a lot of stock to shift.

Prompted by email alerts of the imminent arrival of our very popular recently pressed 'Fresko!' olive oil and our new season Kalamata olives, orders from regular customers started to pour in and we extended our programme of Christmas food and drink events to include some outside the West Country, such as those at Chelsea Physic Garden and Cambridge Science Park. It turned out to be an exhausting but successful climax to our ten years trading. We sold out of olive oil – allowing us to use our 'SORRY… OILED GONE!' stall sign for the first time ever – and all our Kalamata olives. Only small quantities of green Amfissas olives, balsamic vinegar and assorted Greek condiments remained and we eventually managed to offload them onto an obliging, south Devon-based fellow trader. Our decision to abandon selling the business and focus on selling all our stock had been vindicated.

Our customer base had expanded considerably over the course of ten years. It comprised almost 1,000 direct sale customers and over twenty wholesale outlets, most of which were delis, farm shops and independent food stores. The important role of family members and long-time friends who had helped to generate business and acted as local distribution points across the length and breadth of England, as well as Brittany, cannot be overstated. In January 2016, we began informing all our customers by email of our decision to quit. The immediate response was overwhelming. We were inundated with emails, phone calls and cards expressing disbelief, dismay and regret at the demise of Tried & Tasted. A beautiful hand-written card from a customer in Exeter captured the tone of many of the responses. It read:

> *My friends, family, relations and anyone I know who has ever tasted your Kalamata olives and oil are devastated by the news of your retirement. All good things come to an end but the best things will never be forgotten – and your olives and oil were the VERY BEST. Thank you for enriching our lives.*

Similar sentiments continued to follow throughout 2016, giving Mary and me much pleasure and satisfaction but never tempting us to change our minds. We concluded that the ten years of Tried & Tasted had been an absorbing, challenging and fulfilling experience that had enriched our lives. We had learned so much and met so many interesting people, both suppliers and customers, some of whom have remained very good friends. Above all, we felt we had done pretty well for a pair of retired secondary schoolteachers in their sixties who were never prepared to completely sacrifice their lifestyle for the doubtful prospects of a wealthy future.

When Mary and I set out on our Greek venture in October 1997, we could never have conceived that within a few years our lives would become so immersed in the world of olives and olive oil. On the other hand, it would have been hard not to imagine some dabbling. After all, we were going to live in a part of Greece where olive trees occupy a large proportion of the landscape, where olive oil and olive production is still the bedrock of the rural economy and where many livelihoods depend on it. Even where families have embraced tourism as a more profitable alternative, there remains a strong attachment to the soil, the land and the *rizes* (roots), as the Maniots poetically refer to their olive trees. Very few, if any, have abandoned olive farming altogether, and there is barely a moment to take breath between the end of the tourist season and gearing up for the annual olive harvest. It is true that some families have sold olive groves for building development in favourable locations with sea views or within walking distance of seaside resorts, and who can blame them? Olive farming has never been a financially rewarding occupation and some families without other sources of income live a very hand-to-mouth existence. And anyway, many of the foreigners who have houses built insist that as few olive trees as possible are uprooted during construction. They too want to become a small part of the local olive culture.

Traditional harvesting of olives by hand with the minimum of mechanical aids is a relentless, long, drawn-out affair. But it is also a collective process that occupies whole families day by day for many weeks each winter. Families head out into the olive groves soon after dawn, leaving their villages in the custody of cats and dogs. An eerie silence prevails for much of the day until mid-afternoon, when the first signs of weary returnees penetrate the peace and quiet, and the olive press gears up for another session. Olive harvesting is a team effort, with family members performing different roles depending on their age, experience, agility and strength. But everyone is working towards the same goal: a quantity and quality of olives or olive oil that satisfies all and that will generate sufficient revenue to see them through another year.

Working as a group in the open air with the winter sun casting shadows and warming shoulders, limbs being exercised with a purpose, and wide-ranging chatter – exchanging banter and gossip, speculating about the future, sharing common memories from the past – is tiring but agreeable work. The communal picnic halfway through the working day, children joining in proceedings after school and granny sitting on a plastic chair knitting, out of harm's way, help to create an image that belies the unrelenting physical nature of the work. No Zumba needed here! Although it's not so idyllic as it sounds, there are rewards beyond the end product. Above all, this activity creates an annual opportunity for families to reinforce their bonds like very few other occupations allow, for husband and wife, brothers and sisters, aunts and uncles, granddad and granny to work together with a common purpose. Harvesting also provides a powerful link with the past and forebears who engaged in a very similar process when the common way of life was very different to today's. It is an ageless activity – one that has been going on in Greece for maybe 5,000 years – imposing an annual cycle of tasks that governs the lives of farming folk in rural areas.

Euro 2004 Champions.

Chapter 9

TRIUMPH & DISASTER

Warning Signs

In early December 2008, virtually without warning, rioting broke out in Athens on a scale not witnessed since the fall of the military dictatorship thirty-four years earlier. This violent and destructive protest extended over several days and quickly spread to other Greek cities like Thessaloniki, Patras and Chania. As cordons of heavily armed police tried to restrain rampaging rioters, disturbing images of burnt-out vehicles, barricades and ravaged commercial premises grabbed the world's headlines. Central Athens resembled a war zone and this time it wasn't just the work of anarchists and extremists; this was a revolt precipitated by schoolchildren and students. The trigger for this eruption of mayhem was the shooting dead, by a police officer, of an unarmed teenager, Alexandros Grigoropoulos, in central Athens on December 6th. Thanks to mobile phones, social media and prompt TV and radio station reporting, news of the shooting quickly became common knowledge amongst young Athenians. In a spontaneous reaction, they took to the streets to register their utter contempt for the police and a festering despair at their dismal future prospects in a Greece showing early signs of what would become economic turmoil.

Despite being near the top of the league for mass demonstrations and street protests, the intensity of the December 2008 rioting came as a shock to many Greeks, who had experienced an encouraging period of stability, modernisation and prosperity during the 1990s and into the new millennium. Yet, occupation by the Axis powers during the Second World War, the divisive civil war that followed and the repressive regime of the military dictatorship of 1967–74 have left a legacy of suspicion and distrust simmering beneath the surface of Greek society, which is easy to ignite. With the benefit of hindsight, it is perhaps too easy to see the 2008 riots as a perfect storm that had been brewing for some time. The alarming death toll resulting from the summer 2007 wildfires and the exposure of high-level corruption involving German electronic giant Siemens and dubious land deals with the Orthodox Church enclave of Mount Athos had weakened public trust in government.

Thanks to the internet and satellite telecommunications, young Greeks have greater insights than any previous generation into the contrasting lives and opportunities of contemporaries elsewhere in the world, and are increasingly aware of the shortcomings of their own country. They were frustrated by the absence of change and progress. No matter what government was in power, corruption remained endemic, cronyism rampant, and the health service struggling. They also found the education system hidebound, job opportunities declining and future prospects diminishing. What was there to lose by taking to the streets, when the democratic process seemed to promise them so little?

Greece's economic performance in the post-war years was up and down. After a 1960s' economic boom, Greece's economy slowed in the 1970s and stalled in the 1980s. Instead of promoting growth and prosperity – as was widely anticipated within the country – accession to the European Economic Community in 1981 coincided with a period of higher inflation and unemployment, combined with lower productivity and international competitiveness. Public debt increased, numbers working in the civil service rose, regulation and red tape became more widespread, thus disincentivising business development and foreign investment. With the primary goal of obtaining membership of the European Monetary Union (EMU) and adopting the euro, changes in government policy were largely responsible for arresting this decline in the 1990s. However, these changes were not enough: Greece was still being outperformed by its European counterparts.

There is still much debate about whether Greece's adoption of the euro was wise and whether remaining outside the eurozone might have given it more room for manoeuvre and more scope to withstand the impact of the world financial crisis that kicked off in 2008. What is undeniable is the subterfuge and sharp practice that helped to secure Greece's membership of the EMU. Two of the most significant Maastricht criteria governing entry concerned predetermined maximum levels of inflation and budget deficit. In both cases, the Greek government managed to keep these levels artificially low for a critical period. At the same time, another significant criterion, the ratio of public debt to GDP – the total value of the country's annual output – which was supposed to be at or below 60%, was running at over 100% in Greece. But this was overlooked by Brussels because several other member countries had also exceeded the limit. The lingering question is whether this bending of the rules did either side any favours in the long run.

Although joining the EEC in 1981 had not brought the immediate economic benefits and prosperity the country was anticipating, it had elevated Greece's status to a new level and had generated a more confident national mood. From being a peripheral country, albeit occupying a significant geopolitical position relative to the Soviet Bloc and the Middle East, it had become part of the European club and was rubbing shoulders with the main players. Thus, it came as no surprise that Greece registered early interest in adopting the proposed single currency. The prospect of becoming part of a larger, more stable monetary union more than outweighed the arguments for retaining the drachma. In a country where cash transactions – whether large or small – are still the norm, where payment by bank card was rare until relatively recently, and where banks were never fully trusted with people's savings and accumulated wealth – even when they were in dollar or deutsche mark accounts – adopting the euro and all that entailed was a giant leap of faith for most Greeks. On January 1st 2002, Greece became the twelfth member of the European Monetary Union as the first euro banknotes and coins entered circulation. This was the largest ever currency changeover in the world, an incredible logistics and security exercise. Some 7.8 billion notes and forty billion coins were distributed to 218,000 banks and post offices, 2.8 million sales outlets and 302 million individuals across the eurozone.

The exchange rate for each participating country was fixed in advance; for Greece, one euro was equivalent to 340.750 drachmas. Bank accounts and bank loans were automatically converted on the first day of the changeover; the process for coins and notes took a bit longer. By the time Mary and I arrived in Greece for our regular late winter visit, people were still getting used to the changeover. For two months, both euros and drachmas were in circulation, although all change was given in euros. Introducing a new currency in this way was resented by some; shopkeepers complained they were doing the bank's work for them while customers were bemused when they paid in familiar, well-used notes and coins but received crisp and shiny euros in return. For many people on both sides of the counter, the calculation and checking of change proved a headache. As complicated as it seemed, the short transition period ensured that all but diehards had adapted to a greater or lesser degree by the time drachmas ceased to be legal tender on March 1st 2002.

After that deadline, exchange of drachmas for euros had to be done through branches of the National Bank of Greece. Banknotes, for example, had a ten-year period of grace. In December 2004, *Kathimerini*, the Athens daily newspaper, reported that the National

Bank was still exchanging in the region of twenty-five million drachmas a day. In a country with a significant parallel black economy, where many transactions are in cash and unaccounted for, the change of currency posed a headache for many people. How could millions of drachmas, stashed under floorboards, in bank vaults or in mini domestic safes be exchanged without attracting the attention of the tax authorities? Little but often over a long period was the most common solution, resulting in unprecedented daily queues from opening to closing times at branches of the National Bank. It was also estimated that seventy million drachmas would never be exchanged, either lost, destroyed or languishing abroad in the safe deposit boxes of the Greek diaspora or in the leftover small change of millions of tourists.

Both businesspeople and customers needed time to fully adjust to the new currency. It wasn't just a question of correct change but also assessing if the new price in euros was the same value for money as previously in drachmas. Shopkeepers and the like were required to display prices as well as print receipts in both drachmas and euros, and several banks issued a variety of simple gizmos to enable customers to check if the conversion was correct. In common with other countries like Spain and Italy, where people were accustomed to paying for simple things in high-denomination, low-value notes, the introduction of the euro led to stealthy but rapid inflation. A Greek coffee that formerly cost 150 drachmas became fifty lepta (the Greek equivalent of fifty cents and worth €0.50) – a 13% increase – and a lunchtime meal for two at a seaside taverna previously costing 6,500 drachmas became €20 – an increase of 5%. Inevitably, businesses and services tended to round up rather than down and before long the smallest euro coins – the one- and two-lepta – were being virtually ignored, and soon the five-lepta coin would follow suit. Nonetheless, joining the euro coincided with another period of economic growth that created a feel-good factor at home and boosted international confidence in Greece. This allowed the Greek government to borrow money at a lower interest rate but instead of reducing public debt, these loans were channelled towards financing a variety of mega projects connected directly or indirectly with the forthcoming Olympic Games.

This public spending boom was mirrored by a private spending spree based on easily obtainable bank loans. In West Mani the old, beat-up Datsun, Ford and Chevrolet pick-up trucks – the work horses of olive farmers, kept on the road by skilled mechanics and welders – seemed to disappear overnight, replaced by shiny, brand-new Nissans, Toyotas and Mitsubishis. Whereas Greece's export growth was running parallel to that of its European counterparts, imports were rocketing. Abandoned, out-dated white goods, old-fashioned furniture and grubby mattresses, accompanied by discarded bubble wrap, cardboard and polystyrene packaging, became commonplace sights alongside roadside waste bins. They testified to the hidden improvements taking place inside many houses and apartments – and much of it purchased on credit. It was also boom time for house building in West Mani. New houses were popping up like mushrooms after the first autumn rains. Whole hillsides became tainted with housing; nature and the environment were in retreat. Farmers quickly realised that if their olive groves were located in a place with a good view and with easy access to an asphalt road, electricity and telephone lines, then their value had multiplied beyond their wildest dreams. With the selling price of olive oil unfailingly deflated, the urge to sell land for development was hard to resist.

Austrians and Germans had come to live in parts of the Peloponnese in the 1970s and '80s and they were followed by the Brits, Dutch, French and Swedes. Just like Mary and me, most of these new settlers had experienced the delights of Greece while on holiday and fancied more of the same when they retired from work. With property values on the up and up – especially in the UK – and land and building costs in West Mani still modest by comparison, it was an easy decision to make for those whose family and work circumstances allowed. The prospect of being able to afford a stone house with a garden and sea view, newly built to your own specifications in an attractive environment and inviting climate, was hard to resist for those willing to take the risk and undergo the inevitable upheaval.

The first house building quickly triggered an avalanche of related activity as anyone with experience in the sector manoeuvred to get in on the act. Property agents, surveyors, structural engineers, architects and interior designers opened new premises in Kardamyli, Stoupa and Aghios Nikolaos. Builders' yards proliferated and car journeys lengthened because of the increased number of heavy goods vehicles – fully laden with ready-mix concrete or sand, cement, bricks and roof tiles – that crawled along the narrow, winding and hilly local roads. An army of hardworking, experienced Albanian workers arrived on the scene: skilled stonemasons, stone facers, roofers and labourers, almost always under the direction and supervision of Greek project managers but without whom the West Mani building boom would not have been possible.

Some developers created whole new 'villages' out of virgin olive groves. One such is Tzokeïka, named amusingly after its founder Athanasios Tzokas, an architect and designer from Kalamata. It is a complex of newly built stone houses in traditional Maniot style, with a mock Byzantine church and olive press (still under construction), located south of the authentic West Mani village of Riglia and within easy walking distance of Pantazi beach. Some houses were constructed for sale, others for holiday lets and longer rentals. It is also intended that the communal buildings that stand alongside the church will one day house a restaurant and be able to host weddings and baptisms. It's hardly surprising that all kinds of locals – some with precious little building experience – were keen to participate and profit from the building bonanza. If they owned disposable land in an attractive location, olive farmers, restaurateurs, even waiters all tried their hand at building development, sometimes with calamitous consequences. The beginning of the end of the boom came when, instead of building to order with a scheme of regular payments from the client as pre-determined stages were completed, some builders started building speculatively. The results of their rash and risky investment – almost always with borrowed money – can still be seen scattered across the hillsides of West Mani. Empty houses, often no more than windowless shells, waiting for the Greek economy to pick up and for consumer confidence to be restored enough to encourage people to think once again about buying a new home in paradise.

A Sporting Fairy Tale

The upbeat mood that characterised Greece in the early boom years of the new millennium was reinforced by the success of two 2004 international sporting events. One was the performance of the national football team in the European Championships; the other was the unheralded triumph of the Athens Olympic Games. Two years later, Greece narrowly missed out on making it a trio of sporting achievements by losing to Spain in the final of the World Basketball Championships in Japan, having beaten an over-confident USA in the semi-finals. With this burgeoning sporting success spawning widespread confidence and self-belief, was there anything Greece and the Greek people could not achieve? As if to confirm it, Helena Paparizou obtained Greece's one and only win in the Eurovision Song Contest in 2005!

Greece's success at the 2004 European Football Championships is little more than a sporting fairy tale. Greece had only ever qualified for two other major football tournaments and had not won a single match in either. Although they had come top of their qualifying group, they started the tournament in Portugal as 100-1 outsiders, but these odds began to unravel as Greece progressed through the group stage at the same time as fancied winners like Germany, Italy and Spain were eliminated. Greece's arrival at the knock-out phase was the moment when Greeks with only a casual interest in football started to sit up and take notice. But it was the much-vaunted French team of Zidane, Desailly, Thuram, Vieira and Henry that Greece were due to face in the quarter finals. Against a team of such accomplished players, further progress was unlikely. But that had been the situation right from the start of the tournament, the low expectations of fans and pundits dismissed by dogged performances and opportunist goals grinding out victories on the pitch. Greece overcame France with surprising ease and now a semi-final awaited them. By this time, the whole of Greece was in a state of elation.

Lacking the sparkle of earlier performances – due in part, no doubt, to losing their playmaker and talisman Pavel Nedved to injury – the Czech Republic were the next team to be undone by the Greeks' organisation, commitment and disciplined teamwork. After ninety minutes it was 0-0, so the semifinal went into extra time and just before the interval, Traianos Dellas scored the only 'silver goal' in history to put Greece through to a final against the hosts Portugal. Greece now moved into a collective state of euphoria. With its dismal past record, how was it that this team of virtually unknown journeymen players had climbed to the pinnacle of European football? The next seventy-two hours saw an unprecedented demand from Greek fans for flights to Portugal. Whether they managed to get match tickets or not, just being in Lisbon for the final was enough for most of the estimated 15,000 Greek fans who made the journey. And they were not disappointed: a single goal by Angelos Charisteas was enough to condemn the hosts to runners-up and, against all the odds, Greece became European Champions. The reaction in Greece went up yet another notch to delirium status and for the next twenty-four hours, Greeks celebrated like only Greeks can.

Although experiencing divided loyalties, I had followed Greece's fortunes during the qualifying and group stages with more than casual interest, and after England's quarterfinal elimination, my support was unequivocally in favour of Greece. I watched the knock-out phase matches on an assortment of TV screens in local bars and tavernas. Each Greek victory was greeted by a cacophony of noise and spontaneous celebration, but nothing compared to the reaction that followed the referee's whistle that brought the final to a close.

Mary and I were with friends at Fani and Maria's taverna at Krya Vrisi, the uppermost part of the village of Kastania in West Mani. The place was packed and crackling with anticipation. Our restricted view of the small screen made the finer points of the game difficult to appreciate, but it was easy to imagine being amongst the Greek fans in the Estadio da Luz itself. The final whistle precipitated the most manic of celebrations. Friends and strangers hugged and kissed, teenagers set off bangers and fireworks, men unloaded their hunting rifles into the night sky and, most bizarrely, the landlady appeared with an old-fashioned wooden supporters' rattle, which she spun around furiously. It was pandemonium, never to be forgotten by those present, and repeated in villages, towns and cities across Greece and the Greek diaspora.

Over the heady days that followed, Greece gradually settled down, but not until the country had welcomed home its conquering heroes. Their forty-kilometre journey on the team bus from Athens airport to the city centre quickly became a crawl as tens of thousands of adoring supporters waving flags, setting off flares and chanting songs interrupted their progress. They eventually arrived two hours late at the official homecoming ceremony at the open-air, marble-clad 1896 Olympic Stadium, where they received another tumultuous welcome. The team's progress through the tournament had been greeted with mounting astonishment by most Greeks and a widespread belief that the bubble would burst at every next stage. After all, considering their previous miserable record, to have won just one match would have been enough. The team captain and player of the tournament, Theodoros Zagorakis, had summed it up nicely on the steps of the team hotel in Lisbon. Holding the silver trophy aloft for jubilant fans he declared, "*Now I believe it. I don't have to be afraid of having a shower and waking up to find it's all been a dream.*"

The Greek media nicknamed their team *To Pirato* (the pirate ship) in recognition of their ability to 'steal' victories from their more illustrious opponents. Although the style and tactics of Greece's success were roundly criticised, '*Herr Otto*' Rehhagel, the German coach, had fashioned a victorious team from a squad without any superstars. Putting aside intense personal rivalries and passionate club loyalties, all the players had bought into Rehhagel's core philosophy of discipline, organisation and team spirit. They might not have played the most exciting football, but the whole proved to be much greater than the sum of the individual parts. The 'all for one and one for all' bond was memorably demonstrated at the end of the final when the whole team joined hands in a line and performed a series of 'olé' waves for their adoring and ecstatic fans. As Greece was crowned European football champions, many Greeks were daring to hope that the Olympic Games, due to start in five weeks' time, would be just as successful.

Welcome Home

The long-awaited return of the Olympic Games to its homeland was a source of much pride. Lessons had been learned from Athens' failed bid to host the 100th Anniversary Games of 1996, which were awarded to Atlanta. The arrogance, hubris and sense of entitlement of Athens' approach that had so irritated the International Olympic Committee ensured that seeking the 2004 Games was conducted in a very different manner. The key change was the appointment of Yianna Angelopoulos-Daskalaki as the head of the team organising the Athens bid. *The Sunday Times* of August 8th 2004 described her as *'glamorous, ruthless and ambitious'*. She was also rich – married to Theodoros Angelopoulos, the shipping and steel tycoon and one of the wealthiest men in Greece – and well-connected. Despite fronting the successful bid, she was then inexplicably sidelined and amid mounting disagreement, complacency and resignations from the organising committee, vital decisions were not taken and much valuable time was wasted. There was even talk of a reprise of the 2000 Sydney Games if matters didn't improve. But Angelopoulos' recall saved the day. *'While others dithered, the raven-haired dynamo waved away doubts like smoke from her Cuban cigars and with a mixture of dazzling coquetry, chilling menace and fiery patriotism, she cracked everyone into line'* declared *The Sunday Tines*. Greek tabloids even dubbed her '*the Fuherina*'.

Despite Angelopoulos' zealous and uncompromising approach, upgrading and streamlining preparation for the Games proved to be much like turning around one of her husband's fleet of supertankers: a slow, laborious and deliberate process. But just a week before the official opening of the Games, there were only small-scale jobs outstanding, like hanging 20,000 Olympic banners from lamp posts in the city centre. The sheer scope of the Olympic project was breathtaking. A total of thirty-five sporting venues spread across Attica was required for the multitude of different sports that comprise the modern Games. Some were existing structures that were comprehensively renovated, like the main stadium, which hosted the opening and closing ceremonies and athletics. Others were newly constructed, such as the velodrome and the weightlifting arena, which, along with the main stadium, formed part of the Olympic Sports Complex that became the main hub of the Games. As well as sporting venues, the 10,500 athletes needed training facilities and accommodation, there were coaches and officials to house, journalists and TV crews required a media centre to operate from, and a systematic upgrading of Athens' transport system was necessary to avoid the gridlock that Athenians had become accustomed to for a number of years.

To ease air quality concerns as well as speed movement, two new urban motorways were constructed, by-passing the congested city centre and Athens' twin city, the busy port of Piraeus. The Athens Metro was expanded, a new tram system introduced – forty-four years after the last trams trundled beneath the Acropolis – and a new electrified rail link connected Corinth and the western suburbs to central Athens. Totally integrated with these new transport links were two mega projects: a new international airport, north of Athens at Spata, to replace the tired and inadequate one at Elliniko, and a giant new suspension bridge to span the Gulf of Corinth. The security operation was unprecedented for an Olympic Games and included 1,300 CCTV cameras, some of which were mounted on an airship that floated over the capital for fifteen hours each day during the course of the Games. One of the greatest challenges for the organisers was getting athletes, officials and spectators to the right place at the right time. An army of volunteers, the new infrastructure and priority traffic lanes all contributed to easing this logistical nightmare. Despite all the misgivings, the anguish and uncertainty; despite all the doom-laden forecasts from around the world that they would not be ready on time, the Games opened to a great fanfare with the motto 'Welcome Home' on Friday August 13th. An inauspicious choice of date, you might judge, but for Greeks it is Tuesday the 13th that is supposed to be unlucky. Athens – and Greece as a whole – crackled with anticipation, optimism and pride.

The souvenir picture edition of *The Guardian Weekend*'s colour magazine described the sixteen-day Athens Olympics as '*a cauldron of emotions, a vale of tears and an arena for thrilling, unexpected triumphs*'. Even Angelopoulos, with her insatiable energy and optimism, could not have anticipated such a widely acclaimed and successful Games. Once the Games were underway, the focus quickly changed from Athens' readiness and the doping-related, last-minute withdrawal of sprinters Kostas Kentseris and Katerina Thanou (both strong medal hopes for the home crowd), to sporting competition and performance. As the Games unfolded, there was the usual heady mix of success and failure, exhilaration and disappointment, of beaming smiles and tears, courage and pride. Disqualifications caused controversy, hot favourites were vanquished and unknowns came to the fore. 300 events were contested and over 900 medals awarded. *The Guardian* sports writers were divided on the subject of the star of the Games. Yelena Isinbayeva, the women's pole-vault champion, Hicham El Guerrouj and Kelly Holmes for completing rare double victories on the athletics track, and Michael Phelps with his six swimming gold medals all featured at the top of their lists.

With friend Allan, Mary and I spent three days at the Games during the second week of competition. It was an unforgettable experience with so many vivid memories, inside and outside the stadiums. Back in the UK, my ninety-seven-year-old mother was eager to learn all about it. I was in the habit of writing her regular fortnightly letters but the one describing our Olympic experience surpassed anything before or since: it was eight double-sided A4 pages long. As well as containing details of Litsa, our generous host, and Vassilis, our adopted taxi driver, it recalled many outstanding performances that we had been privileged to witness and celebrated the temporary transformation of Athens into a multicultural city with an all-pervading buzz of friendship and goodwill. Greeks revelled in the fact that for two weeks, their capital was the focus of world attention.

The final heart-pounding race of the 2004 Olympic Games, the men's marathon, ended in the white marble stadium in the heart of Athens, bringing the modern Olympics full circle: back to the precise spot where they had been first revived by Baron de Coubertin in 1896. The closing ceremony that followed marked the end of a tense, lip-biting period for Greece and the Greek people. The world had stared them in the face and they had not flinched; they had delivered a memorable Games, almost without a hitch. The universal relief was as palpable as the widespread pride. For many Greeks, irritated by the media rumble that became a storm of doubt and misgiving in the run-up, the success of the Games was a huge boost to their esteem – individually and collectively. At the closing ceremony, Jacques Rogge, the president of the IOC, declared "*These have been unforgettable, dream Games*", invoking a deafening roar from the crowd. Greek athletes had also gained sixteen medals – six gold, six silver and four bronze – in events as diverse as athletics, weightlifting, diving, windsurfing, gymnastics and tae-kwondo.

The bill for staging the 2004 Games depends on who you ask and where you look: a round figure of €10 billion is not far off the mark. The figure compares favourably with the total cost of Barcelona's

Games in 1992 and London's in 2012, and is only a third of the cost of the 2008 Beijing Olympics. Despite all the advance concern about weak ticket sales, most of the Olympic venues were full most of the time and the Games made an operating surplus of €200 million out of a budget of €2.8 billion. The remaining billions were spent on building new, dedicated arenas and sporting venues, far-reaching improvements to infrastructure and telecommunications, and comprehensive security arrangements against terrorist attack. Karolina Tagaris, reporting for *Reuters* in April 2017, revealed that Oxford University researchers who had studied the finances of Olympic Games from 1960 to 2012 concluded that they are the most risky of all mega projects, especially for a small country. Without exception, they always exceed their budgets – in Greece's case, by 97%. How much the debts incurred by hosting the Athens Olympics contributed to Greece's economic crisis and the period of austerity and recession that followed is a much-asked question.

Although all sporting venues were ready for competition by the start of the Games, cost management and control came a poor second to completion deadlines in the last-minute, mad rush of construction. There were too many examples of extravagance and waste and there was minimal forward planning about what to do with facilities once the Games were over. The overriding driving force was to get the Games ready on time, at any cost. Athens' Olympic legacy is a national tragedy, a source of embarrassment, shame and anger. So many of the purpose-built, state-of-the-art facilities are abandoned, dilapidated and unwanted; veritable white elephants that served no purpose once the Games were over. After all, how many Athenians play baseball or softball? How many go whitewater canoeing or kayaking? How many play hockey? Even the arenas for popular Greek sports like beach volleyball and water polo have suffered a similar fate; they are padlocked, graffiti'd, vandalised, litter-strewn and overgrown. The cost of maintenance at a time of economic crisis is not the only factor; grinding bureaucracy and procrastination have also played their part. There are a few exceptions, however. The main Olympic stadium has become the home of AEK, one of Greece's leading football teams; the media centre has been transformed into a shopping mall and the badminton venue has become a theatre cum concert hall. Yet, because little consideration was given to constructing temporary arenas where feasible – as pioneered at the Sydney Games – most remain unloved vestiges of a glorious two weeks in 2004 when Greece was in the world's spotlight and came up trumps.

A Global Crisis

It's a common enough adage in the world of finance that 'when America sneezes, Mexico catches a cold'. That's the way modern capitalism works. In a world that is increasingly integrated, when an economic giant trips up, other countries stumble and the repercussions can be felt worldwide. Some countries are more able to withstand the impact than others; it depends on the strength and resilience of their economies, as well as their political stability and social cohesiveness.

The source of the 2008 global financial crisis was the USA. At the start of the year, although there were signs that things weren't right in some quarters, the prospect of a global economic meltdown was unimaginable, a distant storm that, hopefully, would blow itself out before it reached land. But this complacency led to the biggest, most widespread financial and economic shockwaves that the world had experienced since the Great Depression of the 1930s. At the core of this crisis were Freddie Mac and Fannie Mae, previously unknown to most people outside the USA and sounding more like a vaudeville act than a pair of giant, government-backed mortgage lenders. They were engaged in the high-risk business of lending money for house purchases to people who had always dreamed of home ownership but who, even in the best of circumstances, were likely to struggle to repay what they owed. Default on these loans – known as sub-prime mortgages in the USA – gathered pace as the new millennium unfolded and eventually led to over a million Americans losing their homes. Economic activity in America was slowing down, and the big banks were suffering worrying setbacks. In an effort to cut their losses, some engaged in dubious financial activity, like the discounted selling of 'parcels' of junk mortgages, which exacerbated the situation and eventually led the Federal Reserve to intervene and restore some order. But it was too little, too late.

Normally, similar episodes of financial panic are checked at an early stage and remain regional, but in this case the contagion went viral and quickly became global. Matters came to a head in the third week of March 2008, probably the most tumultuous week Wall Street had ever known, with repercussions in the financial hubs of London, Frankfurt, Tokyo, Singapore and Hong Kong. The collapse of Lehman Brothers, the fourth largest US investment bank with 25,000 employees worldwide and assets roughly equivalent to the annual output of Argentina, was the final straw. The unthinkable had happened; it seemed no business was too big or too revered to fail.

The financial world was in turmoil and staring into the abyss. Without urgent action to support the failing banks and restore confidence, the future looked grim. On October 10th 2008, the G7 group of finance ministers met in emergency session in Washington with the sole purpose of saving the world from the brink of disaster. Even so, stock markets crashed, wiping billions off the value of companies, bankruptcies soared, investment stalled, and much stricter conditions governing loans to businesses and individuals were introduced (often called a 'credit crunch'). Inevitable rises in unemployment followed. No government could ignore the tremors pulsating through the global financial structure; to do so would have risked further erosion of confidence and whatever dire consequences that might bring.

Since 2010, Greece has been cast as the 'black goat' of the European family – that's the Greek way of saying it – and that's one of the least offensive monikers. Others include 'Europe's basket case' and 'European champions of debt'. Core members like France and Germany, who see themselves as upholders of the founding principles of the eurozone, had become increasingly irritated by Greece's waywardness. 'If only it stuck by the rules, brought its debt down and overhauled its welfare, pension and health systems, then its situation would surely improve' was their mantra. Greece was the first of several European countries to go into crisis following the financial whirlwind unleashed by the subprime mortgage fiasco in the USA. In the search for answers to the question 'Why Greece?', the acclaimed American economist Joseph Stiglitz strongly argues that the country's weaknesses were quickly seized upon while other factors, like the absence of an EU stability fund, were ignored. He claims that if such a fund had existed, the debt crises on Europe's periphery would have been more easily managed and less damaging.

In their 2011 book *Understanding the Crisis in Greece*, Michael Mitsopoulos and Theodore Pelagidis delve deep into the underlying causes that catapulted the Greek economy to the brink of collapse. These well-respected academics have produced a detailed, reliable and compelling account of the Greek crisis. Unsurprisingly, they pinpoint massive public debt as being at the heart of the matter, but they also identify and examine many other underlying weaknesses that were so long-established and so entrenched in Greece that they were almost taken for granted. Powerful forces within the country had vested interests in maintaining the status quo and few governments had the confidence or resolve to tackle this inertia.

Not surprisingly, Mitsopoulos and Pelagidis focus on economic reasons to explain Greece's predicament; things like low productivity, excessive regulation, bureaucracy and red tape. Over-manning, slow adoption of automation and IT, and failure to change and update management structures and systems have also played their part. These weaknesses combined to make the Greek economy inefficient by EU standards, rendering it weakly competitive with all but its Balkan neighbours, and its businesses vulnerable to collapse and take-overs. They also point the finger at some of Greece's hallowed institutions, like the slow-moving and cumbersome judiciary, the underperforming state education system, and the country's constitution, with its absence of effective checks and balances, that allows the government to almost always 'get its own way'. They claim that reform of the structure – the building blocks – of the Greek state is long overdue.

Mitsopoulos and Pelagidis also examine three issues that undermine the effectiveness and efficiency of Greece's government, public services and business: patronage, corruption and tax avoidance – all integral parts of Greek life. Patronage is endemic; it's not *what* you know but *who* you know that often counts in Greece. Whether you're seeking a favourable posting for your son's national service or a local government contract, you need a *meso* – an influential acquaintance to manage things in your favour. Hand-in-hand with patronage go cronyism and nepotism, and it is money or rewards in kind that often oil the wheels.

Corruption is a debilitating problem for Greece and exists at every level of Greek society, from the highest echelons of government – for example, the bribery and money-laundering scandal of the 'Siemens Affair' – to ordinary people slipping money to surgeons to ensure their aftercare goes well and any complications are addressed promptly. In a December 3rd *Guardian* report in 2014, Helena Smith recounts the story of a broken lift at the largest public hospital in Athens. When the repairman arrived to fix the problem, he could not believe his eyes: knee-deep at the bottom of the shaft were hundreds of empty envelopes, torn open by doctors to retrieve their 'sweeteners' and then quickly discarded. The widely accepted Greek system of *fakelakia* (little envelopes) seems to have withstood strong external reforming pressures. Evasion of taxes and social security payments is another fundamental issue. Pounced on by populist foreign news media as a primary reason why Greece should not have been bailed out of its economic difficulties, most ordinary Greeks don't view it as a crime and if accused of dishonesty and petty corruption would throw up their arms in horror and disbelief. Opinion is widespread that everyone is fiddling their tax returns in some way or another, so most people follow suit.

But Greece was not the only country heavily exposed to the fallout from the US financial crisis. Portugal, Italy, Ireland and Spain also suffered deep financial and economic stress. But none of these countries – referred to collectively as the 'PIIGS' by the world's media – suffered so quickly, so severely and for so long as Greece. The weaknesses identified by Mitsopoulos and Pelagidis had made Greece especially vulnerable. Thus, it comes as no surprise that the strings attached to the extraordinary and massive international bailout loans that were required to prevent Greece going bankrupt focused on tackling some of those shortcomings in order to create a more robust and sustainable economic framework.

The First to Fall

'*Everyone's furious with Greece – even its own people*'. Thus began an eight-page report from '*the tear-gas filled streets of Athens*' by Stephen Moss and others in *The Guardian* on May 7th 2010. Just three days earlier, a massive march of protest against the conditions imposed on the Greek people by the first bailout loan had ended in the death of three bank workers, suffocated by smoke inhalation after a petrol bomb attack on their place of work. It was an intensely sobering moment for the Greek people, a moment to step back and take stock. How had it come to this?

Greece's eight years in the doldrums began and ended with televised prime ministerial addresses to the nation on small Greek islands at the eastern and western extremities of the country. On April 23rd 2010, by the harbourside in Kastellorizo, the most easterly of the Dodecanese islands, a glum Yiorgos Papandreou announced the country's pressing need to obtain extraordinary financial support to stave off imminent bankruptcy. He had discovered that the previous government had been declaring a public debt of 3.5% of GDP while in fact it was closer to 13%. Although his address contained many stirring words, many exhortations to change and many nautical references, none could disguise the core message that Greek finances were in such a perilous state that they required the EU to provide an emergency rescue package. The Greek ship of state was about to hit the rocks and the moment for bilge pumps, lifejackets and lifeboats had passed; a full-scale rescue operation was required before there were tragic losses leaving precious little left to salvage.

Eight years later, Alexis Tsipras chose the Ionian island of Ithaca to mark the occasion on August 21st 2018 when Greece finally rid itself of the shackles of constraint and dependency imposed on it by the troika of lenders that had assured its survival. From a hill overlooking the harbour of Ithaca Town, Tsipras used much Homeric symbolism to draw parallels between his country's perilous journey towards emergence from the programmes of international financial support, and Odysseus' long and epic journey home to Ithaca after the Trojan Wars. The choice of an island – and the backdrop that mimicked Papandreou's eight years earlier – were clearly not coincidences but part of a cleverly conceived PR ploy.

Between 2010 and 2018, Greece received a sequence of three bailout loans totalling €289 billion. As well as continuing for longer than initially anticipated, their scale and magnitude were unprecedented. The total was comparable to the annual output of countries like Denmark or Malaysia and the market value of global companies like Samsung or Johnson & Johnson. There was a widespread misconception, fueled by global media, that these bailout loans were disappearing into some kind of Hellenic black hole, where they were being manipulated and laundered by unscrupulous politicians and bankers for their own personal advantage, while ordinary Greeks endured punishing austerity. Nothing could be further from the truth. As Yanis Varoufakis, academic, activist, journalist and briefly Greek finance minister points out, most of these loans were used to pay off outstanding debts to German and French banks. These huge transfers of public money barely touched down in Greece before, boomerang-like, they were being redirected back to some of the countries that had contributed them in the first place. Not to their governments or taxpayers however, but to the coffers of giant multinational private banks that had misjudged Greece's ability to repay the loans they had granted and failed to foresee the withering impact of the 2008 financial crisis.

All countries borrow money to balance their books by issuing bonds on the international money markets. Big investment banks and similar institutions buy these bonds at an agreed interest rate over a fixed term. The interest rate is largely determined by the level of risk, a judgement on how able the country is to repay the loan. The higher the risk, the more expensive the borrowing costs. These risks are assessed by credit rating agencies like Moody's, Standard & Poors and Fitch. They are beholden to big finance and have a huge – some would say disproportionate – influence on how easily countries can borrow money.

During a period of economic growth dating from the mid-1990s, when Greece was in confident and optimistic mode, the government borrowed excessively to fund major infrastructure projects and the 2004 Olympic Games. At the same time, individuals also found banks willing and able to lend money at favourable rates of interest, fuelling a consumer boom. All this debt might have been sustainable – and it's a big 'might' – if the US sub-prime mortgage bubble had not burst, or if it had been contained on the other side of the Atlantic. Instead, lenders and borrowers got nervous and Greece's credit worthiness was downgraded. Greek government bonds were reclassified as 'junk', effectively cancelling its overdraft facility and shutting the door to any more loans from normal channels. With interest payments due on previous loans and diminishing means of paying, Greece had little option but to engage in disorderly default (i.e. renege on its loans) or go cap in hand and plead for help from the 'banks' of last resort – the so-called troika. Had Greece resisted the urge to become part of the eurozone, it might have considered devaluing its own currency, a common means of boosting the economy in these kinds of circumstance. However, being tied in to the euro, that option was denied. The debate about whether Greece should have 'bitten the bullet' and exited the euro at this point lumbers on.

The term 'troika' is derived from the Russian word for a carriage pulled by three horses. In Greece's case, it referred to the three 'banks' that rescued it from bankruptcy: the European Commission (EC), the European Central Bank (ECB) and the International Monetary Fund (IMF). The troika was simultaneously resented and feared by the Greek people; after all, in respect of financial and economic matters, it had become the de facto government. Each of the three bailout loans Greece received came with strings attached. With such large sums of money changing hands, that came as no surprise to anyone. The primary aim was to help Greece regain its financial independence and recover its economic strength, but at the same time tackle some of the weaknesses that had made Greece so vulnerable to economic meltdown. Less overt, but possibly more fundamental, was the fierce determination of the EU to preserve the euro as a currency, even if that meant expelling Greece from the eurozone. This background threat was to become a strong bargaining chip. Each bailout loan was released bit by bit by the troika as progress was made on meeting the targets and goals set out in a Memorandum. For the whole eight years of the loan programmes, the troika exercised enormous power over Greece and the Greek people. For any country this would have been hard to take, but for Greece, with its historical claim to being the home of democracy, it was insulting. But what alternatives were there?

The loan programmes allowed Greece to avoid bankruptcy, to repay its debts to French and German banks, to get its public spending under control and to show limited signs of fragile economic growth. But these gains came at an enormous price: eight years of damaging austerity and depression for the Greek people. The conditions imposed by the troika and implemented by the Greek government tore at the heart of Greek society. The facts and figures are stark. At a time when the three bailout loans and accompanying Memoranda were supposed to be reviving the Greek economy, it reduced by a quarter; unemployment reached a maximum of 27.5% in 2013 and still remains at nearly 20%; youth unemployment peaked at a staggering 60% in February 2013; one in three Greeks fell below the poverty line; and, in the same year, 17.5% of the population were living in households with no income. Raw statistics like these, depressing as they are, do nothing to illustrate the anguish and despair permeating Greek society.

A Crushing Impact

It was the urban population of Greece that suffered the greatest hardship during the eight years of austerity. Three quarters of its eleven million people live in towns and cities and nearly one third are concentrated in the two major cities of Athens and Thessaloniki. Whereas country folk have some capacity to sustain themselves in difficult times – by extending their vegetable gardens, for example – city folk are largely hidebound. It was here that belt-tightening became crippling. Thousands of unemployed searching desperately for work, the poor and elderly whose benefits had been slashed, the homeless whose living on the edge became unsustainable, and the sick whose chronically underfunded health service was less and less able to attend to their needs, became the norm in the more downtrodden, less privileged parts of Greek cities. Even the normally comfortably-off middle classes with secure public service jobs for life, in education or the civil service, for example, saw massive job cuts, their wages slashed and conditions savaged, adding to a growing swathe of discontents who could not understand how the boom had so quickly become bust.

The fact that most households survived intact, albeit severely bruised, is a measure of their resilience and the various strands of support that came to their assistance. A 2016 study by the European Bank identified coping strategies adopted by households in financial stress. Some were active, like working longer hours or taking on an additional job, and some passive, such as discontinuing subscriptions, delaying payment of utility charges, defaulting on loan or mortgage payments, and reducing consumption. For those worst-hit city dwellers, austerity meant queuing for food handouts, searching through supermarket waste bins after hours and sleeping rough on the streets. For those in a better situation, it involved relinquishing their homes and moving in with relatives, trading in the car, curtailing spending to bare essentials and substituting the more expensive pleasures they had got used to with more simple ones. The birth rate went down, suicides rocketed and a brain drain of talented young people – Greece's future – opted to seek opportunities abroad. Mass demonstrations, violent protest and graffiti accompanied more sinister stirrings. In Athens, the crime rate escalated, police no-go areas were established and vigilante groups appeared on the streets. Most disturbing of all was the re-emergence of a far-right political movement called Golden Dawn, which succeeded in channelling the widespread despair and discontent and fostering social unrest. At the height of the crisis in 2012 it obtained 7% of the vote in the May elections (nearly half a million) and returned twenty-one members of parliament. Its dark shadow still hangs over Greece.

Neohori's location, far away from the epicentre of Greece's financial and economic maelstrom, did not prevent our neighbours suffering some of its unfortunate consequences. Those most affected were the elderly, people working in the public sector like teachers and health workers, and the sick and needy. Those closely involved in construction also suffered as the building boom came to a standstill. With no new projects forthcoming, builders' yards became redundant and Albanian stonemasons, roofers and labourers were laid off and reluctantly headed back to their homeland. Their numbers were only partially compensated by the arrival of mainly elderly couples taking advantage of their family roots to escape the deprivations of city life. For school leavers, the prospects of finding work without the benefit of connections in the tourist trade were slim. Some took advantage of family relatives and moved to Kalamata in the forlorn hope of better prospects.

Neohori's tight-knit social structure, bonded by long-established extended families, played a crucial role in offsetting the hardships suffered by some villagers and sustaining the community. It has always been so in difficult times. For the majority who work in olive farming and tourism, these were deeply worrying and uncertain times with a need for belt-tightening and introspection, but not ones that threatened their very existence. The signs in Neohori of villagers meeting the challenge of austerity were strangely reassuring. Plots of land within and on the edge of the village were resurrected as vegetable gardens, with some growing single crops like onions, garlic or potatoes, presumably for sale. Whereas it is not uncommon for the bleating of kid goats to fill the air in the months leading up to the Easter festivities, now the gobble of turkeys could also be heard in the pre-Christmas period and the noises emanating from chickens, lambs and even pigs also became more commonplace. And this self-help was not just confined to the village. Paraskevas, from the Neohori Farmers' Co-operative, made several humanitarian trips to Thessaloniki in a lorry loaded with cans of surplus extra virgin olive oil and sacks of potatoes, which were sold at cost price to needy residents.

West Mani district has probably withstood the Greek economic crisis better than most, thanks in no small part to tourism. As North African tourist destinations like Tunisia and Egypt suffered severe downturns due to terrorism concerns, Greek tourism has flourished. A total of thirty-four million foreign tourists arrived in 2019 – three for every one Greek, and the highest total ever recorded. The number of tourists visiting the West Mani resorts of Kardamyli, Stoupa and Aghios Nikolaos reflects this upward trend with a 22% rise in international arrivals recorded at Kalamata airport in 2019, compared with the previous year. The 143,000 passengers were almost exclusively European (78% were British or German) and arrived from origins as diverse as Vienna, Prague, Moscow and Erevan in the east, Dusseldorf, Paris, Amsterdam and London in the west and Copenhagen, Stockholm and Oslo in Scandinavia.

The number of Greek tourists has also expanded. With less disposable income than in the past, making foreign holidays unaffordable, and a motorway that has drastically reduced the journey time from Athens, Messinia has become a popular destination for Greek holidaymakers. The reliable summer weather, the clear, refreshing seawater, the sandy beaches and the stunning backdrop of the Taygetos Mountains have always made West Mani attractive for visitors. To add to this, the local tourist industry has upped its game in recent years by upgrading the quality and diversity of accommodation, of the food on offer in restaurants and of the multitude of other services expected in modern tourist resorts. And all this without compromising the essence of what West Mani has to offer: a stunning natural environment and friendly, engaging, welcoming hosts. Although holidaymakers, especially Greek, have been spending less freely than before, the tourist industry of West Mani and those whose livelihoods depend on it have been able to ride out the economic storm more comfortably than most.

For Mary and me, like most Greeks, our concern centred around money. But in our case, it wasn't day-to-day worries. With our relatively secure UK occupational and state pensions unaffected by the crisis, we were able to accommodate the imposition of VAT rises and additional taxes, such as the annual property tax introduced in 2014. On the one hand we felt fortunate; on the other, we felt uncomfortable that we were able to ride out the crisis more painlessly than many of our Greek friends and neighbours. Even more than usual, we were keen to play down our fortunate financial circumstances.

Although affected by rising prices in supermarkets, filling stations, restaurants and coffee shops, and tough limits on bank withdrawals, it was volatile currency exchange rates that caused us most anxiety. We were confident we could cope with them as far as our monthly international transfers of living expenses were concerned, but large movements of funds from our UK Tried & Tasted business account to pay for olive oil, olives and other food products demanded we pay them much greater attention. Between 2005 and 2015, the value of the GB pound against the euro decreased by 7.5%: a pound worth €1.47 in 2005 could only buy €1.36 ten years later. That meant £1,000 in 2005 bought 310 more euros than in 2010, equivalent to an extra seventy-five litres of extra virgin olive oil – a shortfall we would have preferred to avoid. The GB pound's value had plummeted to €1.16 in 2010, and by 2020, with Brexit fast approaching, was €1.12 – which, with bank charges included, almost equates to parity.

I'm somewhat embarrassed to admit that my standout recollection of the Greek economic crisis was two brief moments of minor fame in the spring of 2010 when I was interviewed over the phone, on air, by Matt Woodley of Radio Devon. Someone had obtained my contact details from the label on a Tried & Tasted bottle and enquired if I would be willing to offer my perspectives on the situation in Greece. At the time the world media was focusing on Greece, where economic collapse and the need for the first bailout loan were prompting mass demonstrations and violent protest in all the cities and towns. The live *Good Morning Devon* interviews lasted no more than five minutes each, during which I tried to give listeners a flavour of the mood of the Greek people facing the grim prospect of economic meltdown. The trans-European link-up was surprisingly straightforward, timed to perfection despite the two-hour time difference and with no technical hitches or bad line. What I found difficult was squaring the anger and chaos in Athens that I was describing with the calm and tranquil outlook from our Neohori terrace.

The Aftermath

In his August 2018 address to the nation on the island of Ithaca, Prime Minister Alexis Tsipras declared, with just a hint of triumph, that "today is redemption day" and the start of "a new era for our country". Few Greeks shared his optimism that now the final bailout loan term was over and Greece liberated from the punishing conditions of three Memoranda, a new, more upbeat era in Greece's modern history would automatically unfold. While European leaders were congratulating Greece on its achievement, declaring that the worst was over but cautioning that there was still a long way to go, *The Guardian's* Larry Elliot was railing against the process that had rescued Greece. In an uncompromising, hard-hitting article on August 19th, he stated that '[the process of rescuing] *Greece has been a colossal failure. It is a tale of incompetence, of dogma, of needless delay and the interests of banks being put before the needs of people*'.

Greece could now begin to seek loans on the open market once again, but until it proves it can stand on its own feet, it will surely find lenders very tentative. Once bitten, twice shy, as the saying goes. And there are strict EU controls in place, designed to prevent any repeat of the situation that led to its crippling meltdown in the first place. Athens will face more exacting checks than any other eurozone member so that Brussels can keep a close eye on Greece's adherence to the EU's budget and its stability and growth targets. It seems Greece will be shackled – with maybe a lighter touch than hitherto – for several years to come.

What is clear is that austerity has not suddenly come to an end. Greece's economic woes will not disappear overnight and any backtracking on reforms – like reversing pension cuts – will be quickly seized upon by EU scrutineers. The Greek people are still numbed by the fate that has befallen them and are well aware that a return to the boom years is as unlikely as it is undesirable. Tsipras' worthy aim to create a fairer, more honest, more just society on the back of modest economic growth was given little chance to succeed. In July 2019, his discredited government was defeated in national elections and Kyriakos Mitsotakis became prime minister and formed a conservative government with different priorities. Greeks were yearning for normality and stability to be restored.

Many Greeks are ashamed that their country, which had such a fundamental influence on the development of Western civilisation, was reduced to the level of a failed South American or African country, begging for help from the international community. Their pride and their confidence in their leaders and politicians have been severely shaken. Public opinion indicated they were fed up with broken pledges, with referendums that were supposed to judge the mood of the people but whose outcomes were discounted, and with violent demonstrations and the resurgence of far-right parties. They lamented their children emigrating to find work, the social disintegration and mounting poverty brought on by austerity, and the deterioration of public services. Equally, they abhorred the overriding power of wealthy oligarchs, many of whom massage their tax liability, and the widening gap between rich and poor.

On the other hand, Greeks welcomed the passing of the constant media attention given to the troika, bailout loans, Memoranda and 'haircuts' (the various attempts to write off some of the Greek debt). They were relieved to see the controversial references to unpaid war reparations by Germany, the very real prospects of 'Grexit', and the threat of expulsion from the eurozone being removed. They were also glad to see the back of the grinding contests of personality, ideology and conviction between leading players like opposing party leaders, Antonis Samaras and George Papandreou, and between Yanis Varoufakis and Wolfgang Schauble, the former German Finance Minister. Most Greeks are happy to see the end of boom and bust and a return to the rest of the world minding its own business. Most would settle for gentle economic growth, a quiet life and a gradual return to normality after such a lengthy period of turmoil.

The first decade of the 21st century had treated Greeks to growing prosperity, sporting triumph and heightened optimism, which the second mercilessly eroded, leaving a trail of broken dreams and disillusion. This poem by Yiorgos Souris, loosely translated from the original Greek, makes a fitting postscript to a chapter on triumph and disaster.

Who has seen such a small country
Unique in all the world
Which spends one hundred
And collects just fifty?

Feeding all the idle unemployed
Having seven Prime Ministers
A Treasury devoid of money
And so many glorifying monuments?

Having clerks as guards
Openly stealing from you.
And while they steal
Who is looking for the thief?

Dreams, hopes and aims
Everything is fake in this land
Our faces have turned into masks
We don't know what shame is

Acute perception, sharp brain
And from great grandfathers and grandfathers
He learns just something but knows everything
Simultaneously a daft owl and a crafty fox

He also wishes – and this is nice –
To pass off as a European
Wearing on his feet
Patent leather on one and a clog on the other

Well groomed, medium stature
The look of a lady killer, a fake Casanova
A little sulking, a little snivelling
A little wretched, a little aggressive

Only bread and cheese and then out for coffee
"Oh well!" and "Oh brother!"
As a citizen, he's a downtrodden servant
As soon as he gets a job, a tyrant he becomes

Alas Hellas
Land of Heroes
With all the children that you spawn
Why so many boorish offspring?

Remarkably, this verse wasn't written in the 21st century but in the 19th – in 1893, in fact – and was referring to one of the Greek state's earliest struggles with bankruptcy. But how it resonates with the recent situation in Greece. For thirty-seven years, Souris was solely responsible for a four-page satirical newspaper called *Romios*, published weekly in Athens. It was the *Private Eye* or *Charlie Hebdo* of its day. He was much admired for his lucid but often humorous writing style and his well-meaning targeting of ineptness, without humiliating or creating enemies. Souris died at home in 1919, aged sixty-six, fretting about who might take on his mantle to expose and confront malpractice and abuse of power wherever it manifested itself, and unsure about the direction Greece's future would take. 100 years later, Greeks have the same uncertainties to contend with.

Monks at the Great Meteoron monastery in central Greece.

Messinian heroes of the Greek Revolution, 1821.

Chapter 10

INTERPRETATIONS OF GREEKNESS

Identity

Only a vague picture of the family that had previously occupied our Greek home in Neohori emerged from the odds and ends they had left behind. Our first rummage through revealed little of value. However, one piece of furniture we inherited – a simple kitchen table that is still in use – contained a single drawer that had obviously acted as the family's filing cabinet. Its contents provided the first reliable clues about our predecessors. As well as playing cards, well-thumbed sepia photographs and long-forgotten Christmas letters and cards with foreign postmarks, it also contained a small assortment of official paperwork, including post-war ration cards, hand-written receipts and ID cards. Family relatives in the village helped us decipher the barely legible details on the official documents and provided us with interesting background information, prompting us to regret not being more inquisitive when we negotiated the purchase of the house with the only daughter and her husband in 1994. The house had been her dowry when they married but her widower father, Yiorgos, known as *o koufos* (the deaf one) continued living there until his death in 1987.

Judging by the scant evidence that remained, Yiorgos had lived a simple, unsophisticated life with few possessions and negligible material wealth. In the living quarters of the house, we also found a battered empty trunk, a rudimentary wooden Orthodox shrine encrusted in candle wax, and a rusty iron bedstead. Within the pitch-black, vaulted arches of the ground floor below, we discovered a wooden donkey saddle with leather harnesses and a jerry can inscribed with 'Gift from the People of the USA' – surely a legacy of the post-war Marshall Plan that saw the USA provide Europe with a massive dose of economic aid to speed its recovery. Yiorgos had lost his hearing while on active service in Albania fighting the Italians during the early part of the Second World War. The war had interrupted his studies at university in Athens and his deafness forced him to abandon his plan to become a schoolteacher. Thereafter, he supplemented the income derived from his olive trees by tutoring village children after school hours, with mathematics as his speciality. His deafness did not seem to diminish him; he was held in high regard by pupils and parents alike, was well respected in the village and acclaimed for his sea fishing skills with rod and line.

Especially during the period in the late '90s when Mary and I were restoring and reconfiguring the house where Yiorgos had spent his lifetime, I occasionally wondered what he would have made of it all. It would surely have come as a surprise that someone not connected with his family was living there, and as a shock that these newly installed inhabitants were not Greek but English. A chance encounter before his death would have probably revealed that we had little in common, apart from our work as teachers and our rural upbringings. Otherwise, I suspect that it would have been our differences that dominated the conversation. Our mismatched generations, our contrasting personal and family histories, our diverse outlooks, attitudes and expectations, as well as contrasting wealth and standard of living, would quickly have become obvious. Our religious beliefs, our political persuasion and our perspectives on the wider world might also have diverged. Yet I fondly imagine that, despite all the differences, there would have remained sufficient common ground to bridge the gap and enough common humanity for us to appreciate our similarities, accommodate our differences and accept our opposing identities. Yiorgos' identity was defined by fighting for his country (some would declare that a person can perform no greater duty), his native tongue, his Orthodox religion and, most of all, his belonging – to his extended family, to his village of Neohori, to the Mani and to Greece, his *patrida* (fatherland). Wherever in the world they live, Greeks retain a strong attachment to their *patrida* and everything it stands for.

All of us have a desire to establish our own individual identity, our distinctive persona that others recognise and relate to. The twin influences of nature and nurture play a big part. At the same time, most people have a desire to be attached to a group or groups where they feel their personal identity fits in, where they feel they belong. At one extreme, these groups can be small and confined to perhaps a pool team or a book club; at the other, they comprise the millions of people who follow a superstar on Twitter, support a football club or belong to a political movement. Greeks find identity a relatively simple matter. A brief but compelling opinion on that subject, delivered by a 'dark, jovial, round-faced' ticket collector on a train from Sikarayia to Alexandropolis in Patrick Leigh Fermor's *Roumeli* summarises it beautifully: "*Greece is an idea, that's the thing! That's what keeps us together – that, and the language and the country and the Church – not that I like priests particularly, but we owe them a lot.*"

So how easy is it to characterise a typical Greek? Opinions vary widely. Some see Greeks as friendly, welcoming, carefree and easy-going, while others view them as loud, boisterous, feckless and opinionated. But beware of stereotypes and caricatures! Identifying Greeks with a presumed norm that oversimplifies those things they are supposed to have in common is sure to misrepresent many. It ignores all those individual characteristics that differentiate them and give them their personal identities. Where you live plays a significant part in creating identity. In Greece, islanders contrast with mainlanders, northerners with southerners, and city dwellers with country folk. Cretan fishermen foraging in the Libyan Sea have different outlooks, customs and traditions to Macedonians and Thracians in the north of Greece and Messinians and Lakonians in the south. Mountain dwellers in Arcadia tending flocks of countless sheep and goats live very different lives to the cotton, tobacco and maize farmers intensively cultivating the plains of Thessaly and Thebes. Athenians, with an unenviable reputation for being brash, overconfident and arrogant, are easily differentiated from other Greeks, while those who have lived and worked abroad or are engaged in the tourist trade often exhibit more cosmopolitan ways. Greeks are a grand assortment of people, but there are certain things that bind this mix together and forge these varied peoples into one.

Who Do They Think They Are?

Most Greeks would like to think that their family bloodline links them directly with Ancient Greeks, so revered for being the source and inspiration of many aspects of Western civilisation. But for the most part that's just fantasy, just wishful thinking. Right from the beginning, ethnic diversity was the norm. The boundaries of modern Greece include ancient sites, where many distinct cultures and societies flourished in the distant past. The very early Cycladic and Minoan island cultures, and the Mycenaean civilisation in the Peloponnese, which followed, are examples. In Classical times, the Achaean and later the Dorian peoples inhabited Greece's heartland and more peripheral parts were occupied by the Epirots, Macedonians and Thracians. And all this diversity existed before the advent of the Christian era.

Ancient Greece was a jigsaw of nearly 1,000 independent political units, most of them centred on cities. Some, like Athens, Thebes, Corinth and Sparta, were big and powerful city states, eager to extend their control and influence; others, like Argos, were small and fearful of their neighbours' expansionist tendencies. At this time, allegiance was first and foremost to a person's city state and that shaped people's identities. So, when did Greeks first consider themselves Greek rather than simply Athenians, Spartans or Corinthians and the like? Change to the use of the terms 'Hellas' and 'Hellenes' – the forerunners of the modern 'Greece' and 'Greeks' – came about as a result of two things. The first was the setting up of colonies around the shores of the Mediterranean and Black Seas and the expansionist conquests by Alexander the Great that followed. Emporion in Spain, Massalia (now Marseilles), Syracuse in Sicily, Paphos in Cyprus and Chersonesos (now Sebastapol) in the Crimea are just a few examples of 400 or so Greek colonies established between 800 and 480 BCE. In this wider Greek world, it became necessary to distinguish between 'true-born' Greeks (Hellenes) and the rest, who were termed *barbari*. The second factor was the considerable threat posed by the powerful and expansionist Persian Empire between 499 and 449 BCE. To repulse this threat, the city-states had no option but to combine forces, which they did to great effect. In doing so, the affiliation to city states slowly diminished as the benefits of co-operation became evident, and Greece and Greekness emerged as a unifying identity.

By the time Greece had become part of the Byzantine Empire during the 4th century, most of the different pre-existing ethnic strands had merged into a more or less homogenous form. At the same time, migrations of people from the north were beginning to add different genetic layers to the demographic mix. Goths and Huns were followed by Bulgars and Avars, and then in the 6th, 7th and 8th centuries, a great influx of Slavic peoples occurred, forcing some of the existing population to flee eastwards across the Aegean Sea to islands and to Asia Minor (now Turkey). Over several hundred years, the Slavs were assimilated, Hellenised and eventually converted to

Christianity, giving rise to much debate about their impact on Greek genealogy. How much of the DNA of modern Greeks is Slavic in origin and how much is pure Hellene, derived from Antiquity?

Many parts of present-day Greece bear the imprint of conquest and occupation during the broad span of history that began with the Romans in the first centuries of the Christian era and ended with the establishment of an independent Greece in 1821. Franks from northern France, Venetians and Genoans from Italy, and Ottoman Turks all imposed their will on some or all of the Greek people for varying lengths of time. The so-called *Turkokratia*, in which Greece was subjected to Ottoman Turk rule for more than 350 years between 1453 and 1821, had an especially profound effect. Even after independence, Greece's stability remained at risk because one and a quarter million ethnic Greeks still remained outside its borders and its fragile existence was being upheld by the then-great powers of Britain, France and Russia. The *Megali Idea* (Great Idea) had been gaining traction in Greece for a while before it was adopted by Eleftherios Venizelos, who pushed it to its limits. Venizelos was a charismatic Greek politician and statesman who was appointed prime minister seven times between 1910 and 1933. He and his supporters were determined to expand Greece's borders to include all ethnic Greeks. Inevitably this involved falling out with its neighbours and Greece was involved in three wars in the ten years between 1912 and 1922.

The two Balkan Wars, in which Greece and its allies confronted the crumbling Ottoman Empire and then Bulgaria, resulted in a doubling of Greece's size. The peace settlements awarded Greece the regions of Epiros and Macedonia in what is now northern Greece, as well as islands in the northern Aegean and Crete. Western Thrace was added in 1920 after Greece's belated and localised involvement on the side of the victors in the First World War. A failed attempt by Greek forces to go one step further and invade Turkish Asia Minor and 'liberate' the ethnic Greeks who had lived there for generations spectacularly backfired. The 1923 peace deal between Greece and

Turkey, brokered by the great powers, sanctioned a huge exchange of populations based entirely on their religion, rather than their ethnicity or language. In an unprecedented episode of resettlement, two million Turks and Greeks were uprooted and forced to relocate in each others' countries. The impact of this programme of forced resettlement on both countries was enormous. By the time of the Second World War, only the Dodecanese islands remained under foreign control, but they were ceded to Greece by Italy in 1947, and the geopolitical map of Greece as we know it today was complete.

Rizes (*Roots*), written and compiled by the late Ioannis Kiskireas, is a comprehensive account of the 20th-century genealogy of families of our village of Neohori; a true labour of love by a man who was born and brought up there and taught at the primary school for many years. This 1998 self-published book – a gift to me from the author – contains numerous family trees, as well as much interesting data about migration from the village during the post-war period. It has proved a great source of information and fascination for Mary and me. Kiskireas reveals that over 500 people – often whole families – have left the village for pastures new. 338 have moved to other Greek cities (mainly Athens and Kalamata) while 178 have emigrated, mainly to the USA and Australia; and all this from a village with a population of barely 250 at the turn of the millennium. The reasons for leaving were common enough: civil war, dictatorship, unemployment and a hard, unrelenting peasant life with little prospect of improvement were some of the causes pushing people to uproot. At the same time, tales of well-paid jobs, better housing, education and healthcare, and more security were pulling people in the same direction. Most who took the decision to emigrate imagined it would be a one-way move with no guarantee of success, but they were reassured by the knowledge that others had done it before them and that they would be welcomed into already-established Greek communities.

Invasion, conquest, migration and assimilation over 5,000 years have all contributed to the genetic make-up of modern-day Greece. And this process continues in the 21st century with the arrival of

Albanian workers and their families, North Europeans seeking retirement in the sun, and returnees – retired Greeks, from Australia, the USA or South Africa, for example – who choose to spend the remainder of their lives in their fatherland, from where they migrated when they were young. In stark contrast are the modern-day waves of desperate, determined, exhausted migrants fleeing war, persecution and poverty, who are arriving in Greece, often by sea from Turkey. The number of migrants, mainly from Syria, Iran and Afghanistan, using Greece as their stepping stone to north-western Europe since 2011, runs into several millions. Although most of them have no wish to remain in Greece, the closure of border crossings has denied them many former routes through the Balkans and forced them to stay put in an accumulation of temporary camps, some official and some makeshift, but all overcrowded and dehumanising.

What Makes a Greek a Greek?

The question of Greek identity has fascinated scholars since ancient times. According to Herodotus, the famous Greek historian (484– 425 BCE), it possessed four main components: shared kinship and bloodline, shared language, shared gods, sanctuaries and sacrifices, and shared customs. More than 2,000 years later, the essence of Greekness remains little changed. It's still all about shared DNA, language, religion and customs. Added to that is its geography – a common climate and close affinity to the landscape and the sea – as well as its thousands of years of common history, with its fluctuating fortunes and shifting borders. All these elements have played a part in shaping what makes a Greek a Greek, in influencing their common characteristics and moulding a national identity. The relative importance of each is difficult to evaluate.

The way Greeks see themselves, how they would like to be seen by others, and how those others actually see them, inevitably courts controversy. Apply that three-way mirror to any nationality and the consequences would be similar, except in the case of Greece, the rift between each perception might be wider. The way a foreigner perceives another nation or people is the product of multiple layers of influences. Some can be first-hand, like living, working or holidaying in a country, but even these direct links are rarely more than superficial, only allowing a veneer of knowledge and insights into the host country. Greece has always prided itself on its welcoming and accommodating attitude to foreigners, yet there is a limit to the level of integration outsiders can achieve; even marriage does not guarantee total assimilation. Most people's perception of a foreign country and its people is a flimsy structure of haphazardly accumulated information obtained from school, holiday visits, diverse media and hearsay. These information blocks are not always as reliable as we might wish and, of course, they change over time.

Filotimo, *leventia*, *pallikaria* and *filoxenia* are four words held in particularly high regard by Greek people, and they offer insights into how Greeks like to see themselves. They have been part of the Greek language for centuries, are difficult to translate into other languages, and even Greeks can find disagreement about their exact meanings. The first three represent idealised versions of Greekness, more especially male Greekness. *Filotimo* in particular embodies complex notions of manhood that include honour, dignity, pride and selflessness. *Leventia* and *pallikaria* are more concerned with traditional warrior virtues like virility, bravery, courage and gallantry, and are applied particularly to young men. In his instructive but harrowing book *Inside Hitler's Greece*, Mark Mazower captures their essence when he comments on the communist guerrillas' decision to resist the occupying Axis forces in the Second World War. He declares it was '*an assertion of everything that was most admirable in the Greek spirit: a fierce nationalism, a refusal to calculate where matters of honour were concerned, a stoic acceptance of enormous hardship and a determination to act together against overwhelming odds*'. In more recent times, the meanings of these emblematic terms have mellowed and their usage changed. Today you might hear an elderly woman thanking a *palikari* who helped her across the street, carried her shopping bags, or offered her his seat on a crowded bus. The fourth term, *filoxenia*, has a simple dictionary definition of 'hospitality' but again, its meaning is deeper and more complex. Literally it means 'friend to a stranger' and that involves an obligation taken seriously by all Greeks: to offer hospitality whatever the circumstances and regardless of colour, gender, age or creed, without expecting anything in return. This popular tradition helped to lessen the impact of austerity in a host of different ways during the deprivations of the 2010–18 economic crisis.

No author considering the issue of Greekness can afford to ignore exploring the relative importance of Antiquity and Byzantium in shaping a common Greek identity. It involves a dilemma – a kind of split personality – and begs the question: are Greeks European orientals, oriental Europeans or a complex mixture of both? In his book *Roumeli*, Patrick Leigh Fermor commits nine pages to a detailed examination of the issue. The formation of national identity is an ongoing and evolving process that involves shared experiences, collective memories, aspirations and achievements. In more recent times, the formative roles played by the opposing influences of eastern and western traditions have become less of an issue as Greeks have embraced more of the European side of their character.

There is little doubt that the Greek language has been a strong unifying force for 2,000 years or more, but perhaps more fundamental has been the role of the Christian religion in the form of the Greek Orthodox Church. In his 2018 booklet *Getting to Understand the Greeks*, Dimitris Calandranis states that *'Faith is profoundly rooted in the souls of Greeks'* and that *'mass is not only a religious performance but a reminder of their history'*. Greeks have a great attachment to the Orthodox Church; it's one of the essentials of being Greek. That is not to say that Greeks are more devout than other Christian peoples, but in Greece the Church plays a more fundamental role in the lives of individuals, communities and the state, and it infiltrates every aspect of a Greek's life, from birth to death.

No visit to Greece can pass without noticing explicit signs of the Greeks' fidelity to their Church and its teachings. Religious paraphernalia dangle from the rear-view mirrors of taxis or from the windscreen blinds of buses, and passengers cross themselves as they pass churches and the many assorted roadside shrines that commemorate lives lost in road accidents – or is it near-misses? Men grow beards for forty days to show respect for the death of a loved one, widows dress in black, and religious icons accompanying photos of deceased forebears can be found on walls behind the counters of countless shops, offices, cafés and restaurants. The local priest plays a significant role at all formal community events, whether they are religious or secular. One of his busiest days of the year is September 11th, when he presides over ceremonies to mark the first day of the new school year in every school in his 'parish'. Even though they may only attend church on saints' days, holy days, baptisms, weddings and funerals, few Greeks would ever consider renouncing their umbilical attachment to the Orthodox Church. Maybe the Greeks are more God-fearing than most Christians, or is it that they attribute – in part, anyway – the survival of Greekness to the durability of the Orthodox Church, and thus have an unbreakable loyalty to it as an institution?

First Perceptions of Greekness

Perceptions of Greekness by outsiders are gathered in many different ways. In my case, two black and white films viewed during my youth, before I had visited Greece for the first time, were responsible for forming my earliest impressions of that country and its people. I only got to see *Never on Sunday* at the second attempt; an X-rating by the British Board of Film Censors, my woeful teenage efforts at deception and an unbending doorman at the Regal cinema in Wells, Somerset, combined to prevent me seeing this engaging film when it was first released in 1960. It tells the story of an American tourist who tries unsuccessfully to reform an indomitable prostitute with a heart of gold when he visits the port of Piraeus. The sexual revolution had yet to gain traction in Britain when *Never on Sunday* was first shown, and its showing aroused some controversy.

Melina Mercouri's appealing portrayal of the feisty main character with her free spirit, her joie de vivre and universal popularity amongst the Piraeus waterfront locals gained her great acclaim. Although she swam in the harbour with a shoal of exuberant shipbuilders, persuaded a reluctant young sailor to lose his virginity and appeared topless, except for a skimpy black bra, in a few fleeting frames – enough to disturb the sexual equilibrium of an untutored adolescent boy – this was extremely mild eroticism when compared with 21st-century norms. No matter how much the box-office success and critical acclaim of *Never on Sunday* hinged on Mercouri's magical performance and Manos Hadjidakis' musical score, a major spin-off was the introduction to a worldwide cinema-going public of some essences of Greekness. Although not all have survived intact to the present day, it successfully portrayed the camaraderie, solidarity, spontaneity, irascibility of Greeks; their love of socialising, live Rembetika music, impromptu dancing, and overindulgent eating and drinking when a special occasion demands. I was charmed and intrigued.

Another film, *Zorba the Greek*, followed shortly after and also became a worldwide hit. All of a sudden, through the magic of cinema, Greece was demanding the world take notice. Based on Nikos Kazantzakis' novel, directed by Michael Kakoyiannis with musical score by Mikis Theodorakis, this black-and-white 1964 film achieved great acclaim from critics and cinema audiences alike. It was a huge box-office success. Alexis Zorba, played by Anthony Quinn, is a lovable rogue with an insatiable lust for life, an unfailing optimism and an unquenchable self-confidence. It took me a few more years to realise that these were quintessential Greek characteristics. His persona contrasts vividly with the shy introspection of Basil, a white-suited English author played by Alan Bates whom Zorba befriends on a ferry to Crete. Basil intends to revive the fortunes of his father's lignite mine and rather reluctantly enrols Zorba's help, little anticipating the bizarre situations that would befall them.

Zorba – *What will I do without your company?*
Basil – *Cheer up! We'll get together again.*
Zorba – *No, you'll stay with your books.* [He raises his glass.] *Good health!*
Basil – *Yours, Zorba!*
Zorba – *Dammit boss! I like you too much not to say it. You've got everything except one thing: madness. A man needs a little madness, or else...*
Basil – *Or else...?*
Zorba – *...Or else he never dares cut the rope and be free.* [Pause.] *Are you angry with me?* [More pause.]
Basil – *Teach me to dance, will you?*
Zorba – *Dance? Did you say dance? Come on my boy! Together! Let's go!*

These lines from the final scene of *Zorba the Greek* capture the contrasting Greekness and Englishness of the two main characters. With the failure of Basil's plans, Zorba persuades him to invest in a timber felling scheme, which involves the construction of a zip wire rig to bring logs from the mountain top to the sea. A trial run, blessed by priests and attended by most of the local population, ends in disaster with the spectacular collapse of the rig, sending spectators fleeing for their lives. Zorba and Basil are left alone by the shore to devour the spit-roast lamb and red wine intended to celebrate a great success. Instead, they gloomily digest their utter disappointment and contemplate their uncertain futures. Suddenly Basil's inhibitions are discarded; he throws his jacket to the ground and loosens his tie, and with arms around each other's shoulders, they dance the *Syrtaki* with its ever-increasing rhythm as the camera zooms out and the credits roll. It's a wonderful joyful moment that never ceases to raise the hairs on the back of my neck. It demonstrates the way close contact with another country and its people can have a profound effect on a person's attitude and behaviour, and hints that a touch of madness might be a characteristic that Greeks are secretly quite proud of.

Viewed for the first time in my teenage years, *Never on Sunday* and *Zorba the Greek* strongly influenced my early perceptions of Greece and Greeks. They were the spark that set alight my longstanding love affair with the country and its people. Many films featuring Greece have followed in their wake but, for me, none have succeeded in capturing the essence of Greece like those two. *Shirley Valentine* came close and *Mediterraneo* too; the two *Mamma Mia*s created a feelgood factor and a yearning for Greek sunshine, but *Captain Corelli's Mandolin* was a huge disappointment – a monumental missed opportunity to reflect the soul of Greece, like *Cinema Paradiso* did for Italy and *Jean de Florette* did for France.

It was only after several summer holidays in Greece that I felt the urge to find out more, and books – almost all in the English language – provided me with the means. I started with fiction – John Fowles' *The Magus* remains one of my top ten novels of all time – and then moved onto travelogues like Patrick Leigh Fermor's *Mani: Travels in the Southern Peloponnese* – a classic of its kind to which I have returned many times – and memoirs like Dilys Powell's *An Affair of the Heart*. I've ended up delving deeper and deeper into my adoptive country by reading learned tomes of non-fiction depicting and analysing modern Greek history. Roderick Beaton's illuminating *Greece; Biography of a Modern Nation* has been my most recent read.

Along with Lawrence Durrell and Henry Miller, Patrick Leigh Fermor formed part of a trio of the 20th century's most acclaimed English language writers, all exercising their craft in Greece in the years immediately before and after the Second World War. They were part of a loose-knit group of intellectuals, artists, poets and writers who were inspired by each other and by many aspects of Greece. In their different ways, they vividly portrayed Greece and Greeks at a turning point in history; a Greece long since changed by the forces of urbanisation, modernisation, Europeanisation and mass tourism.

Yet many of their acute observations and comments still resonate today, more than seventy years after they were first made. Their books are indispensable reading for anyone disposed to get to the heart of Greekness.

Lawrence Durrell had persuaded his widowed mother to abandon 'dreary' England in 1935 and move her family to the Greek island of *Kerkyra* (Corfu). Here, for six years in his twenties, Lawrence developed his literary craft and his affection for all things Greek. He published three books set in Greece, *Prospero's Cell* being the most acclaimed. Written in the form of a journal, it describes his idyllic, somewhat bohemian, worry-free life with his first wife Nancy. Durrell's graphic descriptions of visits to ecclesiastic and historic sites are rich and appealing and his evocative observations of a host of colourful locals and their customs and folklore often capture the essence of Greece and Greekness.

The American author Henry Miller spent nine months living in Greece just as the ugly portents of a second World War were echoing around Europe. Considered by some critics as a masterpiece of travel writing, *The Colossus of Maroussi* is a rambling but never dull account of his stay that courts controversy and divides opinion. The Colossus of the title does not refer to an ancient monument but to the poet and raconteur, Yiorgos Katsimbalis, who lived in the Maroussi district of Athens and who Miller greatly admired for his animated and imaginative story-telling. Often digressionary, with countless musings about people and places, *The Colossus of Maroussi* is rarely predictable. Miller's visits to Classical sites are described in a quirky, unconventional, almost spiritual way, requiring a prior knowledge to really appreciate their obliqueness. His travels are punctuated with encounters with an eclectic mix of people. His candid tales of these episodes are both entertaining and perceptive and, despite his blunt, opinionated and fearless style, his enthusiasm for Greece and the Greeks remains unbounded.

Characterised by the BBC as a cross between Indiana Jones, James Bond and Graham Greene, Patrick Lee Fermor – Paddy to his friends

– transcends all other authors in the breadth and depth of his writing about Greece and the Greek people. He was certainly more qualified than most. He had distinguished wartime service in Crete, was a fluent Greek speaker and had travelled widely in Greece – making use of his considerable network of acquaintances – before he and his wife Joan had a house built and settled in Kardamyli, West Mani in the 1960s. He moved outside his close coterie of friends in search of authentic Greeks and through his command of the language, his self-assurance, his easy sociability and his genuine interest in ordinary people's lives, backgrounds and opinions, he was able to burrow beneath the surface of the folklore, customs and traditions he encountered on his travels. Furthermore, his accomplished travel writing, described in *The New York Times* as opulent, erudite and anecdotal, '*conjuring up people and places with loving precision*' is what sets him apart from his contemporaries.

Leigh Fermor wrote two seminal volumes about Greece. *Mani* (1958) featured the eponymous peninsula in the southern Peloponnese; the other, *Roumeli* (1966) recalled his experiences while travelling in northern Greece. Both vividly portray Greece and Greeks in simpler, more leisurely times when the pace of change was unhurried. In amongst Leigh Fermor's insightful and intriguing accounts of people and places, he often examines their historical, cultural, political and social contexts. Both are essential reading for those who wish to understand more about the development of Greece as a nation state and those distinctive traits that characterise Greek people.

Face-to-Face with Greece

Mary and I experienced our first real taste of Greece in the summer of 1969, just a year after we had started work as teachers. Our holiday began with a short stay in Athens that was as exhausting as it was exhilarating. This was due in part to sleeping in the cooler open-air on the roof-top of the Hotel Argos. For young travellers at the time, this was the fashionable thing to do, but it proved stubbornly unrestful. The early morning ferry from Piraeus proved a welcome and refreshing tonic after four days of urban heat, choking air, ceaseless traffic noise and swarming crowds. Our much-anticipated sojourn on the island of Hydra was proving difficult to resist. The prospect of a decent night's sleep was no doubt part of the attraction.

As the sun slowly climbed above the semicircle of hills that form an imposing backdrop to Athens, we settled down to enjoy the gentle rhythm of the ferry's passage through the waters of the Saronic Gulf, the Greek ensign flapping vigorously at the stern and the horizon seeming to constantly shift and realign. Leisurely stops at Aegina and Poros prolonged the journey time, but shortly before midday we entered the impressive, steep-sided cove and natural harbour around which Hydra town has grown. It's the only settlement of any size on the island. The two-week idyll that followed captured many indelible images of Greece for us and our group of friends. Two impressions remain undiluted by the passage of time: the spontaneous hospitality and the locals' casual attitude to time and time-keeping.

Dave Phelps, an old school friend, had belatedly joined us on Hydra. Halfway through our stay, he and I agreed to explore the rugged interior of the island, which rose up steeply behind our lodgings at the topmost limits of Hydra town. We set off at daybreak to make the rough climb before the full force of the sun's rays became too debilitating. Even so, it was nearly two hours before we approached the imposing walled monastery of Profitis Elias and some welcome shade, from which to admire the breath-taking panorama of the Argolid Gulf and the mountainous Peloponnese beyond. In the near horizontal morning sunlight, the contrasting zones of bright and shade conspired to enhance our appreciation of the folds and creases of the ancient landscape that spread out before us. It was while in this trance that an adjacent old wooden door creaked open and a bent and bearded monk appeared, grasping a brass tray on which were two glasses of water and a plate of almond biscuits.

Our breathless arrival had obviously been noticed from within, and the age-old Greek custom of *filoxenia* extended to us in a simple and gracious manner. I have never forgotten that first experience of spontaneous Greek hospitality that I have been the grateful recipient of many hundreds of times since. *Filoxenia*, in all its various forms, constitutes something fundamental, something instinctive about being Greek.

One of the delights of holidays that take you away from the routines and demands of home and work is the opportunity to relegate the way time can rule our modern lives. During our stay in Hydra, time became redundant; when we were hungry we ate, when we were tired we slept, when we were thirsty we drank and when we got too hot we cooled off in the sea. The parabola of heat intensity from a 'chilly' dawn through the noonday peak to dusk and the cooler evening and night-time hours hijacked our body clocks. It coaxed us into becoming more nocturnal beings and compensated for our loss of night-time sleep by inducing lazy hours of snoozing in the shade during afternoons. The Greeks have long followed this survival regime during the summer months of the year, paying little attention to their clocks and watches, save to make sure they don't miss a bus or ferry, a film or a concert. Otherwise, lateness is endemic in Greece; something all Greeks take for granted and accept as standard. Whether it's an appointment with the notary public, a baptism or a dinner engagement, Greeks know that turning up on time will probably mean waiting for others to arrive before anything can begin.

This casual disregard for time that can be so irritating to foreigners was brought home to us on our last night on Hydra. Eager to conclude our holiday in style, we and our friends turned up mid-evening at *Tou Yiorgou* (George's), our favourite waterside taverna. We were quickly accommodated, our order for fresh fish was taken and a delicious mix of salads, olives, bread and wine was brought to the table. All was hastily consumed and carafes of wine replenished when the service stalled and everything came to a halt. Ten minutes passed without any sign of the grilled fish and despite assurances from the waiter that they were nearly ready, further minutes passed and still no fish appeared. With patience running out, a more robust enquiry, which reminded the increasingly harassed waiter that he had promised the fish would be served in two minutes, stopped him in his tracks. With a defiant smile peeling across his face, he held up a Churchillian two fingers, and declared triumphantly, "Two Greek minutes!" No sooner had the resulting uproar calmed down than a large stainless steel platter of steaming grilled fish appeared, dressed in the traditional manner with an emulsion of hot olive oil and lemon juice – *ladolemono*, as the Greeks call it. The prospect of a noteworthy last night on Hydra had been restored.

Aspects of Greekness

When Mary and I arrived in Neohori in October 1997 after the first trans-European road trip in our Leyland-DAF van, we were understandably excited and wary in equal measure at the prospect of establishing a second home in southern Greece. By this time, we had become familiar with the geography of the area and the summer delights it offered to holidaymakers, but much else remained unknown. Of course, we had gathered information, both deliberately and casually, in advance of our arrival but nothing had prepared us for the explosion of learning about Greece and Greekness that would follow. As we made contact with local people – both Greeks and expats who had settled there before us – and started building friendships and relationships, the more we learned about our adopted home. That, in turn, motivated us to delve into books, TV, newspapers and eventually the internet, to further enhance our knowledge and understanding. Our earliest attempts to adopt the Greek language were also proving helpful in our efforts to integrate with the local community.

In the fifty-five years I have known Greece intermittently at first hand, but more especially in the twenty-three years living part-time in Neohori, I have accumulated numerous thoughts and opinions about Greekness, most of which are positive. None are unique to Greece, none apply to all Greeks in equal measure, and yet a few have a commonality, regardless of gender, age, occupation or background. A trawl through the previous chapters in this book will reveal some that I shall not dwell on further. Yet there are others that particularly resonate with me. My interpretations of Greekness are personal – sometimes shared with others and sometimes not – and they are definitely not intended as a comprehensive examination.

* * *

Few would dispute that Greeks have a great lust for life, which manifests itself in its most vibrant form when there is something to celebrate. No opportunity is spurned and it's never done by halves. Religious feast days, public holidays, name days, baptisms and weddings are all excuses – if any were needed – to do what Greeks do best: to celebrate with carefree abandon. Mary and I were more than surprised when our younger son Peter announced in 2011 that he and his wife-to-be Amanda were intending to get married in Greece, but we could understand their motivation. If they wanted to make the most of their special day, then choosing a country with an unmatched reputation for knowing how to celebrate, where the summer weather is wholly reliable and where local people would be sure to embrace their every need, seemed to make very good sense. And so it turned out. From the midday civil ceremony at the town hall in Kardamyli and a lunchtime reception at Dioskouri restaurant nearby, to the late afternoon marriage procession through Neohori led by Panayiotis on his violin, and the evening reception hosted impeccably by the Marambeas family in their now-defunct Marabou Restaurant, no opportunities were missed to make it an unforgettable day.

Panagyria (gatherings) are perhaps the best example of how Greeks can celebrate. Often timed to coincide with August 15th – an important date in the Orthodox calendar when the Dormition (or Assumption) of Mary, Mother of God, is commemorated – these annual village celebrations provide a very popular excuse to party, whether you are a devout Christian or not. It is also an opportunity, when every village is full of summer visitors, for families and friends to reconnect and for villages to raise money for local causes. Neohori is a little different; it holds its *panagyri*, which ranks as one of the most anticipated of all the village's annual celebrations, on the evening of the last Saturday in July. Hundreds of people gather together in the open air on long lines of plastic chairs and tables set out in formal lines on the spacious forecourt of the main church. Nourished by copious quantities of roast pork, assorted salads and bread, furnished with ample supplies of beer and wine, entertained by an energetic live band and needing little encouragement to dance, revelers celebrate as Greeks have done for generations. Being able to dance traditional dances is an essential part of being Greek; elegant, nimble and accomplished dancers are held in high regard and are always eager to show off their flair and skill.

Two other Greek words that also prove difficult to adequately translate are *kefi* and *parea*. Between them they capture the essence of Greek celebrations. The dictionary defines *kefi* as 'good mood, fun or enjoyment', but it's more all-embracing than that. It is also about enthusiasm, excitement and 'making merry', something conspicuously evident when Greeks are celebrating. *Parea* describes a group of friends who get together to enjoy each other's company. This simple pleasure is highly valued amongst Greeks and, as much as anything, involves talk, something beautifully summarised by Leigh Fermor in *Roumeli* as '*an* [Greek] *addiction* [...] *conducted with invention and great narrative gifts, the knack of repartee, the spirit of contradiction, the questioning of authority, mockery, self-mockery, satire and humour.*'

Kariovouni, a small village tucked away in a steep-sided valley in the mountains above Aghios Nikolaos in West Mani, has a population of only six elderly folk during the winter. But in the summer months it comes alive as empty houses fill up with families returning to their roots for their holidays. Dominating the village are two giant plane trees that have benefitted from the perpetual spring water that issues from the rocks nearby. A marble plaque high on a stone wall records the planting of these trees in 1918 and I imagine that the village *syllogos* (association) had little hesitation in deciding to mark their 100 years' existence with a birthday party. It would not have been Greek to do otherwise.

Thus, on Sunday July 29th 2018, Mary and I, with Greek friends Yiorgos, Elektra and Vassilis, were privileged to join families from far and wide with Kariovouni connections to celebrate the lives of two centenarians that had overseen so many episodes of village life. The prologue was led by dancers in traditional costume accompanied by musicians under the shade of the smaller of the two trees in the tiny square behind the church. They were followed by a solemn blessing conducted by the village priest and short speeches by local dignitaries. The main event was a splendid sit-down meal in the open air under the spreading branches of the other plane tree for the 200 or so people who had gathered for this special occasion. The atmosphere was joyful and relaxed as the food and wine flowed; *parea* and *kefi* were everywhere to be seen as people reconnected with family, friends and former neighbours, and the musicians and dance troupe conspired to produce some impromptu extra entertainment. No doubt for some, the celebrations continued well into the night. And all to recognise the long life of these two towering natural specimens that form such an integral part of the village – a veritable expression of Greekness and a tribute to the forethought and organisational skills of the village leaders.

* * *

Many Greeks seem to possess a suspicion of authority, sometimes bordering on contempt, which can be expressed in different ways. At one end of the spectrum, it simply amounts to casual disobedience.

Dimitris Calandranis sums it up neatly in his 2018 booklet *Getting to Understand the Greeks*: 'Freedom [...] is conceived differently by a Greek. Being free [...] means they can do whatever they think is right, and sometimes "right" is what the majority does, regardless of whether it is law-abiding or not.' Greeks seem to have an inbred reluctance to abide by low-level laws, rules and regulations, even when they are designed to encourage personal safety and collective wellbeing.

Smoking provides a good example. For many years Greece has been at the top of Europe's smoking league table. One of the reasons for this has been the low price of tobacco products, many of which are manufactured in Greece using locally farmed tobacco. The smoking ban in public places, introduced as part of an EU initiative in September 2009, was virtually ignored in Greece and has never been effectively enforced. Although tobacco consumption has halved in recent years – possibly due more to financial, rather than health, concerns – smoking in public places is still commonplace. Ashtrays remain the norm in restaurants, bars, cafés, and even on beach-bed tables, while people smoke openly and with impunity inside and outside public places and proprietors and managers rarely intervene. The new government, elected in July 2019, has pledged to enforce the smoking ban in public places, promising large fines for non-compliance. Even so, it is unlikely that the number of Greek smokers will shrink to European norms any time soon.

That Greeks have a universal reputation for being easy-going and laid-back is hard to deny. Yet at odds with this – and certainly more contentious – is their reputation for being impulsive and quick to react. Morning gossip in that Greek male bastion, the *cafeneion*, can sometimes quickly unravel into a high-volume, short-lived, verbal free-for-all with tempers raised and rash statements and accusations no sooner uttered than regretted. Are Greeks especially temperamental, hot-blooded and easily roused? I have no doubt that similar altercations happen all over the world and yet, in my opinion, they don't gather intensity as swiftly or dissipate so quickly as they can do in Greece.

On one memorable occasion, Mary and I were present when calm proceedings rapidly deteriorated into pandemonium. This time it was not in a *cafeneion* but in the notary public's office in Aghios Nikolaos, where we were trying to negotiate the sale of a small parcel of our land. The potential buyer became incensed when he learned that the cost of officially transacting the deal was going to far exceed the agreed value of the land. The speed with which he transformed from composed client to ranting complainant was staggering. He jumped to his feet, waved his arms vigorously, loudly proclaimed the injustice of the system and accused the affronted notary and the Greek state of flagrant profiteering. It was an astonishing performance, brought to a peaceful conclusion by the cool and conciliatory intervention of the notary's assistant. We left in embarrassed silence without any agreement, but within days – as often in Greece – another way was found to enact the deal.

Some would see a tenuous link between Greeks' tendency to have a short fuse, their suspicion of authority and their disobedience of low-level regulations with behaviour at the other end of the spectrum: their rebelliousness. Greeks have a reputation for protesting and demonstrating. Resistance to 400 years of Ottoman Turk rule, to military occupation by German, Bulgarian and Italian forces during the Second World War, and to seven dictatorships during the 20th century alone have clearly left their mark. During the ten years of the economic crisis arising out of the 2008 global financial meltdown, many Greeks saw reason to express strong opposition to their predicament by parading through central Athens and other big cities in large numbers, waving banners, chanting slogans and seeking to influence government policy and public opinion. And sometimes a peaceful demonstration can quickly mutate into a riot. TV news reports that feature images of smashed windows, torched wheelie bins, Molotov cocktails being hurled at police cordons, and banks and government buildings being stormed ensure the rest of the world looks on in disbelief.

Yet not all demonstrations in Greece deteriorate into mindless mayhem. In February 2008, Mary and I were on a bus taking us from Athens to Kalamata after a flight from the UK. We had almost reached the halfway stage of the journey when we encountered a road block at Tripoli: farmers were protesting against rising fuel and fertiliser costs and had parked a cordon of black-flagged tractors across the motorway, closing it to traffic in both directions. Burning tyres were belching black smoke into the cloudless sky but there was little other threat to road users. In fact, there was a kind of carnival atmosphere, with the farmers emboldened with ample supplies of translucent liquid – was it ouzo or tsipouro? – and drivers seemingly unfazed by the disruption to their journeys. Judging neither face masks nor headscarves necessary to protect their identity, the protesting farmers were quite content for a TV crew to conduct interviews and for the conciliatory police to arrange for our bus to turn around and find another route to continue its journey. It was a fine example of orderly, peaceful but effective civil disobedience, something practised by most Greeks more than once during the course of their lifetimes. They start early in life; young children accompany parents on demonstrations and before long, many have gone on to participate in school and university demonstrations, sit-ins and lock-outs. In this way, protest becomes a way of life.

* * *

Greeks have an obsession with money and wealth. It is a big deal for Greeks, and not just because of the impact of the financial crisis and the resulting austerity that put a squeeze on so many people's pockets. Whereas Brits are mostly cagey about their personal financial affairs, with even close family and friends sometimes unaware of an individual's relative wealth, Greeks are much more transparent and open. Demonstrating affluence is expected of successful Greeks, and much respected if generosity and philanthropy flow from it. If they have wealth, they tend to flaunt it in the manner of oligarchs, film stars, TV celebrities and sports stars the world over. Greeks are inclined to brazenly enquire about your financial status not long after first meeting you. My first conversation with a next-door neighbour, shortly after moving into our Neohori house, promptly turned to money. Vangellis was eager to learn how much we had paid for the house and what my monthly pension was. My inadequate Greek, my inept mental conversion of British pounds to drachmas, and the fact that we were shouting our conversation from terrace to terrace not only confused our neighbour but probably convinced him I was deliberately prevaricating.

No talk of Greeks and money can avoid the subject of tax and tax avoidance. For much of the world's popular media, Greece's economic crisis was largely of its own making. It simply boiled down to too much government borrowing and the Greek people's reluctance to pay their taxes. What dissuades Greeks from paying their rightful dues is a profound distrust in the government – whatever its complexion – and the civil service to administer their taxes in an open, honest and even-handed way. Malpractice and corruption are suspected at all levels. At the same time, the tax collecting system in Greece has been weak and under-resourced, with workers, especially the countless self-employed – 34% of the total workforce in 2017, according to the World Bank – easily able to avoid paying tax with little fear of being caught. With cash payments for goods and services big and small being the norm in Greece until very recently, tax avoidance became endemic and difficult to budge. Everyone was doing it, so why would even the most honest and upright of citizens choose to do otherwise? But things are improving as conditions imposed on Greece by its lenders during the economic crisis are having an impact.

Generosity is one of the most prized of all Greek characteristics. By the same token, tight-fistedness and meanness are abhorred. Many examples of natural, simple, spontaneous acts of generosity have punctuated our time in Greece. A jug of wine arriving unannounced from a Greek friend on the other side of a crowded taverna; a still-warm, half–round of *spanakopita* (spinach pie) or a freshly-made, steaming bowl of *rizogalo* (rice pudding) arriving on our doorstep from neighbours; a bulging bag of freshly picked lemons in response to a casual remark to our plumber's mother about the magnificent yield of her back-yard tree, were just three we experienced during our first six months in Neohori. No favour or assistance can be given, no admiration or praise tendered, without the recipient feeling a strong urge to offer something in return. The simple act of tightening a stainless steel nut with a spanner to stop a kitchen tap spurting water every time it was turned on sent Koula, an elderly neighbour, into a blind panic. How was she going to repay me for this simple act of kindness? Eventually she chose a solitary can of Coca Cola, probably intended for her grandson. No amount of pleading diminished Koula's resolve and, to escape without further delay, I accepted my reward with as much grace as I could muster.

* * *

Greece's natural environment is one of the richest, most diverse and most appealing in Europe and one of the reasons why foreign visitors are so attracted to the country. Sadly, many Greeks do not seem to appreciate it in the same way. It is hard to understand why they are so dispassionate about the value of their stunning natural environment and so complacent about preserving it. Threats to Greece's environment come in the usual forms. Vehicle emissions and carbon-burning power stations diminish air quality, and ever-present litter, fly-tipping, and indiscriminate building development damage the natural landscape and devalue its beauty. Overfishing, inadequate sewerage treatment and disposal, and burgeoning tourism endanger the marine environment – crucial to a country so wedded to the sea – while deficient waste collection and disposal and half-hearted recycling are certain to become some of the most pressing environmental issues in Greece over the next decade.

Changing public attitudes is vital if everyday environmental problems like litter, fly-tipping and low levels of recycling are going to be addressed. Despite the commendable efforts of volunteer-led environmental action groups like *Kathari Mani* (Clean Mani), not a lot has changed in the twenty-two years since Torrington friends Mike and Trisha spent a few days with us in Neohori in the summer of 1998. They had returned to Athens after ten days island hopping and were heading south by train on the six-hour journey to Kalamata, where we had arranged to collect them. They had obtained seats opposite an elderly Greek couple and when they started to unpack their picnic lunch, Mike and Trisha did likewise. Despite the language difficulties, friendly offerings and exchanges of food and drink soon followed and a convivial atmosphere prevailed. As each item was consumed, Trisha collected up the containers and wrappings in a carrier bag that she intended to dispose of in a rubbish bin at journey's end. However, once the picnic lunch was concluded and the leftovers packed away, the old Greek lady beckoned unmistakably to Trisha to hand over the waste bag. Without a moment's hesitation Trisha complied, only to look on aghast as the old lady wound down the compartment window and lobbed the bag into the passing countryside.

Answers to all these environmental problems exist and, in some cases, Greece is well-equipped to make the most of them. Harnessing the sun and wind to generate renewable energy is one answer to Greece's overdependence on electricity generation by burning costly and polluting fossil fuels. But whereas wind turbines forming ranks of arm-waving white giants on mountain skylines throughout Greece have become a common sight in the last twenty years, the adoption of solar power has lagged behind. But there are plans to change all that, with DEH, the national electricity provider, publishing plans in April 2020 to build two giant solar energy farms on a brownfield site at Megalopoli in the central Peloponnese, and thus allow the gradual phasing out of the lignite-burning power stations nearby, which have been belching out pollution into the Arcadian sky for close on fifty years. Together with another major solar power development near Kozani in northern Greece, the aim is to generate nearly 300 MW of solar power annually. Sadly, this will amount to only a fraction of Greece's electricity consumption, but it is a step in the right direction.

* * *

The path towards overturning patriarchy and establishing some gender equality in Greece has been slow. Greek women only began to obtain greater rights and freedoms in the second half of the 20th century, when the right to vote was granted in 1952. The 1983 Family Code legislation marked a watershed that guaranteed equality between spouses, eased the strict conditions for divorce and outlawed the age-old custom of marriage dowries, while in 2006, domestic violence in all its forms was criminalised. Traditionally, the Greek man's role is to earn money and be the breadwinner and provider; the woman's role is to support her man, massage his ego, overlook his indiscretions, wash and iron his clothes, cook his dinner, make his coffee, raise his children, manage the home and family and – most demanding of all – cope with his mother, her mother-in-law. As recently as 2017, EU research ranked Greece the lowest of all the twenty-eight EU countries for gender equality. The study found that Greek women were discriminated against in many different ways: they earn less, their access to key employment sectors is restricted, and their roles – even in education, healthcare and social work, where they are well represented – are rarely at the highest level.

However, there are signs that things are changing. Katerini Sakellaropoulou was elected the first female president of Greece in January 2020, and Maria Lepenioti fearlessly presided over the three-member criminal court that, after a five-year trial, convicted the far-right, ultra-nationalist Golden Dawn party of being a criminal organisation and sentenced its leaders to thirteen-year prison terms in October 2020. They represent fine role models. The gender pendulum in Greece still swings in favour of men but many of today's young Greek women have higher aspirations, more opportunities and greater determination to break the mould than their mothers and grandmothers ever had. More than ever before, they are more educated, more emancipated, more travelled, more informed and more determined to be judged and valued on the basis of merit rather than gender. Optimism amongst young women for a more egalitarian future has never been greater, but few think it will be anything other than a long struggle.

* * *

Many other common Greek traits, attitudes and cultural norms help to form a picture of Greekness. It's a jigsaw puzzle with many different pieces, some big, some small, and some that refuse to fit together easily. A quick scan of websites like *quora.com*, which boldly seeks 'to share and grow the world's knowledge' through online questions and multiple responses can sometimes be rewarding. The question 'What are the characteristics of Greek people?' generated lots of detailed online opinions from Greek Greeks, as well as those living in Cyprus and the diaspora. Not surprisingly, there was considerable agreement that included some characteristics and behaviour that I have neglected. Respondents claimed that Greeks are loud, and that they yell, gesticulate and complain a lot; that they are very family-oriented with a love of children and a great respect for old people; that they are superstitious – witness the enduring power of the evil eye; that they are supremely proud of their cultural heritage; and that, compared with other nationalities, they are intuitively friendly. I would add a few more esoteric traits. In my experience, Greeks possess a different appreciation of personal space, and some have scant regard for privacy; they have a deep-seated and unbounded self-confidence that persuades them that no task is beyond their capability; they have a deep mistrust of their neighbours, the Turks – something that goes well beyond the French calling the English '*Rosbifs*' and the English calling the French '*Frogs*' – and they have a tireless capacity to cope with the bureaucracy and red tape that are an integral part of life in Greece.

Becoming Greekish

The final scene in the film *Zorba the Greek*, where Basil suddenly exhorts Zorba to teach him to dance, offers a fleeting glimpse of how people can change through contact with another country. Up until that moment, Basil has remained an archetypal, self-restrained English gentleman, when suddenly he abandons his inhibitions and dances the *Syrtaki* with Zorba. My Greek dancing leaves a lot to be desired and I've never been an archetypal English gentleman, but there are ways in which my time in Greece has changed me; nothing radical or profound, but in small ways that become noticeable in certain situations. I still spend half the year in the UK with all its fundamental influences and there are other factors that may be responsible, at least in part, for these changes – things like my retirement from employment and my slow passage into old age that both have an ongoing impact on my outlook and wellbeing.

Since I started dividing my time between the UK and Greece, I believe my all-round wellbeing has attained a new level. I have never been more at ease with myself, with the people around me whom I love and cherish, and with the world at large. That's not to say that I'm in a permanent Zen state where nothing irritates or angers me, but those moments are rarer than they have ever been. Living part-time in southern Greece with the sea on my doorstep plays a big part. The sea's changing moods are visible at all times from our terrace; its calming sereneness when it reflects paths of sunlight or moonlight at the close of day or night contrasts with its rare but daunting storm-induced anger – easily audible several kilometres from the shore, even on a windy day. A ruler-straight and pencil-thin south-western horizon dividing the sea from the sky on a calm, clear day has a habit of transporting me effortlessly to another world beyond, to people and places where different languages, different customs, different ways of life flourish: Sicily, Algeria, the Balearic Islands and Morocco. The Greek sea also possesses unparalleled power to refresh and revitalise body and mind, and the freshwater springs in the bays of Stoupa and Kalogria enhance that effect. An early morning or late evening summer swim, when I have the sea virtually to myself, is an unfailing tonic.

Greek light is an extraordinary force of nature that has inspired and enhanced the work of many writers, poets, artists and photographers. Not only the fierce, intense, bright light cast down from the heavens by the midday sun, but also at dawn and dusk, when the sun's less perpendicular rays seem to gather a palette of muted pastel colours from the earth's atmosphere. The mesmerising magic of Greek light manifests itself in many different ways. The fantastic array of geometric patterns projected by the sun through the prism of the crystal-clear sea onto a sandy seabed is one, and the pink-tinted, snow-covered peaks of the Taygetos Mountains illuminated by a setting sun after a calm, unfettered winter's day is another. These sensations are uplifting in a spiritual kind of way. Even without bright sunlight, the dark profiles of mountains, peninsulas, headlands and islands picked out by the rays of a rising or setting moon can be equally stunning.

The Mediterranean climate's propensity for sunshine, heat and clear blue skies, and its aversion to cloud, mist and rain, provides an indispensable backdrop for this state of carefree wellbeing. Similar terrestrial and coastal landscapes provide comparable opportunities in North Devon, but their full enjoyment is so dependent on good weather, which is often in short supply. Yet on a fine day without wind, rain, low cloud and poor visibility, the experience can be just as uplifting – but it only serves to reinforce how fortunate I am to be able to do the same on the other side of Europe, where fine weather is the norm even in winter. What a fillip blue sky and sunshine are! I am invigorated on a daily basis by the power of the Greek sun, its heat, its light, its health-giving properties and its ability to make me feel good, like a grey, overcast sky – and cold, murky Atlantic seawater – never can. And after the sun sets, I am equally enchanted by the phases of the moon across a month of uninterrupted night skies, accompanied by occasional conjunctions of planets, infinite constellations of stars, and meteor showers like the Perseids in August and the Geminids in December. Observing these routine cosmic events where light pollution is at a minimum and when cloud cover only rarely interrupts viewing never ceases to fill me with awe and wonder.

In Greece I live a simpler life. I spend most of it in the open air and my days are longer, especially in summer, when an early rise and a late finish become the norm. The Mediterranean diet that Mary and I now espouse in the UK as well as Greece ensures my daily intake of food has never been so healthy. I also sense a subtle change in my metabolism; my body, now much more able to withstand high temperatures, is more vulnerable to the cold and damp than it has ever been. Life in Greece has also provided opportunities to uphold my mental health. Learning the Greek language, renovating our traditional village house, creating a pleasure garden from a derelict site, and setting up and running a boutique olive oil and olive business for ten years have all been projects that have challenged Mary and me and kept our brains active and in good working order.

While I have resisted the temptation to join in the morning coffee and gossip sessions in the village *cafeneion* and have never adopted *komboloi* (worry beads) as an accessory, there are small changes in my behaviour and attitude that can be attributed to our time in Greece. For one, I have become much more tactile, something first learned from French friends greeting us with handshakes and cheek-kissing, which has progressed to hugging and the adoption of that very Greek expression of affection, the gentle stroking of the arm or back. An afternoon siesta (*ipnaki* in Greek) has also become an integral part of my lifestyle. Adopted in the first instance to help withstand the intense heat of high summer, I now indulge myself every day whether I am in Greece or the UK, and regardless of the season. I feel I have also become more carefree; the shrug of the shoulders accompanying the rhetorical statement "*Ti na kanoume?*" (What can we do?), denoting resignation to one's fate, has become common practice. I have also become less concerned about my behaviour conforming to accepted norms and less likely to abide by minor regulations. While in Greece, I often park my car with scant reference to pedestrians, other road users or parking restrictions; I never stop my car at pedestrian crossings (it would be certain to cause a traffic accident); I am more likely to push in at the front of a long post office queue if I only have the briefest of transactions to make; and using bar and café toilets as a non-customer coming directly off the street has become second nature.

One of the gains from this period of my life has been my transition into a European at a time when many Brits have voted to move in the opposite direction. This has not only been the consequence of living in Greece and coming to terms with its social, cultural and political differences, but also of making firm friends with an assortment of other nationalities – Austrians, Dutch, Swiss, German, French, Swedes – doing the same thing. The numerous road trips Mary and I have made across Europe travelling back and forth to Greece have also contributed to my view that we Europeans have so much more that unites us than divides us. My horizons have been indelibly broadened by these contacts and I no longer see things from a purely British viewpoint. I'm more metrified (178 cm tall, weight 91.4 kg, waist 92 cm, shoe size 43), more open-minded, and more convinced than ever that an integrated, united Europe benefits Europeans and is a force for stability and progress in the wider world. I deeply regret Brexit.

Yet, our time in Greece has also heightened my appreciation of many things in the UK that most Brits take for granted. Both countries have national health services provided free of charge at the point of need but there are marked differences between the two. Probably the most notable for Brits is the absence of general care of patients in hospitals. Whereas the clinical procedures in Greek hospitals are conducted in a broadly similar manner with a high level of professionalism and expertise by both doctors and nurses, the day-to-day wellbeing of the patient in the ward is down to the family, who often keep a bedside vigil day and night. They are responsible for all the non-medical needs of the patient, including providing food and supervising personal hygiene, a far cry from standard practice in the British NHS. It's a cultural difference, the way it's always been done.

Dividing my life between two countries does have its drawbacks. The upkeep of two properties, the carbon footprint of travelling to and fro two or three times a year and the temporary estrangement of family and friends are just some obvious examples. In some cases, we have to work harder to compensate, like making more effort to communicate regularly. In our early years in Neohori, we had no choice but to write letters or use the single, public pay-phone and take our turn in the queue; now emails, messaging, WhatsApp and Skype make communication so much easier and better. In other cases, we just have to accept that it's the price to pay for choosing to do what we do. For example, it would seem that growing vegetables in the near-ideal conditions that exist in southern Greece is a no-brainer, but I've tried it and it doesn't work. Our part-time presence ensures the timing is never right. That lack of permanency also compromises my willingness to participate as a volunteer; few organisations supporting local community activities or groups can be effective with volunteers who are present one minute and absent the next. Or am I just massaging a guilty feeling about not paying back some of the incredible good fortune that has characterised my life? However, I judge these drawbacks as minor compared with the gains. Belonging to and feeling comfortable in two such different communities is a great privilege and one I could never have imagined happening when I first became acquainted with Greece when I watched *Never on Sunday* nearly sixty years ago. There's no chance I'll ever be even 10% Greek, but neither will I ever again be 100% British. I am proud to have become just a little bit Greekish.

Great Mulleins on the roadside near Nomitsi, West Mani.

Bibliography

This bibliography contains books that I have read or consulted before or during the writing of *Greco Files*. The year of publication relates to first editions. Several books have been revised and/or reprinted, and, in some cases, by other publishers. I have provided a very brief summary of books that are out of print or not easily obtained. I appreciate the division of titles into categories is inexact but consider it more useful than a simple alphabetical list.

Local History - Neohori

Ρίζες (Roots) – Ioannis Kiskireas – Bergina Publications – 1998.
   A comprehensive, graphical record of the genealogy of families in Neohori, West Mani, with accompanying lists of families who have migrated and those that have died out. In Greek.
Ατούρι (Hide & Seek) – Ioannis Kiskireas – self-published – 2001.
   An intimate study of the lives, customs, traditions and folklore of the people of Neohori. In Greek.

Mani Guides & Travelogues

Mani: Travels in the Southern Peloponnese – Patrick Leigh Fermor – John Murray – 1958.
Deep Into Mani – Peter Greenhalgh & Edward Eliopoulos – Faber & Faber – 1985.
Mani – Greek Traditional Architecture – Yanis Saitis – Melissa Publishing House – 1990.

The Mani – Bob Barrow – Thomeas Travel Services – 1998.
From the Edge of Greek Space – Frederick Gearing & Mariekaty Georgota – Statchi – 2002.
Inside the Mani – Matthew Dean – self-published – 2006.
Colonel Leake in the Mani – Martin Jones – Book Guild Publishing – 2012.

Greek History

The Flight of Ikaros: Travels in Greece during the Civil War – Kevin Andrews – Weidenfield & Nicholson – 1959.
Modern Greece: A Short History – C. M. Woodhouse – Faber & Faber – 1968.
Eleni – Nicholas Gage – Ballantyne Books – 1983.
A Traveller's History of Greece – Timothy Boatswain & Colin Nicholson – The Windrush Press – 1989.
Inside Hitler's Greece – Mark Mazower – Yale University Press – 1993.
Salonica: City of Ghosts – Mark Mazower – Harper Perennial – 2005.
The Great Sea – David Abulafia – Allen Lane – 2011.
Greece: Biography of a Modern Nation – Roderick Beaton – Allan Lane – 2019.

Olives & Olive Oil

Olives: The Life and Lore of a Noble Fruit – Mort Rosenblum – Absolute Press – 1997.
Olive Oil – Charles Quest-Ritson – Dorling Kindersley – 2006.
Extra Virginity – The Sublime and Scandalous World of Olive Oil – Tom Mueller – W.W. Norton – 2012.

Gardens

Flowers of Greece and the Balkans: A Field Guide – Oleg Polunin – O.U.P. – 1980.
Making a Garden on a Greek Hillside – Jaqueline Tyrwhitt – Denise Harvey – 1998.
Greece, garden of the Gods – Jennifer Gay – Athens News Publications – 2004.
A Dry Gardening Handbook – Olivier Filippi – Thames & Hudson – 2008.

Bibliography

Greece's Economic Crisis

Understanding the Crisis in Greece – Michael Mitsopoulos & Theodore Pelagidis – Palgrave Macmillan – 2011.

Greekonomics: the eurocrisis and why politicians don't get it – Vicky Price – Biteback Publishing – 2013.

Modern Greece: What Everyone Needs to Know – Stathis Kalyvas – O.U.P. – 2015.

And The Weak Suffer What They Must? – Yanis Varoufakis – The Bodley Head – 2016.

Adults in the Room – Yanis Varoufakis – Random House – 2017.

Memoirs, Travel Writing, Commentaries & Biographies

Colossus of Maroussi – Henry Miller – Colt Press – 1941.

Prospero's Cell – Lawrence Durrell – Faber & Faber – 1945.

An Affair of the Heart – Dilys Powell – Hodder & Stoughton – 1959.

Roumeli: Travels in Northern Greece – Patrick Leigh Fermor – John Murray – 1966.

A Fair Exchange – Gillian Bouras – McPhee Gribble – 1991.

Trekking in Greece – Marc S. Dubin & Michael Cullen – Lonely Planet – 1993.

Greece: A Literary Companion – Martin Garrett – John Murray – 1994.

The Olive Tree: Travels in Greece – Katherine Kizilos – Lonely Planet – 1997.

Hellas: A Portrait of Greece – Nicholas Gage – Efstathiadis Group – 1997.

Eurydice Street: A Place in Athens – Sofka Zinovieff – Granta Book – 2004.

92 Acharnon Street – John Lucas – Eland Publishing – 2007.

Blue Skies & Black Olives – John Humphrys & Christopher Humphrys – Hodder & Stoughton – 2009.

Patrick Leigh Fermor – Artemis Cooper – John Murray – 2012.

On the Unhappiness of Being Greek – Nikos Dimou – Zero Books – 2013. (First published in Greek in 1975.)

Getting to Understand the Greeks – Dimitris Calandranis – Anagennisi – 2018.

Fiction

The Magus – John Fowles – Johnathan Cape – 1966.

Captain Corelli's Mandolin – Louis de Bernières – Secker & Warburg – 1994.

Birds Without Wings – Louis de Bernières – Harvill Secker – 2004.

The Island – Victoria Hislop – Headline Publishing Group – 2005.
The Thread – Victoria Hislop – Headline – 2011.
Skios – Michael Frayn – Faber & Faber – 2012.
The Sunrise – Victoria Hislop – Headline – 2014.
Cartes Postales from Greece – Victoria Hislop – Headline – 2016.